LEWIS WOLFGANG BRANDT is Professor of Psychology at the University of Regina.

A psychology that cannot explain how human beings develop psychological systems, theories, research methods, techniques, and treatments falls short of its goal. In this book, Dr Brandt investigates how close to the goal various systems come. Beginning with a discussion of his own premises, which are largely based on his own experience, he proceeds to consider the premises of various schools of psychology – behaviourist, psychoanalytic, gestalt, phenomenological, genetic, and dialectical-materialist. Brandt demonstrates how each is bound by a number of frameworks in which psychologists are caught. He discusses the roles played by different language backgrounds, interests and value systems, conceptualizations of the natural sciences, tastes, and religious systems, in determining the kind of psychology any given psychologists follow and try to promote.

The author's approach in this book combines phenomenological and psychoanalytic approaches on the basis of their common hermeneutic approach. He draws upon a number of European works, chiefly German and Russian, not available in English, key sections of which he has translated. This book, therefore, is a unique introduction to recent German and Russian psychology for unilingual English readers. It will be of interest to a wide audience including practising psychologists and psychiatrists, philosophers of science, and those in the fields of social and theoretical psychology, and of systems and methodology.

LEWIS WOLFGANG BRANDT

Psychologists Caught:
A Psycho-logic of Psychology

University of Toronto Press
Toronto Buffalo London

© University of Toronto Press 1982
Toronto Buffalo London
Printed in Canada

ISBN 0-8020-5539-7 (cloth)
ISBN 0-8020-6508-2 (paper)

Canadian Cataloguing in Publication Data

Brandt, Lewis, 1921–
    Psychologists caught
    Bibliography: p.
    Includes index.
    ISBN 0-8020-5539-7 (bound)   ISBN 0-8020-6508-2 (pbk.)
    1. Psychologists – Psychology. 2. Psychology –
    Philosophy. I Title.
    BF 38.B72   150.19   C81-094733-4

I dedicate this book to my forebears, all of whom were Jews and without whom this book would never have been written.

*Wissenschaft wird vom Menschen gemacht. Dieser an sich selbstver-
ständliche Sachverhalt gerät leicht in Vergessenheit, und es mag zur Ver-
ringerung der oft beklagten Kluft zwischen den beiden Kulturen, der
geisteswissenschaftlich-künstlerischen und der technisch-naturwis-
senschaftlichen beitragen, wenn man ihn wieder ins Gedächtnis zurüc-
kruft ... Naturwissenschaft beruht auf Experimenten, sie gelangt zu ihren
Ergebnissen durch die Gespräche der in ihr Tätigen, die miteinander über
die Deutung der Experimente beraten.*

Science is made by human beings. This after all self-evident state of
affairs falls easily into oblivion. It may, however, contribute to the
decrease of the frequently bemoaned abyss between the two cultures,
that of the artistic sciences of the mind and that of the technical natural sciences, if one calls this fact back to memory ... Natural science
rests on experiments; it arrives at its results through the discussions of
its practitioners who consult with one another about the interpretation of the experiments.

Werner Heisenberg, *Der Teil und das Ganze*
(*The Part and the Whole* – mistranslated as *Physics and Beyond*)

Preface

My wife, Elisabeth Pasztor Brandt, whom Kishon had obviously not met when he referred to his as 'the best wife of all,' contributed more to this volume than anyone else. We wrote not only chapters 8 and 10 together, to the point where we can no longer tell which thoughts, formulas, and sentences are more hers or mine, but she also contributed ideas to every other aspect of this book and helped with much of the piddling work required to get a manuscript into its final shape. All of this she did in addition to providing us with delicious meals, taking care of our house and yard, and pursuing her own professional work as a speech pathologist and communication consultant.

Gerald R. Farthing, Arthur Wiener, and Leendert P. Mos read the entire manuscript in an earlier draft form and made useful comments. My former student Gerry Farthing was the most critical of the three and encouraged very considerable changes and rearrangements. We spent many hours together discussing and clarifying various issues. Leo Mos still objects to my presentation of Calvinism and its relation to Puritanism in chapter 9. I suggest that my perspective is concerned with the effects of Calvinism – in whatever distorted form – on Anglo-American psychology, while he focuses on Calvin's original writings. Chapter 9 was also read in an earlier version and commented on by Kurt Danziger and Charles G. Costello. Gerhard Kaninski, whose influence on my approach to psychology will become evident to the reader of this book, contributed specifically by some critical comments on a first draft for the original paper (Brandt and Brandt 1972) in which Elisabeth and I started the ideas which led to the present chapter 8. My thanks go to all of them.

I am also grateful to Eileen Brownridge, who undertook the enormous task of starting a subject index for this book from early draft chapters while busy on her own master's thesis. I wish to thank especially John St James for his conscientious and understanding copy-editing of the final manuscript.

Theodore C. Hein II read a later draft of the manuscript and pointed out some errors which I corrected. Our work on his PHD thesis was particularly useful to me in learning more about 'cognitive behaviourism.'

The list would become too long if I were to include the names of all the colleagues and students who through discussions and correspondence made me question my assumptions and thus led me to new conceptualizations. The names of some of them will appear in the chapter in which I try to set the stage on which the rest of the play takes place.

Parts of chapter 3 appeared earlier in the *Canadian Psychological Review*, parts of chapter 4 in the *International Journal of Psychology*, and parts of other chapters in *Psychologische Beiträge*, and are reproduced here with the permission of the respective journals.

This book has been published with the help of grants from the Social Science Federation of Canada, using funds provided by the Social Sciences and Humanities Research Council of Canada, and from the Publications Fund of University of Toronto Press, to whom I am deeply grateful.

I cannot possibly tell how much I owe to the most fantastic of German psychologists, Ernst August Dölle.

LWB

Contents

Figures

Frame of Frameworks

Different schools of psychology	considered from various perspectives				
	behav-iourist	diamat	genetic (Piagetian)	gestalt-phenom-enologic	psycho-analytic
Behaviourism	95-101	108	106	105	102-4
Dialectical-materialist psychology	108	93-5	106	104	102
Genetic (Piagetian) psychology	108	108	92-3	104	102
Gestalt-phenomenology	108	107	106	88-92	102
Psycho-analysis	108	107, 202-3	106	104	85-8

inter-personal relations (ch. 6)	research methods (ch. 7)	sociology of knowledge (ch. 9)	English and English	L W B	other sources
120-8	133-6 138-41	206-22	95	24, 209	95, 201
119-20	132-3	204-6		204	93-4
118-19	132				201
117-18	131-2	195-200	88		89, 201
115-17	131	190-5	85	24, 79	201

Abbreviations and Symbols

diamat   dialectical-materialist (psychology), dialectical materialism

E   experimenter

S   subject (except in S–R)

S–R   stimulus-response

v   or

~   not

$\neq$ not identical

$\equiv$ equivalent (not identical)

$\not\equiv$ unequal, not equivalent

p   'person'– an impression someone has formed of someone

X(pY)   the impression individual X has formed of individual Y (first-hand personicating resulting in X's 'person' of Y)

X[pY(pZ)]   the impression X has formed of Z on the basis of what Y told X about Z (second-hand personicating resulting in X's 'person' of Z)

X{(pY) • [pY(pZ)]}   the impression X has of Z on the basis of both X's impression of Y and of what Y told X about Z (second-hand personicating in which X's 'person' of Z is influenced by X's 'person' of Y)

X(pX)   the impression X has of him/herself, his/her self-concept

Introduction

Introduction
Knowledge is a belief that the believer believes to be more than a belief.

0.0   This book consists of an investigation of the psychology of psychologies and psychologists. Bakan (1971), Bannister (1968), Kaminski
(1970), and others have, for some time, called for such a psychology. At
the end of the final chapter, entitled 'Psychology as a Pluralistic System,' of the *Einführung in die Psychologie* (Introduction to Psychology)
Thomae (1969) wrote:

> The 'psychology of psychologies' must therefore also not shrink from recogniz-
> ing [*erkennen*] and/or exposing the relativity of the methodological standpoint
> one has chosen ...
>   After such a critical distancing from the 'perspectivity' (Graumann 1960) of
> one's own standpoint, the differences among various psychological theories
> prove to be differences in the evaluation of certain approaches and forms in
> collecting information. These differences are thus not so much concerned with
> the opposition of 'true' and 'false' knowledge [*Erkenntnissen*] or 'true' or 'false'
> theories. The issue is rather which significance is attributed to the individual
> groups of information.
>   Since the attribution of significance is the result not only of rational consid-
> eration but also of motivational processes (attitudes, inclinations, needs, basic
> convictions), critical self-reflection, i.e., a certain form of the 'development of
> consciousness' becomes an indispensable requirement for the work of the
> investigating as well as of the practising, of the beginning psychologist as well as
> of the psychologist who has been active in the field for years. (p. 167)

0.1   The psychology of psychologies is a meta-psychology. The first problem consists therefore in finding psychologies which can be used as
frames of reference for a meta-psychology. According to Thomae's

above statement, they must be cognitive, critical, and self-reflective, and deal with motivational processes.

0.1.1 One psychology which meets these requirements and makes use of corresponding methods is psychoanalysis. It began with the psychology of a psychologist. Freud derived psychoanalytic psychology from his own self-analysis. Since then every psychoanalyst begins his or her studies of psychology with his or her own analysis. Freud had asked the logical question: 'Why do you want to exclude your own psychic processes from the regularities which you acknowledge for [the processes] of the [individual]?' (1920, p. 245). Consequently, the psychology of the psychologist always precedes the psychology of others in psychoanalytic psychology. However, psychoanalytic psychology does not investigate psychologists qua psychologists but qua individuals. It also does not investigate psychology as such. While I shall make use of some psychoanalytic concepts in my investigation and also investigate psychoanalysis as one school of psychology, my main method will be a different one.

0.1.2 Behaviourism is, in the words of one of its founders, *The Psychology of the Other One* (Meyer 1921); it deals with 'the thing observed' (Stevens 1935), and rejects reflection as 'arm-chair psychology' (Scripture 1895). Hence it is not concerned with the psychology of psychologists and psychology, though it presents itself as a nomothetic science and might as such attempt to establish general laws about the 'behaviour of psychologists.' To my knowledge, no behaviourist has as yet done so.

0.1.3 The cognitive schools of psychology – gestalt-phenomenology, genetic-Piagetian psychology, and dialectical materialist (diamat) psychology – make no distinctions between psychologists and other human beings. Of the three, gestalt-phenomenology seems to me the most appropriate for my investigation. It is reflective and its researchers have frequently used their own observations as psychologists in their research.

For those readers who are unfamiliar with the methods I am using in this book, I give a brief background introduction to phenomenology, dialectics, and hermeneutics.

0.2 According to my use of phenomenology, there exists only one truth: the truth of my experiences. By this I mean that it is beyond doubt for me that *I perceive* (see) the typewriter in front of me, (hear) its humming noise, (sense) the warm and smooth keys, (taste) the tobacco in my pipe, (smell) its smoke, and (sense) my somewhat stiff neck. While I am writing about this experience, *I conceive of* these experiences. That too is beyond my doubt. I do not claim that typewriter, tobacco, and pipe exist. I can *bracket* their *existence*, which means that I can leave the question of their existence unanswered.

Of my pipe I can see only the bowl. I see only certain *aspects* of it. Yet, I experience it as a whole pipe. It is given to me in my experience, namely, it presents itself to me as a three-dimensional thing. When I take it out of my mouth, I perceive different aspects of it: I sense it as hot and I see its stem.

When I took it out of my mouth, I changed my *viewpoint* and with it my *perspective* in relation to the pipe. As I now hold it in my hand, I also change the *framework* within which I perceive it.

I always perceive in the present. I cannot perceive the past or the future. I can only conceive of, only conceptualize past and future. The fourth dimension, time, is given to me only in my mind. Through the addition of the time dimension to the three dimensions of perceiving, the number of possible *perspectives* and *frameworks* in thinking becomes practically infinite.

All thinking takes place at and from some point in space-time. It also takes place in some conceptual framework. I can think of my pipe as something to relax with or as something that makes the air sticky and occasionally causes holes in my suit. I can also think of it as an expensive habit. Each of these thoughts places the pipe in a different frame of reference. Some of these frameworks overlap.

Like Sir Karl Popper (1970) 'I admit that at any moment we are prisoners caught in the framework of our theories; our expectations; our past experiences; our language. But we are prisoners in a Pickwickian sense: if we try, we can break out of our framework at any time. Admittedly, we shall find ourselves again in a framework, but it will be a better and roomier one; we can at any moment break out of it again' (p. 56). Any framework and any perspective hides some aspects while opening new vistas for other aspects. All perspectives result from *approaches* originating at some point, some *standpoint* in space-time. This means that I must always take a stand.

I shall try to uncover more and more hidden aspects. As Karl Mannheim (1927) stated: 'a first step toward correction [of any single approach] consists in trying to increase the efficiency of thought by striving to think from several positions and to grasp the world on the basis of several principles' (1964, p. 489).

In the course of striving 'to grasp the world on the basis of several principles' I shall also evaluate those principles. This requires 'stepping into someone else's framework in order to evaluate it' which presents 'very special difficulties' (Kuhn 1970, p. 232).

As I compare different frameworks I take a meta-perspective on perspectives and step into a meta-framework. I shall try to describe my perspectives and frameworks always as clearly as possible. In other words, I shall always attempt to make my *assumptions explicit*.

0.3   I shall approach the issues I deal with via hermeneutic circles. Habermas (1971) describes the *hermeneutic circle* as follows:

> The interpretation of a text depends on a reciprocal relation [*Wechselbeziehung*] between the interpretation of the 'parts' through an originally diffusely preunderstood 'whole' and the correction of this pre-concept by means of the subsumed parts. A modifying force can feed-back from the 'parts' to the prejudged whole on whose foil they are interpreted only because they have already been interpreted independently of that hermeneutic anticipation. The complex preunderstanding of the entire text has, certainly, the place of a variable interpretive schema into which individual elements are arrayed in order to make them understandable. But the schema can make its subsumed elements understandable only to the extent to which itself can be corrected by these 'data.' (p. 216f.)

I shall use the hermeneutic circle frequently to describe concepts by means of a *phenomenal analysis*. The latter consists of analysing phenomena into their constituting parts and elucidating their various aspects. A phenomenal analysis thus takes the place of a definition.

0.4   My approach is also largely *dialectic*, by which I mean that I conceptualize the world in many respects in terms of contradictions which negate each other – like Faust seeking to become the benefactor of mankind through improvement of its lot and its freedom by signing a covenant with 'the spirit who always negates.' The resolution of contradictions, by recognizing the unity of opposites and by evolving from thesis and antithesis, leads to new contradiction and conflict. In this sense, any analysis – phenomenal analysis as well as psycho-analysis – is infinite.

0.5   I shall now apply my methods to defining or rather describing what I mean by 'science' and 'psychology.'

0.5.1   I use 'science' to refer to *Wissenschaft*. As Russell (Russell and Roth 1958) stresses one basic difference between Anglo-American and

German-speaking psychologists is 'the difference between the terms 'sciences' as understood by [the former] and *'Wissenschaft'* as understood [by the latter]. The two words are by no means synonymous' (p. 226). *Science* (Latin: *scientia*, meaning knowledge), which Pribram (1976) considers 'the pursuit of understanding,' consists for me in *problematizing the taken-for-granted*. Such questioning leads from old to new *meanings*. Science, as distinguished from technology, is, for me, a human linguistic activity dealing with meanings, *the meaning something has for some human beings within a given context or framework at a given time*. Science, as I mean it, does not aim at changing reality through actively interfering with it but through re-conceptualizing it – in line with Faust's translation of St John 1:1 by 'in the beginning was meaning [*der Sinn*].'

Consequently, I consider science not to be bound to any particular method. The most scientific method is in any given instance the one which is most appropriate for the investigation of the problem one wishes to study. In particular, the methods which are usually most appropriate in the *Naturwissenschaften* are usually inappropriate for research in the *Geisteswissenschaften* (sciences of the products of the human mind, i.e., of Popper's [1973] World 3).

0.5.2   I consider psychology the *Geisteswissenschaft* which investigates such conscious and unconscious processes as human perceiving, thinking, feeling, willing, and acting, the interactions between these processes and their meanings to individuals, and the verbal and non-verbal communications and relations among individuals.

I relegate the study of animal 'behaviour' to ethology in order to avoid the anthropomorphizing of rats and the ratomorphizing (Koestler 1967) of human beings. I leave the study of physiology to physiologists until a new metascience combining psychology and physiology can be meaningfully developed. Hence, psych(soul)ology, as I understand it, investigages *minds* and not brains.[1]

---

1 I know that sexual fantasies can lead to consciously perceivable physical phenomena of sexual arousal and wonder why I have never seen this mentioned as evidence for psychosomatic connections. I also know that a common cold or broken leg influences my thinking and feeling. Such connections are very different from those between seeing the needle move on an EEG or GSR recorder and hearing someone tell me his thoughts. The

---

0.6   In chapter 1 I apply the above-described methods to a description of how my present approach to psychology developed. I do not follow a straight temporal line but present different aspects of my overall conceptual framework. Consequently, I again and again change my perspective. Like the book as a whole, the first chapter resembles a kaleidoscope. The same parts form different wholes from shifting perspectives. The end result may remind some readers of Picasso's *Arlequin au violon*. Some people like that picture, others don't. Most people find it at least interesting.

In chapter 2 I argue that the language in which one thinks largely determines one's way of conceptualizing psychology.

In chapter 3 I attempt to show how different research-motivating interests and their underlying values lead to different ways of pursuing psychology.

In chapter 4 I present two basically different views of the physical world and show how each one leads to different psychological systems.

In chapter 5 I apply psychoanalytic, gestalt-phenomenological, genetic-Piagetian, dialectical-materialist, and behaviourist psychology to psychologists constructing theories in the respective frameworks and evaluate each of these psychologies in terms of the others.

In chapter 6 I show that these different psychologies imply different relationships between the respective psychologists and the people whom they study.

In chapter 7 I discuss the consequences of those different relationships for research and particularly for conducting laboratory experiments.

In chapter 8 my wife and I analyse what we call 'personicating,' namely, the process of forming impressions, in so far as it concerns psychologists forming impressions of other people in clinical and experimental settings.

In chapter 9 I relate psychoanalytic, gestalt-phenomenological, diamat, and behaviouristic psychology to their historical sources in the sense of a sociology of knowledge.

In chapter 10 my wife and I illustrate a number of ways in which psychologists are alienated, that is, have lost their identity, and we try to present possible reasons for that alienation.

---

latter are mere correlations which provide me with no understanding of psychological processes.

In chapter 11 I suggest that, instead of continuing the search for an elusive 'scientific truth,' psychologists may enjoy their science as an artful game.

I conclude that the resulting ethical principle is fair play.

1 The Author-Psychologist Caught in His Own Net[1]

---

1 The purpose of this chapter is to help the reader join me in the framework within which this book is written.

The Author-Psychologist Caught in His Own Net
2b v ~2b?

γνῶθι σεαυτόν

γένοιο οἷος ἐσσί

1.0.1   A number of circumstances raise questions about my existence. They beg the question as to whether I exist in terms of Popper's (1973) World 1 of physical objects, World 2 of experiences, or World 3 of creations of human minds, or of Brandt and Metzger's (1969) transphenomenal, phenomenal, or encountered 'reality.' To be specific: Am I merely a character in *Tragende Wolken* (Carrying Clouds), the comedy my father wrote and directed and in which my mother played the leading female part when I was six weeks old, or am I more than a figment of their imagination? What was my mother expressing when she wrote to me that sex did not mean to her what it means to most women? What should I conclude from my calculation that I was conceived on New Year's Eve, if at all? What about the fact that I have no forefathers with my family name but that Brandt is my father's pen-name and that I was further named after Mozart and Beethoven and told by my father that Goethe was my 'spiritual' grandfather? Do I exist merely in my father's only novel, entitled *Flucht und Ziel* (Escape and Aim), which was never published? Since my parents disappeared and were presumably killed in a German concentration camp with no grave and not a record or trace left of them, what empirical evidence have I that they ever existed? Did I, an only child, play during my childhood with an imaginary playmate or *was I* the imaginary playmate of the children my mother did not have? Did I later for hundreds of hours lie on couches of various psychoanalysts whom I neither saw nor heard? Have I been listening silently for hundreds of hours to analysands who could not see me, whose faces I could not see, and who wondered who I am? Did they not talk to an anonymous transference object? Do the examinations I have been grading not throw some doubt on my belief that I have been teaching university students psychology? Was I a German whom the

Hitler government expatriated and made stateless because I am a Jew who never learnt Hebrew and never studied the Torah and the Mishna?

1.0.2   These questions and the fact of my asking them may provide the reader with some frame of reference for the subsequent chapters. I am a phenomenologist who brackets existence while investigating experiences and assuming as many perspectives as possible. Via changing perspectives new and different aspects are discovered. I am a psychoanalyst who interprets the hidden meanings of free associations in order to make unconscious motives conscious. I am a dialectical materialist who acknowledges contradictions and conflicts as well as the unity of all determinants including opposites. As a psychoanalyst I acknowledge my individual history as one determinant. As a dialectical materialist I acknowledge the history of the society in which my individual history is embedded as another determinant. As a phenomenologist I consider psychoanalysis and dialectical materialism as two different perspectives revealing different aspects of me, of psychology, and of the world.

In this chapter I do not intend to write my autobiography. I intend to set the stage for the various perspectives from which I discuss different psychologies later in this book. A perspective, be it perceptual or conceptual, always derives from a given standpoint. In the following pages I shall attempt to describe how I arrived at the standpoints from which I later view different psychologies. Of course, these descriptions themselves imply standpoints to which the reader must add his/her own. By adopting as many different standpoints as possible the number of facets which appear in focus increases. Such an increase in facets-brought-into-focus I consider an increase in objectivity. Objectivity can never be complete. In order to get as close to it as I can I shall frequently change my standpoint and approach the same issue from various angles. Thus, my account may at times read like free association, at times like a critical analysis, and occasionally like my personal history. I hope that, if the reader has some patience, a meaningful whole will appear, just like with Delaunay's paintings, which seem at first sight to consist merely of square patches of different colours. As one continues to look patiently one recognizes a roof here, a steeple there, then houses, now entire streets, and finally a whole city.

1.1

1.1.1   On my father's side my ancestors may have come to Germany with the Roman armies before there was any Germany. My maternal forefathers came to Germany in the sixteenth century after they had been expelled from Spain and Portugal. All of them were Jews. However, my mother was raised as a Lutheran. Before marrying my father, who had formally resigned from the Jewish congregation, she resigned from the Lutheran church. They brought me up without any religion. I thus was a Jew and not a Jew and am a German and not a German.

I was their only child. I was born in Berlin and raised by my parents and a nurse in close vicinity to my maternal grandparents, at whose flat I spent much of my childhood. My father was a writer and actor, director, and producer, first for the theatre and then for the radio. My mother was an actress. But when I was seven years old my father was in a train accident and my parents were no longer any of the above. Shortly after my father recovered the National-Socialist government came to power. It declared us Jews and not Germans and all my father was allowed to do was to write without publishing what he wrote. I was left with a father who was a writer and no writer and a mother who was an actress and no actress.

My parents spoke German to me. When they did not want me to understand what they were talking about they spoke French or English until I too knew those languages. Language and culture were of primary importance in my home. My parents spoke *Bühnendeutsch* (stage German) and that was what I had to speak. Dialects were fun but were not to be used in everyday communication. My father was a perfectionist and my mother's and my speech had to be perfect, just as my letters had to be later in style, spelling, and handwriting. One of his maxims was, '*Wer immer strebend sich bemüht, den können wir erlösen*' (Him who strives in eternal effort we can save), from Goethe's *Faust*. But, as I learnt with tears, striving by itself was not enough. It had to result in perfection, my father used to remind me by quoting, 'I will not let thee go, except thou bless me,' from Genesis 32:26.

My father was very free in the expression of love and affection but did not tolerate any expression of anger. In the diary my mother kept about me during my first year and a half she mentions my father and I screaming at each other. I have no memory of any such scenes. She also reported that I 'consciously' used the pot at nine and one-half months, was 'almost clean' at thirteen months, and cried and showed signs of guilt at seventeen months when I had not asked in time to be taken to the toilet. But she did not mention that she breast-fed me or anything about weaning, thought the diary contains regular entries about what she fed me and how much I weighed. She always wrote in the jagged German characters which look cold and stern while my father wrote in a very rounded, warm Latin script. On the many pictures I have of my parents my mother almost never smiles while my father often does.

My parents had an extremely close relationship which they did not give up even when my mother could have saved her life by leaving my father during their abortive attempt to escape from Hitler Germany. They were caught together and probably died together in a gas chamber. They shared everything: their artistic and intellectual interests, their political views, their pacifism, their work in the theatre, their poetry recitals in concert halls, even kitchen work when because of the anti-Semitic laws we no longer had a maid. They tried to include me in that relationship through joint activities and insisting that the three of us belonged together. But I did not feel that they really needed me. I was part of the Brandts and I was not.

1.1.2 The question of where I belonged arose again and again in my life. Brandt was the legalized pen-name of my father. Thus I had no other relatives by that name. Moreover we had almost no contact with my father's relatives, the Meyers, and saw little of my mother's large family, the Jacobys, except for her parents. During the Second World War the Hitler government forced us to revert the family-name change, declared us officially as Jews, and finally expatriated me. I now was no longer a Brandt or a German. I was officially stateless and in fact a homeless orphan.

I had none of this consciously in mind when I wrote a paper on the self-concept (1967a) or when I worked with my wife on the chapters on alienation and personicating for this book. But my concern with these issues may well be related to the fact that my self-concept has frequently been in conflict with other people's concept of me. Not only did the German government of Hitler consider me to be a Jew when I did not, but so did the other inmates of the refugee labour camps in which I was interned by the Swiss government during most of the Second World War, and so did my Roman Catholic supervisor in the translation department of a New York bank where I worked while studying psychology. Long after having been declared stateless, and even after having first assumed and then again rejected U.S. citizenship, and after having finally become a Canadian many people still consider me a German.

After graduating from the Interpreter School of the University of Geneva with a diploma in English, French, and Spanish I was hired as a research analyst, not an interpreter or translator, for the prosecution of German war criminals at the Nuremberg Trials. The Germans there took me for an American though I had not yet been to America. When I subsequently did the work of an editor for an international news agency in Zurich I was not allowed to call myself an editor and have the corresponding privileges because my salary was below the official range for news editors. Meanwhile I have been trained and worked for many years as a psychoanalyst, but am not allowed to call myself one because I did not graduate from an institute recognized by the International Psychoanalytic Association.

As I am writing this I suddenly understand why, as soon as I first heard about it, I became interested in 'fuzzy set theory,' the theory about sets whose members are members of the sets to varying degrees, and which attempts to resolve paradoxes of which my life has been full and which I discovered again and again in psychology as the following chapters show. But the relativism of fuzzy logic was not part of the principles with which my father raised me.

1.2   My father's values were absolutes. Pacifism included my not being allowed to play either with tin-soldiers, as most boys did in Germany at the time, or with toy guns. For my perfectionist father perfection was not something to be proud of but something taken for granted. Anything was to be done perfectly or not at all. There existed no gradings. Accordingly my parents sent me whenever possible to schools without any grading systems and without any grades.

I went to a Montessori school for my first four years of schooling. Since it was not located in our immediate neighbourhood, I went there by myself either by public transportation or by walking for about half an hour through the streets of one of the world's largest cities. Independence and responsibility were further promoted by the Montessori system in which the pupils learn individually at their own speed and on their own initiative with few group activities. As a consequence I had few friends. In the fourth year I became part of a group of six children who stayed after regular school hours to learn English. When, by the end of that year, the Nazi government dissolved all Montessori schools in Germany I spoke English fluently and knew how to extract square roots. But I was again separated from the few peers with whom I had established some closer relations.

Six months earlier we had moved from the apartment in which I was born to a house in an entirely different part of that immense city. We knew no one in that neighbourhood until I started going to the local *Gymnasium*. This school was almost the complete opposite of the Montessori school: regular subjects, homework, examinations, and grades. I quickly forgot my English as the cirriculum did not include it but consisted of French, Latin, German (of course), mathematics, biology, physics, chemistry, geography, history, drawing, and athletics. Here the foundations were laid for my later interest in the theories of Einstein and Heisenberg. But my favourite subject at the time was geography. When my schoolmates read children's books I read the diaries of polar explorers and, later, books on astronomy. I thought of becoming an explorer of the earth or of the universe. Little did I imagine then that I would become an explorer of the human mind.

While the emphasis in the *Gymnasium* was on human and natural sciences my parents introduced me to the arts. We read plays together and went to museums. My father sang Beethoven and Schubert *lieder* and my mother accompanied him on the piano. I learned many poems by Goethe and Schiller by heart, often studying the interpretation with my father. No wonder that I became interested in psychology first through the novels of Hermann Hesse, with whom I later corresponded until his death and who invited me twice to his house at Montagnola. At that time I had no idea that his novels represented Jungian psychology. No wonder either that at the end of this book I attempt a synthesis of science and aesthetics.

In 1937 my parents sent me to Switzerland because we were Jews. They stayed in Berlin because we were Germans. My father believed that by 1940, when I would graduate, the German people would have rid themselves of Hitler. He believed that most people were inner-directed as he was and as he had raised me. I cannot remember his ever punishing me without a long explanation about the consequences of the action for which he punished me. The punishment was not for my 'behaviour' but for its results. My parents never deceived me but wanted me to understand their actions fully. I cannot have been older than five when they told me that Santa Claus was my father in disguise. When, around that time, a stranger mentioned that children were brought by the stork I said that my mother had told me that I came from her stomach. This stress on rationality led on the one hand to my later need for psychoanalysis and on the other hand to my interest in various forms of cognitive psychology.

The school in Switzerland to which my parents sent me was, like the Montessori school earlier, 'anti-establishment.' It was a coeducational boarding school governed jointly by the pupils and the teachers; it had no grades and no examinations; all the housework was done by the children, who ranged in age from five to eighteen; the language of instruction depended on the mother tongue of the respective teacher and could be German, French, or English – thus all of us had to be at least bilingual. I was now for the first time part of a large 'family.'

This 'family,' or *Schulgemeinde* (school community) as it called itself, was not without internal and external conflicts and contradictions. Its egalitarian principles clashed on the inside with the favouritism the director showed to some children, and on the outside with the villagers who rumoured that boys and girls showered together in our school. Its idealism and pacifism contrasted with Hitler's Germany where the parents of most of the children lived. The free educational system was in conflict with the university entrance examination most of us expected eventually to pass.

To make sure that I passed the matriculation examination I was sent for six months to a special preparatory school, a 'cram' school, the exact opposite of the *Schulgemeinde*. The examination lasted a full week and consisted of six written and ten oral parts covering eleven subjects. As I got the highest grades in my weakest and the lowest marks in my strongest subjects I found out once and for all the role of chance in testing.

1.3 While cramming for that examination I developed a friendship with the daughter of friends of my father. I shared with her my interest in Hindu and Chinese philosophy, in Einstein and Hesse. The Viennese young lady introduced me to some contemporary English writers and to the music of Richard Wagner. But we were soon separated as I went to work for a farmer in another part of Switzerland. Twenty-three years later, when I had signed my first contract as an instructor of psychology, I flew from New York to Denver to marry Elisabeth H. Pasztor. She had earned a PhD in communciation methodology and speech pathology. Since then we have collaborated in most of our work, including the writing of this book. As we discuss its issues – or anything else – we speak English, German, or French, whichever is most suitable for the expression of a given idea.

What could be more paradoxical than working fourteen hours a day, seven days a week, for a farmer right after passing a university entrance examination and meeting a middle-aged retired actress who worked there because she liked the countryside? Only to be introduced by her to yoga, Marx, and a psychologist who spent his life demonstrating that everybody can be creative! But that encounter was very brief too as the Swiss government now interned me in a labour camp. There I spent all my spare moments studying from books first Spanish and then Russian, the two most widely spoken languages I did not yet know.

Since coming to Switzerland I had exchanged letters with my parents and my grandfather twice a week. While still in school I was without news from them once for about two weeks. By the end of that period I received a letter from my father that they had stopped writing when my handwriting had become sloppy and resumed the correspondence only after it improved. When I had been in labour camps for about two years the correspondence from Berlin stopped again. This time it was final. As I learnt from friends and relatives after the war, my grandfather had been deported at age eighty-three and my parents had subsequently attempted to escape from Germany and had been caught at the border by the Gestapo. Four years earlier, when they visited me at school I had tried to talk them into staying in Switzerland, but they had not wanted to leave behind my mother's father who was living with them. They feared that the Nazis might use reprisals against him.

1.4 I finally succeeded in getting out of the labour camp by being admitted to the Interpreter School at the University of Geneva. When I had learnt Spanish and some Russian by myself I had wanted to understand how people thought in other languages. Now my language studies were no longer theoretical but became practical. They were supplemented by studies in international law, human geography, diplomatic history, and constitutional law and history. I obtained special permission to declare English instead of German as my first language and French and Spanish as secondary languages. Only after arriving in New York did I find out that, being of German mother tongue, I could not work as a translator or interpreter for the United Nations. But this did not stop my concern with language and thought which the reader will encounter throughout this book.

At Geneva I met again a former schoolmate who had meanwhile become very interested in Jungian psychology. With him I had my first few psychoanalytic sessions. I also met a group of Trotskyites. They too were refugees from Germany, where some of them had been politically active before Hitler came to power. We met regularly to discuss current events and analyse them in Marxian terms. Once we went together to a large meeting of German refugees of varous socialist convictions. The failure of the meeting to come to any kind of agreement was one of my first disillusionments about democracy. Another one occurred when I visited the Grand Conseil de la République et Canton de Genève (legislative assembly of the province of Geneva) where I found every kind of childishness and no rational debate.

As soon as the war was over the Swiss police pressured me to leave the country. I had only two alternatives: to return to Germany where my family had been murdered, or to emigrate to the U.S.[2] in spite of what Hermann Hesse had written to me: 'I am convinced in Germany live today vastly more [people] who are moved and inspired in mind than in all of America, north and south taken together.' When I was offered the job at the Nuremberg trials by the U.S. War Department Hesse wrote: 'I can only approve of and congratulate you on your decision to return to Germany and not to go to America.'

The trials made me think a lot about justice. I had gone to Nuremberg with the suspicion that von Papen, who vacated the prime minister's seat to help Hitler into it, and Schacht, who provided the money to keep Hitler in power and finance the war, would be acquitted. They both were. Smaller fry were hanged. Von Papen and Schacht were the only upper class defendants in the International War Crimes Trial.

1.5   I could fulfil two long-standing wishes while I was at Nuremberg. During a one-week vacation I visited Paris. I saw the city, the Louvre, Versailles, theatres, museums, and many places few foreigners get to see. I met again the head of the little Marxist group from Geneva who now told me about some of the Stalin horrors. On the train back to Nuremberg, I got into a conversation with an Indian mining engineer who told me that all Hindu writings from the Vedas to Tagore must be read without commentary because they have only one true meaning: the one the reader finds in them.

My other wish had been to find out how well I could act. I approached the stage director of the Nuremberg theatre and asked him whether he could recommend a drama coach. He offered to give me acting lessons himself. To my great surprise I discovered the different roles I was able to play, roles which I had not thought were in me.

When he offered to hire me as assistant stage director, a New York Jew who had been the attorney of a theatre chain in Berlin after the First World War and whom I had met at the trials convinced me to

---

2   From my Canadian perspective, as from that of the united states of Mexico and of any country south thereof, America is a continent. Hence, I refer to the country in between as the U.S. and to its citizens as Yankees.

---

leave Europe for the U.S. My decision not to become a German again was also prompted by finding that the young Germans I met had never heard of Einstein, Freud, or Hesse. Thirty years later, when these are again familiar names to Germans, I still do not regret my decision. The veiled re-unification propaganda of West Germany and the sabre-rattling of both Germanies remind me too much of Hitler and all aspects of Germany which clash with my values and convictions. Moreover, I could not live with their bureaucracy.

My concept of the U.S. was, like Hesse's and that of other friends I left behind, rather negative. We thought of the country as having a highly developed technology and no culture, as socially extremely backward and politically very conservative, with a so-called two-party but in fact a one-party system which supported any anti-communist dictatorship, and as a society in which people were judged only by what they owned. But once I had decided to move there I was also determined to become part of that nation and not to remain among German-speaking immigrants. In Switzerland I had always known that I had to leave the country as soon as the war was over. When I went to Germany to the war crimes trials I did so for a one-year job and to see how that country had changed. When I went to New York I went there reluctantly but nevertheless to stay.

Now was the time for me for some much needed self-exploration. I seemed to have reached the end of my wandering in the outside world. I wanted to settle and sort out my inside world in order to make some kind of peace between the two. I started psychoanalysis.

Very shortly I met a young woman from the Middle West with no German background who had written a bachelor's thesis on Rilke, the twentieth-century German poet. She introduced me to Bach's and Beethoven's chamber music, and was interested in the kind of culture which I had not expected to find among U.S. natives. I fell in love with her, married her, and told my analyst that I did not need him any longer. When he expressed doubts about the sudden answer to all my questions I replied that I had expected such doubts from him.

His doubts proved only too soon to have been justified. He referred me to another analyst, a Hungarian Jew, who also spoke German and who, as a student of Steckel, had learnt that the most important strength of a psychoanalyst is a very broad general knowledge.

1.5.1   The friend who at Nuremberg had convinced me to leave Europe had told me soon after my arrival in New York that in order to have a satisfactory life I had to obtain an American university degree. Since I had to work forty hours per week to support myself, my choice of a major was largely dependent on the credit I received for my European education. On the basis of the latter Columbia University admitted me directly to its MA programme in French literature. As soon as I had completed the course work and passed the comprehensive examination, and before beginning research on a thesis about Rousseau and Nietzsche, I wrote letters to 180 colleges asking for a teaching position. I received many flattering replies regretting that the department had no opening, but not a single job offer. Only years later did I learn that university departments generally reject unsolicited applications for teaching from complete strangers – even if the department has an opening. I believed that there simply were no open positions for university teachers of French language and literature, and that it was thus useless to continue working for the MA.

1.6   My first marriage lasted less than three years, that is, some months less than my first work as an analysand. I realized during that analysis that I had pursued languages and literature in an attempt to explore the workings of the human mind. I had now gained some acquaintance with another road toward the exploration of the workings of the mind. I decided to become a psychoanalyst. One of the requirements I already had: a relatively vast background and knowledge.

1.6.1   Again practical considerations played an important part in my selection, this time of a programme in psychoanalysis and simultaneously of one in psychiatry. I wanted to study both at Vienna (Austria) but discovered that the psychoanalytic institute there had given in to pressure from the American Psychoanalytic Association not to accept students in psychoanalysis who were U.S. citizens and who had not first completed psychiatric training. I was by now a U.S. citizen and thirty-three years old and could not afford to go through psychiatric training before studying psychoanalysis. As a consequence I was looking for the fastest way of becoming a psychoanalyst in New York while supporting myself through a full-time job. I found that with twelve undergraduate credits in psychology I could be accepted to both the psychoanalytic training institute founded by students of Theodor Reik and the graduate psychology programme at the New School for Social Research. Since both offered their entire programmes at night, I could continue working during the day.

1.6.1.1   I obtained the undergraduate credits at the City College of New York. In the introductory course, which was based on the textbook by

Gardner Murphy (1951), I heard for the first time about gestalt psychology and Piaget. I deeply regretted that I had never attended one of Piaget's lectures, which I could easily have done when I studied at Geneva. There was little emphasis on behaviourism in the courses I took at City College and much critique of it at the New School, whose psychology department had been strongly influenced by Max Wertheimer and was still unequivocally gestalt oriented. Among my teachers were Wolfgang Köhler's collaborator Hans Wallach, Mary Henle, Irvin Rock, Solomon Asch, and Helen Block Lewis, the Witkin collaborator and psychoanalyst. There were no rats at the New School and I developed no taste for them. Much later, I was fortunate to meet the leading contemporary gestalt psychologist, Wolfgang Metzger, and to collaborate with the great old man on both his and my territory.

Meanwhile my psychoanalytic work, which in terms of intensity, frequency of sessions, and depth was not a true analysis, had reached a point where my analyst suggested that we stop the sessions and that I continue with someone else, preferably a woman, when I could afford a regular analysis. This analyst had also suggested that I not continue studying at the New School beyond the MA because of the extremely high demands for admission to the Ph D and the high failure rate in that programme.

In 1957 I received the MA from the New School. At the same time I had reached the point in my psychoanalytic training where I could begin to do psychoanalysis under supervision. I did so, started a regular analysis with Marie Coleman Nelson, and registered at New York University in a Ph D programme in educational psychology. One of my reasons for choosing this programme was that it took a very different perspective from that of psychoanalysis and that, at the same time, I was going to learn something about real human beings – the gifted, the retarded, and the physically handicapped – namely, about aspects of human functioning about which I so far knew almost nothing.

1.6.1.2 I was now involved in psychoanalysis as an analysand, a student, an analyst, and a supervisee. I conceptualized psychoanalysis as an educational and growth process (Brandt 1966a) designed for emancipating human beings from unconscious impulses which were ruling them, and thereby increasing the number of choices people have to decide freely their own lives. I did not conceive of myself or others as mechanically 'responding' to 'stimuli.' *The prediction and control of human actions is*, in view of my entire past, *an undesirable temptation of an obsessive-compulsive individual to achieve the impossible.* An individual life consists for me of situations, some of which one conceptualizes as opportunities which s/he makes use of.

One such situation arose at a conference on the 'self.' After a short conversation a stranger asked me whether I was interested in teaching psychology in his department where he had an opening. I had not thought previously about teaching but had wished I had some regular salary so that my financial concerns would not interfere with my work with analysands. His offer also seemed appealing because teaching would present a gratifying balance to the frustration of having to listen for hours without saying anything. It would decrease the temptation to give my analysand premature interpretations merely because I wanted to say something too and not merely listen, and because I wanted to show off. It would be an appropriate outlet for my exhibitionistic needs. I once had wanted to become an actor like my parents and had taken acting lessons at Nuremberg but had not made a career of it. Teaching in a university was right for me. It fitted my concept of my self.

1.6.1.3 The concept of my self changes in unending analysis and synthesis. While writing this book I recognized that here too I am following in the footsteps of my father. At his home I grew up with the idea that the right to live as a human being had to be earned through some creative contribution to mankind in the arts or in science. The great example was Goethe, who combined both and to whom I had been introduced by my father when I was a small boy. My father had then shown me around the house in Frankfurt where Goethe grew up and the one at Weimar where he wrote and died. My parents and I had read and seen many of his plays together. I now found out that Goethe was the precursor of phenomenology and gestalt psychology. He represented the high point of German culture.

I never felt that I could be creative in any of the arts. I did not consider translating, which I had done for a living, truly creative. I enjoy writing, which I can do easily in German, French, and English. The explorer spirit of my boyhood which guided me through solitary bicycle hikes in Germany and mountain climbs in Switzerland, through the museums of Paris and London and the Prado, through the works of Marx, Nietzsche, Laotse, Buddha, Plato, Hesse, the Old and the New Testament, was now directed quite single-mindedly at the exploration of the human psyche. Through both psychoanalysis and phenomenology these explorations became analytical and critical. The method of these two approaches is not experimental, but rather that of archaeology, the first scientific method I had learnt about when my father showed me around the Egyptian, Babylonian, Greek, and Trojan collections in Berlin and told me how Schliemann had found Troy and Mycenae. My first published psychological creation resulted from unearthing a hidden memory of Freud. I traced his idea that Judaism was the Egyptian religion in which Moses had been raised to an essay by the German poet and historian Friedrich Schiller (Brandt 1960).

Psychoanalytic and phenomenological explorations are conducted through communciation. Communication uses language. Communication is also our only means for overcoming loneliness and alienation. When I had experienced the height of loneliness and alienation, namely when my first wife left me, I had seriously turned away from the lonely study of language and literature to psychoanalysis and the study of psychology. I was not interested in a psychology which experiments with people and animals without true communciation, without the use of language. I next wrote about my discoveries of the role of language in psychoanalysis (1961a).

Seen from another perspective, my writings are attacks. They are verbal attacks, just as my father attacked me verbally when he punished me for having destroyed his poetic creation by whistling in the house. He did not hit me but ordered me to reflect upon the consequencs of my action. My writings are verbal attacks on established ideas, on what others take for granted. All psychoanalytic interpretations are attacks on defences, just as archaeological digs are attacks on the earth and the past it hides beneath its surface. But the aim of such attacks is not to destroy. It is to open up new vistas, to discover fresh aspects of life.

Freud, the gestalt psychologists, and the phenomenological psychologists wrote in German. As a translator, and particularly having read Dostoyevsky in Russian, I am aware of the losses and changes in meaning brought about by translation. *'Traduttore, traditore'*: a translator is a traitor. I therefore read German psychology in German. I soon became aware of entire areas of psychology untouched by my English-speaking colleagues. I decided to take on the task of introducing German-language psychology to North America – an aggressive enterprise in the face of Yankee resistance to anything foreign, and particularly in view of the fact that German-language psychology is highly critical of behaviourism.

1.6.2   When I received my first teaching appointment I married Elisabeth Pasztor. She had just finished her Ph D with a thesis on German-English translation. Some years earlier I had found out that she too had come to the U.S. I now again conceptualized a situation as an opportunity to be used constructively. It was an opportunity for reducing my loneliness and alienation, for communication and intimacy. I had recently terminated my second analysis, which had extended over almost four years, and was in a psychoanalytic group in which I was to continue my analysis for a while. In my individual and group analyses the issue of aggression played an important part.

1.7

1.7.1   This issue came up soon in a different context: race riots, the Vietnam war, and the murder of the two Kennedy brothers and of Martin Luther King. Elisabeth and I opposed the Vietnam war from its beginning and became actively involved in the peace movement. U.S. policy, internal and external, and behaviourism are in my mind closely intertwined. Both aim at the control of other people – not at understanding them. The American Psychological Foundation, an arm of the American Psychological Association, was not interested in my translating foreign psychology into English but only in exporting its psychology of control to other countries. Just as any experiment represents a self-fulfilling prophecy, U.S. policy represents from my perspective a self-fulfilling prophecy, creating more and more 'communists' in fighting 'communists.' Just as self-fulfilling prophecies result from not reflecting upon one's actions, so both behaviourists and U.S. politicians disregard their own actions. If either take their actions into account, they consider them to be 'responses' to 'stimuli' or 'the only alternative.' Such an approach results in paradoxical situations.

To avoid creating self-fulfilling prophecies in my work with analysands I set up a weekly counter-transference seminar with two colleagues. The three of us discussed for three years our psychoanalytic work and helped one another in recognizing our roles in it. We focused on how our own unconscious, unresolved conflicts interfered with helping those who had come to us for help in self-understanding. These intimate encounters were one of the most insightful growth experiences I ever had. They ended only when Elisabeth and I emigrated to Canada.

I had meanwhile obtained my Ph D on the basis of a thesis in which I had performed a content analysis on the free descriptions of their problems by applicants to some psychoanalytic clinics where I had worked. I avoided self-fulfilling prophecies by using pre-existing data. I learnt to take nothing for granted and to be sceptical about statistics from my *Doktorvater* (supervisor), Louis E. Raths, when he taught us that, if three pencils cost 15¢, one pencil costs 5¢ if, and only if, the price of all three pencils is the same and there is no special sale. Raths's life interest was the development of values through experience.

1.7.2   At Regina, in the Canadian prairies, this form of closely working together with colleagues could not be resumed. However, I was going to develop there a quite different kind of intimate relationship from which I still derive deep gratification.

After long, serious considerations Elisabeth and I had decided not to have any children. While she works mostly with small children and their parents, I work exclusively with adults. I consider my students as adults and treat them as such. I quite likely would do the same with my children if we had any. My own childhood memories do not contain much to guide me in treating children as children. As a consequence, the only children to whom I can relate are other people's children who are no longer children but are young adults.

With some of my graduate students I developed intimate friendships. We discuss their and my work together. Those who have become full-fledged psychologists and moved away correspond with me and visit us when they come to Regina, as we visit them in their new places. Those who now have their own families have made us part of them so that their children have become our grandchildren in some way. My former students who share their lives, their gratifications, and their frustrations with us, and who with their spouses share ours, have greatly contributed to the lessening of my alienation.

One of them in particular has contributed to this book, though others have too through discussions in my seminars. Gerald Farthing, who returned to this province, though not to Regina, after earning his Ph D at the University of British Columbia, read the entire manuscript and made many useful critical comments.

1.8   In January of 1968, while we were still in the U.S. I had become convinced that our anti-war efforts were fruitless. The internal and external use of force by Washington reminded me so much of Hitler's rise to power that Elisabeth and I decided to turn down an unexpected and, in terms of my interests, very attractive offer I had received from Duquesne University and to leave the country. This meant not only giving up a number of jobs but also dissolving our practices, leaving a beautiful home and garden, and leaving a number of good friends behind. On the other hand it meant living up to our convictions. Three years later, my convictions made me resign from the American Psychological Association.

1.8.1 When we moved to Canada I had for the first time in my life chosen an identity. We had travelled in Canada extensively before, visited Regina before moving there, and had made a conscious and free choice. Without the assistance of another analyst I was now going to consolidate my identity.

1.8.2 We had moved to a country which is no melting pot, but a multicultural mosaic. One can be a Canadian without giving up one's roots, nay by even strengthening them.

1.8.2.1 As I tried to resume the ties with my immediate roots I recognized that my image of my parents had become blurred. It was by now a conglomeration of my direct memories, of bits and pieces pulled together from their letters and diaries, from what others who had known them had told me, and from what various analysts had reflected to me on the basis of my free associations. The complexities of what I came to call 'personicating,' the formation of impressions about others, became clear to me. I was assisted in the process by Elisabeth and by the work of Gerhard Kaminski, whom we later had the pleasure of visiting at Tübingen.

1.8.2.2 Seeing that I could not achieve closure in this direction, I turned to a wider aspect of my roots. I delved into German-language psychology and corresponded with colleagues in Austria, Switzerland, East and West Germany. Lothar Sprung from East Berlin and Klaus Horn from the Sigmund Freud Institut at Frankfurt supplied me with critical ideas and many otherwise almost unobtainable publications. During lecture tours I discussed issues of common interest with many European colleagues. The medical psychoanalysts Battegay, Benedetti, Lorenzer (cf. my 1979b), and Mitscherlich (cf. my 1979a) treated me always as an equal, which helped my feeling of identity. Some German-language colleagues were so familiar with English-language psychology that they introduced me to some aspects of it of which I had not even heard in North America.

1.8.2.3 Thus I heard in Europe for the first time about Heinz Kohut's work on narcissistic personality disorders. Realizing that here was an aspect of my self which I had not yet explored I spent some time with another analyst at Innsbruck while teaching in the department of Ivo Kohler and learning of his diverse interests. Those analytic sessions – my only ones in German – led to some of the insights in this chapter.

1.8.2.4 Finally I got to the deepest root: In order to push the open-ended process of search for identity further I had to make a Sartrian choice in favour of authenticity – I had to accept being a Jew. After learning that according to Reconstructionist interpretation the 'chosen people' consists of those who themselves have chosen to be Jews, I was ready to make that choice.

Faith is not a matter of choice. I cannot choose to accept Judaism as a religion. But, as I now discovered, Jewish men differ in two non-religious respects from any other group of men: they constitute the only group of men who for about three thousand years have learnt to read and write, and who for about two thousand years learnt more than a single language. I begin my exploration of psychologies with a chapter on the role of language. The following chapters contain values, views of the world and of human beings, and emotions, as well as a casuistry (in the non-derogatory meaning of that word) which have been handed down to me through generations of Jews living in Germany. One of the last links in that chain was my maternal grandfather, the pharmacist, the eternal scholar, the businessman who supported my parents and paid for my schooling in Switzerland, the lover of music and literature – the one to whom I ran as a boy when I wanted unconditional acceptance. He who had his two children raised as Lutherans returned under Hitler – contrary to my parents – to Judaism. He was authentic.

1.9 Like my personal history, this book contains many contradictions. It is one sign of having resolved some of one's anal conflicts that one is no longer obsessively seeking to 'eliminate' all contradictions. Contradictions and conflicts with their frustrations are part of *la condition humaine*. As my companion, wife, and collaborator, Elisabeth, has taught me: 'It is a very imperfect world!' And as I hear her wonderful free laughter I am reminded of my uncle's typically Berlin remarks when I phoned him on his eighty-seventh birthday at the hospital: 'I sure will get out of here, but I like to get out alive.' I am reminded of the only solution to our problems, the solution which unites me with Nietzsche and Hesse and with generations of persecuted Jews: not to take oneself too seriously and to laugh at my own foolishness.

2 Psychologists Caught in Different Linguistic Frameworks

Psychologists Caught in Different Linguistic Frameworks
My friend has no sex.

2.0   All sciences require language: for reasoning, for reporting research for communication and critical discussion among scientists. Languages differ in vocabulary, that is, in available concepts, and in structure. Consequently, the perceptions and conceptualizations of their users differ (Humboldt 1836; Whorf 1956; Lee 1959). In Anastasi's (1970) words: 'The nature and breadth of concepts available to an individual in solving a problem or performing an intellectual task obviously vary ... with the language he has been taught' (p. 900). If one believes that a psychologist is 'an individual' and if psychologists do not merely blindly 'run experiments' but happen to be 'solving a problem or performing an intellectual task,' then Anastasi's statement applies even to psychologists.

Anastasi made the above statement in relation to situations in which others are presented with problems and intellectual tasks by psychologists. The conceptualization of those problems and intellectual tasks is, however, in itself a problem and an intellectual task and will 'obviously vary ... with the language [the psychologist] has been taught.' In other words, what kind of issues psychologists consider relevant (cf. chapter 3), what theories (cf. chapters 4 and 5) and methods (cf. chapter 7) they apply, and how they relate to other people (cf. chapters 6, 8, and 10) vary with the language (or languages!) they have been educated in.[1]

---

1 In many countries only people who have learnt more than one language are considered 'educated.'

2.1   It is difficult for a unilingual individual to grasp how much of a frame of reference a language represents, how much his or her perspectives result from language. Most Anglo-American psychologists are unilingual and do not seem to realize the implications of Anastasi's statement. They also are unaware of some of the idiosyncrasies of English.[2] In this chapter I shall try to make Anastasi's point more understandable to unilingual psychologists by providing them with a number of examples of some of the differences between different languages.

2.2

2.2.1   *Ich bin ein Mensch.* Я человек. Psychology is the science of the *Mensch*, человек. The German word *Mensch* and the Russian word человек can be translated into English by 'human being' or 'man,' and into French by *être humain* or *homme*, but neither language possesses a single unambiguous word corresponding to *Mensch* and *tchelovyek*. 'Human being' and *être humain* are verb-adjective combinations which are not common in everyday colloquial speech. 'Man' and *homme* are not sexually neutral because they designate not simply a *Mensch* but also a male *Mensch*. Thus, the use of the word 'man' for *Mensch* has led in recent years to lengthy discussions concerning 'sexism,' with corresponding changes of words like 'chairman' to 'chairperson' etc. – discussions which appear somewhat ridiculous to me, whose mother tongue could not lead to such disputes.

2.2.2   In the preceding chapter, I wrote about my *Eltern*. This German word, meaning 'parents,' has no singular like its English translation. In German one cannot speak about a parent without indicating the sex. One must speak about both parents or about one's father or one's mother. *Eltern* are inseparable. A parent of unidentified sex does not exist in German. In French neither *Eltern* nor parents exist. *Mes parents* are my relatives. The French word *parents* is defined in the *Larousse* dictionary as 'those from whom one descends.' In everyday usage, it includes

---

2 It is probably no coincidence that two Anglo-American psychologists who discussed some of the limitations set by language and presented examples from several languages, William James and Robert MacLeod, were both phenomenologists, i.e., they were aware of the significance and meaning of frameworks and perspectives. Most non-Anglo-American psychologists read at least one language besides their mother tongue fluently, as evidenced by the references in their publications.

---

uncles and aunts. It has two forms in the singular, one masculine, *un parent*, and one feminine, *une parente*, meaning a male and a female relative respectively. The Spanish word for parents is *padres*. It means also 'fathers' both in the secular and in the clerical sense. Thus, the French word *parents* and the Spanish word *padres* have very different connotations which they share neither with the English word 'parents' nor with the German word *Eltern*.

2.2.3   Just as *ein Mensch* and a parent can be male or female, many other words denoting people do not indicate in Chinese, Cree, Indonesian, or English what the individual's sex is. Whereas English distinguishes between an actor and an actress, a waiter and a waitress, or a host and a hostess, a friend, a worker, a teacher, and a psychologist can be either a woman or a man. The recently evolved use of 'they' to refer to a single individual makes it possible to talk at length about someone without revealing the sex of that individual. This is impossible in many other languages which have separate words for male and female friends, workers, teachers, psychologists, etc. (German: *Freund / Freundin, Arbeiter / Arbeiterin, Lehrer / Lehrerin, Psychologe / Psychologin*; French: *ami / amie, ouvrier / ouvrière, instituteur / institutrice, le psychologue / la psychologue*). In addition, the indication of sex is not limited to nouns but extends to adjectives, articles like 'the' and 'a,' and, in Russian, even to verb forms like 'was,' 'went,' and 'pondered.' On the other hand, these languages do not use words like 'males' and 'females' which distinguish sex but do not differentiate between humans and rats.

2.2.4   Of general relevance to social psychology are the relationships among people. While in English everyone is addressed by 'you' – which recently also has come to mean 'anyone' – and no distinction can be made between addressing an individual or a group, other languages differentiate between speaking to a single individual or several people and between different relationships between the speaker and those being addressed. These distinctions vary greatly among different languages. Thus, in French a distinction is made between addressing an individual with whom I am intimate and one with whom I have a more formal relationship, but the word used for addressing a single individual in a formal relationship is also used for addressing several people irrespective of the relationship. In German different words exist for addressing one or several people with whom one has an intimate relationship, while the formal form of address does not differentiate between the number of people spoken to. The distinctions are clearest in Spanish, where four different forms are used for addressing: (1) a single individual in an intimate relationship (*tu*), (2) several people in a close relationship (*os*), (3) an individual in a formal relationship (*usted*), and (4) several people in a formal relationship (*ustedes*). While these distinctions characterize the closeness of the relationship between the speaker and those spoken to, in Japanese distinctions are made on the basis of status.

In English interpersonal relations are further blurred by addressing new acquaintances immediately by first name and calling 'friends' those whose last names one does not even know.

When frictions arise in such relationships is it really irrelevant that the English speaker is 'mad' at the other, that is, insane when angry, while the German-speaking individual is *böse*, which means 'evil,' and the Francophone is *fâché*, meaning 'sorry'? Is their attitude towards the feeling and expression of anger the same? How would a unilingual psychologist even realize that such questions can be asked?

2.2.5   Even more important for psychology is the relationship between the experimenter and the other participants in an experiment. This relationship is characterized in English by calling the other participants 'subjects.' This term clearly denotes a hierarchical relationship. 'Subjects' are inferiors who owe loyalty to a sovereign, 'person[s] subject to political rule' (Fowler and Fowler 1964; for a detailed discussion cf. Lorenz 1977). They are subjected to the experimental method freely chosen by the psychologist. In German the other participants in psychological experiments are referred to as 'partners in the experiment' (*Versuchspartner*) or as 'experimental people' (*Versuchspersonen*), neither of which implies a difference in status between the experimenter and others. Thus, English psychological jargon implies a different position within psychology of the psychologist and of other people (cf. chapter 6).

2.2.5.1   Moreover, 'subject' can designate a man, a woman, a child, and an animal. Not too rarely does the reader of a psychological journal article in English realize only after several paragraphs that the experiment was carried out with rats. This can simply not happen in German. *Versuchspartner* and *Versuchspersonen* are always human beings. The word for animal subjects is *Versuchstiere*. But the distinction between humans and animals goes further. In both French and German, different words must be used for the mouth of a human being and that of an animal. In French human and animal hair are differentiated by different words. German has different words for 'eat' depending on whether a human being or an animal does it. Both these languages contain different words for teaching something to a human being and to an animal.

Since all of these words are used in connection with the psychology of learning, it does not seem surprising that French and German psychologists do not conduct as many learning experiments with animals and do not as easily generalize from animal experiments to human beings as their Anglo-American colleagues. Nor may it be coincidental that a separate and distinct animal psychology called 'ethology' was started and developed by German-speaking scientists who do not consider themselves actual psychologists.[3]

2.2.6　　Of particular relevance for cognitive psychology seems the lack of different words in French for 'consciousness,' 'conscience,' and 'conscientiousness.' English has only one word 'to know' where French distinguishes between *savoir* and *connaître* and German between *wissen, kennen,* and *erkennen*. It is very difficult to explain to a unilingual English speaker the difference between an *Erlebnis* and an *Erfahrung*, both translatable only by 'experience,' or between *Verstand* and *Vernunft*, which are both translated as 'reason.' Perhaps this explains the lack of interest among Anglo-American psychologists in the psychology of thinking and the psychology of subjective experience.

All languages are limited. The attempts to overcome some of those limitations, for example by using words from another language like *Gestalt, Anlagen, Zeitgeist, Weltanschauung*, are never too successful. Someone at home in the language from which such words originate finds frequently that they are misunderstood by users of another language community. The limitations become particularly serious when they are shared by a number of languages, so that even multilingual psychologists and other scientists do not notice them. I wonder how much confusion among various groups of scientists is due to the fact that such important words as 'to determine,' 'to decide,' and 'to establish' (German: *bestimmen, entscheiden, feststellen*) can refer to both active causation and passive registration of events, and that a given context need not elucidate which of the two meanings applies.

3　Konrad Lorenz, the most widely known ethologist, has an MD degree and a PHD in zoology.

2.3   One of the problems common to English, French, German, Spanish, and other standard European languages (Whorf [1956] referred to 'Standard Average European,' which he abbreviated SAE) is that they express processes by nouns instead of by verbs. By speaking about 'a process,' 'the development,' 'the growth,' etc., we freeze 'the movement' into 'something' stationary and thereby abstract from its 'flow.' We objectify or reify what is proceeding, moving, growing, developing, and treat, at least linguistically, those 'movements' as if they were things or objects. The same applies to any 'change' taking place over shorter or longer periods of time like 'events,' 'episodes,' 'actions,' and, obviously, 'behaviour.' This petrification of 'motion' seems to me an enormous handicap of SAE which, as this paragraph demonstrates, cannot be avoided in these languages. It seems that, for example, in Hopi one can express 'movement' without resorting to the same kind of words which are used for things.

2.3.1   On the other hand, the fact that even our relationship to things can be expressed – and possibly also experienced – in different ways is evident from a comparison of Germanic and Romance languages with Russian. Where the former use the very 'to have' without implication of ownership, as in 'I have a cigarette,' the Russian says 'cigarette at me,' simply indicating the approximate location of the object. Not even the word 'is' appears in the Russian sentence. It may be no coincidence that the problem of 'the "is" of identity' was first discussed by Korzybski (1933), who learnt Polish and Russian before English. Language without the verb 'to have' and without a present tense of the verb 'to be' is almost impossible to imagine for people who know only Germanic and/or Romance languages.

2.3.2   When abstract concepts, particularly hypothetical constructs which are obvious human inventions and which, in SAE at least, are also expressed by nouns, are combined with 'is,' reification becomes quite dangerous because psychologists like other scientists tend to forget that they are no longer speaking of phenomena. When we say that someone 'has an archaic superego' or that 'a habit is' extinguished, we freqently overlook the fact that 'superego' and 'habit' are mere ways of conceptualizing what we have observed but are not 'something' observable. This linguistically supported unconcern for the difference between perceivable objects and events on the one hand, and hypothetical constructs on the other (and the confusion between the latter and generalizations from observables including emotions), greatly hampers 'the progress' of science and of the science of psychology in particular. When anxiety is called a hypothetical construct, though one can definitely perceive it in oneself and often also in others, and when the word 'dog' is called an abstraction because it does not refer to any specific dog, the psychological and scientific issues involved in what I am concerned about are entirely confused. A hypothetical construct is an idea created by someone to explain observed events. The hypothetical construct is describable but not observable. It can be done away with if it is not found useful for the explanation of the events which it was intended to explain. This happened in physics with 'phlogiston,' which had been invented to explain why certain substances burn. If one does not realize that such a hypothetical construct does not denote an existing thing, one holds on to the word and cannot give it up. If the word is assumed to denote something that 'is' or that someone 'has,' one cannot simply forget about it. 'Is,' 'has,' and the nouns standing for hypothetical constructs thus prevent science from progressing to new conceptualizations.

2.3.2.1 One particularly dangerous word is 'fact.' It comes from Latin *factum*, meaning 'made.' Facts are made by people who believe that something is a fact. But facts are not something. As Hanson (1969, p. 172) stated: 'Of those of us who so readily speak of observing the facts, looking at them, collecting them, etc. – and most of us *do* so speak – has any ever asked what observation of a fact would be like? What do facts look like? In what receptacle might we collect them? I can photograph *objects* like x-ray tubes, or *events* like fluorescence, or *situations* like the set-up of an x-ray diffraction experiment. But what sort of photograph would a photograph of a fact be? Asking the question in this way is like biting the forbidden apple. Facts can never again be regarded in the fat, dumb, and happy way we looked at them before.' In other words, we do not 'perceive' facts but we 'conceive of' something as a fact. Not only in everyday life, but even in scientific publications by psychologists, 'perceive' is used where 'conceive of' would be correct and would make it clear that one does not describe something observable but an idea in one's mind.

2.4 The 'unbelievable sloppiness of typically American definitions of terms,' of which Metzger complained (personal letter of 21/4/71 to me), also comes to the fore in the use of 'I feel' for 'I believe' or 'I think,' even in scientific psychological publications. The confusion between *perceiving* and *conceiving* or *conceptualizing*, and between *feeling* and *believing* or *thinking*, may be related to the emphasis on the study of learning at the expense of research on perception and thinking among Anglo-American psychologists. The confusion is a peculiarity of English usage which does not correspond to any parallel expression in German.

In order to make the implications of linguistic frameworks clearer to those readers who know only English and to demonstrate the relevance of language for psychology I shall critically[4] present some concrete examples.

2.4.1   The confusion concerning the word 'believe' is reflected in Rokeach's work on 'belief systems' which led to the construction of the widely used 'Dogmatism Scale.' In his theory of 'belief systems' Rokeach confounds existential beliefs like 'I do not believe in flying saucers,' which means 'I do not believe that flying saucers exist,' with value judgments of the kind 'I do not believe in communism,' which does NOT mean or even imply 'I do not believe that communism exists,' but which, to the contrary, means 'I DO believe that communism exists, but I do not approve of it.' Only in the English vernacular, and neither in German nor in French, can 'I believe in communism' or 'I do not believe in communism' be expressed by using the word 'believe,' and can such statements thereby be said to express a 'belief' instead of a value judgment or likes and dislikes.

Though Rokeach (1960, 1968) attempted to clarify his concepts by examples, he did not dispel Foppa's (1967) complaint about 'explanatory systems based on ambiguous concepts and relationships' (p. 190). Rokeach's examples rather beg than answer questions. The illustration of 'primitive beliefs, 100 per cent consensus' by 'I believe this is a table,' 'I believe this is my mother,' and 'I believe my name is so-and-so' (Rokeach 1968, p. 6) contains a large number of ambiguities. Does 'I believe this is a table' mean 'I believe this is not a stool' or 'I believe the correct English word for this is "table"' or 'I believe I am neither hallucinating nor dreaming but my perception is that of a real table'?

---

4 'Critical' comes from the Greek word 'to discern.' In German *kritisch* still has the same meaning, as in Kant's three 'Critiques' (of pure reason, practical reason, and judgment) and in Holzkamp's (1972) *Kritische Psychologie*. In English it means 'faultfinding' rather than 'discerning,' which may, in part, account for the dearth of critical psychology in North America. I use the word 'critical' here in its original Greek meaning.

Psychologically, these three meanings of 'I believe this is a table' are certainly not identical. Nor do Rokeach's other examples throw more light on his concept. Does 'I believe this is my mother' mean 'I trust my memory with respect to the woman whom I remember to have mothered me as far back as I can remember' or 'I believe that I was told the truth when I was told that this woman gave birth to me'? The latter meaning represents an 'authority belief' which, however, forms a separate category in Rokeach's system. This confuses the issue even further. So does 'I believe my name is so-and-so' which represents an arbitrary relationship between an individual and a name which people can change. If it is to mean 'I believe that my parents named me so-and-so' then it too is an 'authority belief.' And so is 'I believe in God' which Rokeach classified as 'primitive beliefs, zero consensus.' Or 'I believe in God' is based on a mystical experience and then is psychologically indistinguishable from 'I believe that the table I visually and haptically perceive exists independent of my experience of it.'

The lack of clear definitions of various 'types of beliefs' may account for the fact that Rokeach's (1960) 'Dogmatism Scale' failed to pass his own first attempt to validate it and was subsequently validated by him only with the help of his students who were familiar with his hypothesis (pp. 102f.). His whole theory of 'belief systems' rests on and collapses with the vagueness of his definitions. Such a theory would require a phenomenal analysis of beliefs which might result in the distinction between the taken-for-granted, the questioned, the doubted, and the disbelieved.

2.4.2   Osgood's 'Semantic Differential' reveals clearly that its inventor was unilingual. In what is held out to be a 'comparative study of cultures' (Osgood 1964) appears not a single example of a word used in a language other than English. In order to know what non-English-speaking participants were asked to indicate on the Semantic Differential Scales, and to judge whether any meaningful comparisons between different language groups can be made, one needs, however, to know which words were actually used by the field-workers who did the research for Osgood. One scale is identified by Osgood as 'sweet-sour.' Yet this opposition does not exist in French, which is one of the languages in which the Semantic Differential Scales are said to have been used. The common opposites in French are *doux-amère*, which means in English 'sweet-bitter,' and *sucré-aigre*, which means 'sugared-sour,' while the opposition of *doux* and *aigre* strikes a French-speaking individual as very awkward and clearly incorrect. Another problem arises with the translation into French of the dimension 'tall-short.' French has no word which corresponds to the general usage of 'tall.' Instead, French uses *grand* for people and *haut* for buildings. But *grand* means also 'great' and *haut* means also 'high.' Thus, when the predicate *grand* is attributed to a human being out of context – as is the case on the Semantic Differential – it can mean that the individual is tall, great, or both (cf. Brandt 1972a, 1978).

2.5   The problem of translating, which raises serious doubts about the meaning Osgood attributes to the 'measurement of meaning' in his 'comparative study of cultures,' crops up again and again in English translations of foreign language psychological works. Frequently, basic concepts of a theory have been translated into English by words with quite different connotations from those used by the foreign psychologist. Such mistranslations have sometimes led to far-reaching misunderstandings of a psychological system. These misunderstandings are then propagated through discussions and popularizations of those psychologies in their distorted form by psychologists who are not familiar with the originals but rely entirely on translations. Two psychologies which are widely misunderstood by unilingual Anglo-American psychologists and non-psychologists alike are those of Freud and of Piaget.

2.5.1
2.5.1.1 Freud's basic concepts were seriously distorted in the English translation of the corresponding terms (Brandt 1961a, 1966a, 1977a). By referring to *das Ich* as 'the ego' instead of 'the I' (the French translation reads correctly *le moi* and the Spanish correspondingly *el yo*), Freud's concept is emptied of its existential immediacy and becomes a mere abstraction. The term 'id,' which ought to have been rendered in English as 'it,' cannot be related to Nietzsche's explanation of 'it thinks.' The English title 'Analysis Terminable and Interminable' of Freud's paper dealing with 'finite and infinite analysis' has led to ridicule of psychoanalysis which is justified only in terms of the mistranslation. The translation of process terms by structural ones and of active grammatical constructions by passive ones resulted in conceptualizations of psychoanalysis as a mechanistic instead of a dynamic theory. Thus, the open-ended emancipatory development expressed in Freud's *'Wo Es war, soll Ich werden,'* which means 'Where it was I ought to become,' has been turned into a technological 'Where id was, there shall ego be,' leading to the erroneous impression that psychoanalysts are technicians who can replace one structure by another. The correct translation 'Where it was I ought to become' shows that psychoanalysis

is much closer to 'Humanistic psychology' with Allport's emphasis on 'becoming' and Maslow's idea of 'self-actualization' than the promoters of 'The Third Force' ever admitted.[5]

Psychoanalytic theory and practice have always stood in a dialectic relation to each other. During his lifetime Freud altered his theory on the basis of observations in his psychoanalytic practice and his technique on the basis of changes in his theory. In both psychoanalytic theory and practice language plays an absolutely central role, as illustrated particularly in *The Psychopathology of Everyday Life*, but also in *The Interpretation of Dreams* and all other examples of Freud's self-analysis and analyses of others. The *exact* wording of an utterance, including slips of the tongue and other errors, as well as the tone of voice forms the raw data for analysis (cf. Lorenzer 1970, 1973, 1976). Even the slightest change in the wording of an utterance is psychoanalytically of relevance and significance, so that any change in the translation may lead to a serious misunderstanding of the inferences drawn from an analysand's remark.

Freud's consciousness of language expressed itself also in the content and in the form of his writings. In a paper on the contradictory meaning of the primal words (1910) he analysed specifically some aspects of various languages, among which he knew French and English well enough to write and publish articles in these languages. For the form of his German works Freud received the Goethe-Preis, the highest German literary distinction.

2.5.1.2 Piaget's first book (1923) dealt with language, *La langage et la pensée chez l'enfant*. It was followed up by years of research and innumerable publications on concept formation and the development of intellectual structures. All the more deplorable are the many distorted renderings of his basic concepts. By translating *l'intelligence* as 'intelligence' the translators have given the impression that Piaget is concerned with abilities as they are expressed by the English word. As the whole debate

---

5 The idea of 'becoming' and 'self-realization' originated neither with the 'Third Force' nor with Freud. It was already expressed in exactly the same terms by the sixth century BC Greek poet Pindar, namely 'Become the one thou art,' and has been repeated by thinkers through the ages. It appears in Pindar's words in several of Nietzsche's works.

---

around IQ tests demonstrates, 'intelligence' is considered to be quantifiable and measurable. Above all, 'intelligence' is considered largely inherited and invariant, as indicated by IQ. However, *l'intelligence* is a structure of the mind which Piaget compared to two other structures, namely perception and habit. None of these structures were considered by him to be invariant. It is exactly their development through maturation and interaction with the environment which Piaget made the object of his lifelong research. Though he considered them as structures, he did so from a higher-order perspective as he did not regard them to be rigid. On the contrary, *l'intelligence, la perception,* and *l'habitude* were all three considered to be activities. A better translation into English of *l'intelligence* might be 'the intellect,' though this word too has connotations which differ from those of the French term. The latter corresponds most closely to the German word *Verstand*, for which no identical term exists in English.

2.5.2   There exists a dialectic relation between mistranslations and the introduction of different conceptualizations into Anglo-American psychology. As translations into English are made by behaviourists, non-behaviouristic concepts are couched in behaviourist language. Other behaviourists then conceptualize the foreign systems in behaviourist terms and are unable to become aware of conceptual differences.

2.5.2.1   The 'behaviourization' of Freud has been promoted by the translation of *Trieb* by 'instinct' instead of 'drive,' and of *freier Einfall* by 'free association' instead of 'spontaneously occurring ideas.' Psychoanalysis could thus be linked to 'Associationism' and 'S-R Psychology.' The result was such misrepresentations as the widely circulated *Primer of Freudian Psychology* by Hall (1954).

2.5.2.2   The 'behaviourization' of Piaget strikes a bilingual reader like myself not only in the above-discussed translation of the qualitatively changing activity *l'intelligence* by the quantifiable ability 'intelligence,' but particularly by the translation of *conduite* by means of the two basic behaviourist terms 'behaviour' and 'response.' Piaget defined *conduite: 'Toute conduite, qu'il s'agisse d'un acte déployé à l'extérieur, ou intériorisé en pensée, se présente comme une adaptation, ou, pour mieux dire, comme une réadaptation'* (1947, p. 10).[6] Such a readaptive act is certainly not a 'response.' The 'behaviourization' of Piaget is carried further by also translating *mouvements* and *motricité* by 'responses,' while using 'behaviour' indiscriminately as a translation of *conduite, comportement,* and *tâtonnement.* The general understanding of Piaget is also not promoted by the use of different English words for one and the same French word (e.g., *emboîtement* is variously rendered by 'formation,' 'fitting,' 'joining together,' and 'classification,' but never by 'nesting' which is the literal and in all instances most appropriate translation) and vice versa.

The 'behaviourization' of Piaget can further be recognized in the Anglo-American attempts to quantify his concepts and to apply his ideas to education. While the logician Piaget, whose lifework has been *l'épistémologie génétique,* that is, the understanding of the development of cognitive activities and processes, has usually been presented to Anglo-American students of psychology and education as a child psychologist, his works reveal not a technical but a hermeneutic interest. Piaget was not interested in speeding up learning, in changing behaviour, but in understanding the activities of the human mind.

The above examples illustrate various ways in which psychologists can be caught in linguistic frameworks and particularly so when they are unilingual and, in addition, unaware of their limitations. In Piaget's terms unilingual psychologists are egocentric, are aware of only a single point of view, namely the one inherent in the language they are familiar with and use, and are correspondingly not even aware of the possibility of different perspectives taken by different languages and their speakers. This egocentrism can, as I have tried to show in this chapter, be overcome only to a very limited extent by reading translations of works written from different viewpoints, because such translations frequently bring foreign – in at least two meanings of that word – theories and research in psychology in line with the Anglo-American behaviourist framework.

---

6 'Every *conduite* [move], whether it be externalized as action or internalized as thought, reveals itself as an adaptation or, rather, as a readaptation.'

2.6 But the problem of linguistic egocentrism, of the lack of objectivity and relativism in Piaget's terms and of perspectivity in phenomenological terms, can also not be solved by simply ignoring all psychological works which have not been published in English, like the works of the Soviet Union's leading psychologist in the 1950s, Sergei L. Rubinstein, which have been translated into twelve languages but not into English. Rubinstein's is by no means a unique fate. Wolfgang Metzger's definitive work on Gestalt psychology in all its aspects (i.e., going far beyond its application to perception) has been translated into a number of languages other than English. When I inquired with a European publisher about books in psychology which had not been translated into English and for which not even the translation rights had been sold, he sent me a list of 110 original French titles of books published by just one publisher.

The problem of the linguistic isolation of unilingual Anglo-American psychologists can, however, also not be solved – as many of them would wish – by having other psychologists publish their research in English. Though there exists a strong tendency in that direction, as illustrated by *The Japanese Journal of Psychology, The Scandinavian Journal of Psychology, Psychological Research* (which used to be *Psychologische Forschung*), and other English-language psychological journals from non-English countries, such a turn to scientific and particularly scientific psychological communication in a single language will lead to tunnel-vision within psychology but not to an increase of the visual field. These reflections lead me to

2.6.1 *The linguistic paradox* If, in order to communicate more universally, all psychologists resort to publishing in one and the same language, psychology will become less instead of more universally applicable to human beings.

Like all other scientists and human beings in general, psychologists must accept limitations. I have tried to show that each language has limitations and that no two languages share entirely the same limitations. The reduction of all of psychology or any other science to one universal language – be it English, mathematics, or any other – cannot but eliminate vast areas of human experience which cannot be 'understood'[7] by those outside a given linguistic reality. The best any psychologist can achieve is always a limited 'understanding' of human experiences and actions.

2.6.2   For those readers who, without being able to read German, wish to
familiarize themselves somewhat with recent developments in German-
language psychology, I wrote the chapters and book reviews indicated
by an asterisk (*) in the bibliography at the end of this book. I similarly
indicate other books in English which summarize aspects of German-
language psychology.

---

7 I use this word here in the sense in which Dilthey distinguished between
verstehende and *erklärende* psychology and which has been expanded by
Jaspers.

---

3 Psychologists Caught in Different Value Frameworks

Psychologists Caught in Different Value Frameworks
Navigare necesse est vivere non est necesse.

3.0 In the most widely used English-language psychological dictionary (English and English 1958) 'frame of reference' is defined as 'a system of standards or values, usually merely *implicit*, underlying and to some extent controlling an action' (emphasis in original). In line with stated aim of this book I shall attempt in this chapter to make some of the standards and values underlying the actions of psychologists explicit.

3.0.1 Standards and values need not be ethical standards and values. Values in the broadest sense underlie all human activities.[1] Human activities, in distinction from automatic or impulsive behaviour, can be conceptualized in terms of means and ends. We work towards ends using certain means. Both ends and means are chosen in any particular instance from among a variety of possible ends and means. By choosing one goal and one set of means over other possible ends and means one demonstrates that one values the end one works toward over other possible ends and the means one uses over other possible means. Every choice or decision with respect to means and ends usually involves explicitly or implicitly

---

1 Lorenzen (1974) suggested distinguishing between 'motion' in the physical sense, 'processes' taking place within organisms, the instinctual or automatic 'behaviour' of animals, and intentional 'activities' of human beings. Science is in this sense a human activity. Psychology is consequently the human activity which consists of the investigation of, among other issues, human activities.

---

several different value systems: utilitarian, financial, emotional, ethical, etc.

Psychology, like any other science, is a human mental and practical activity (Holzkamp 1968). By pursuing psychology psychologists demonstrate that, at least in terms of some value system, they value psychology as highly as or more highly than other possible activities. This does not exclude that different psychologists value different aspects of psychology and pursue psychology in terms of different values.

3.0.2   In this chapter I want to discuss only some limited aspects of the issue of values in psychology. I am not going to deal with ethical values, which will be mentioned within a different frame of reference. I am concerned here with the frequently mentioned issue of the relevance of psychology (Deese 1969; Holzkamp 1970; Silverman 1971; Mitscherlich 1971; Hornstein 1973; Sprung 1976 – to refer to just a few psychologists on both sides of the forty-ninth parallel, the Atlantic, and the Iron Curtain) and with what Habermas has called *Erkenntnisinteresse* (cognitive interest). According to Rubinstein (1974) 'value is the relevance of something in the world for human being' (p. 290). What is relevant to me I value and vice versa. But it need not be relevant and valuable for someone else. Nor is relevance (value) independent of circumstances. Something may be relevant in one context and not in another. I shall, therefore, address myself specifically to the two questions: 'relevant to whom?' and 'relevant for what?'

3.1   NOMOLOGICAL VERSUS HERMENEUTIC SCIENCES (HABERMAS)
3.1.1   What an individual psychologist or other scientist considers relevant depends largely on her or his interests in pursuing that science. Habermas (1971) distinguished two basic kinds of 'cognitive' or 'knowledge-constitutive interests': the technical, which aims 'at the comprehension of an objectified reality' and its 'possible technical control,' and the practical, which aims 'at the maintenance of the intersubjectivity of mutual understanding, within whose horizon reality can first appear as something' (p. 176). Habermas considers the latter practical because its goal is to reach consensus among scientists on the basis of some traditional self-understanding. If the understanding of the world proceeds by self-reflection, critique of individual rationalizations and collective ideologies, of commonly accepted myths, Habermas speaks of emancipatory interest: 'The experience of reflection articulates itself substantially in the concept of a self-formative process ... In

self-reflection, knowledge for the sake of knowledge comes to coincide with the interest in autonomy and responsibility.[2] For the pursuit of reflection knows itself as a movement of emancipation. Reason is at the same time subject to the interest in reason.[3] We can say that it obeys an *emancipatory cognitive interest*, which aims at the pursuit of reflection' (1971, p. 197f. – original emphasis).

3.1.2   Habermas points out that the different cognitive interests are related to different sciences and to different scientific methods. The differentiation is made along the distinction between *Naturwissenschaften* (natural sciences) and *Geisteswissenschaften* (mental sciences or human sciences, roughly corresponding to J.S. Mill's 'moral sciences'). Habermas refers to the former also as 'nomological' and as 'empirical-analytic' and to the latter as 'hermeneutic sciences.' The *Geisteswissenschaften* include philosophy, history, theology, jurisprudence, philology, aesthetics, and the social sciences. They rely most heavily on hermeneutics, that is, on the interpretation of verbal and non-verbal communications. Psychology is considered by some a natural science and by others a *Geisteswissenschaft*. In the German-speaking countries many psychologists have a *Dr. rer. nat.* (doctor of natural sciences) while others have a *Dr. phil.* (PhD).

According to Habermas the natural sciences pursue a technical interest. Their principal method is the controlled experiment.[4] The *Geisteswissenschaften* pursue a practical interest through the hermeneutic method when they interpret texts on the basis of accepted rules. 'A critical social science, however, will not remain satisfied with [producing nomological knowledge]. It is concerned with going beyond this

---

2 'Autonomy and responsibility' translates *Mündigkeit* which comes from *Mund* = human mouth and means literally 'majority,' 'of age,' i.e., having a voice in public.

3 *Vernunft*, i.e., reason in the sense of reasonable.

4 The problem of categorizing becomes quite evident here. From the discussion in chapter 4 the question may arise whether to consider theoretical physics as a natural science in the sense of *Erfahrungswissenschaft* (science based on experience, empirical science) or as a *Geisteswissenschaft* pursuing a hermeneutic interest.

---

goal to determine when theoretical statements grasp invariant regularities of social action as such and when they express ideologically frozen relations of dependence that can in principle be transformed. To the extent that this is the case, the *critique of ideology*, as well, moreover, as *psychoanalysis*, take into account that information about lawlike connections sets off a process of reflection in the consciousness of those whom the laws are about. Thus the level of unreflected consciousness, which is one of the initial conditions of such laws, can be transformed' (1971, p. 310 – translator's emphasis).

3.1.3　In order to apply my understanding of Habermas specifically to various approaches in psychology I formulate his categorizations as follows. The technical interest is directed at changes in the physical world including observable human behaviour. The hermeneutic interest aims at greater understanding of the world including one's own actions and those of others. The emancipatory interest has as its goal the liberation of human beings from rationalizations and prejudices and thereby the increase of options among alternatives. Correspondingly, I shall refer to 'technical psychology,' 'hermeneutic psychology,' and 'emancipatory psychology.' While the three kinds of interest are not mutually exclusive, one of them may clearly dominate the pursuit of psychology by any given psychologist or school of psychology. One's definition of 'science' and of 'psychology' will be related to one's interest in psychology.

3.2　TECHNICAL PSYCHOLOGY The technical interest in science expresses itself in the mention of 'science and technology' in the same breath and the lack of a distinction between the two. While many Europeans at least attempt to differentiate between science and technology, such a distinction is usually not made by Anglo-Americans. The latter consider science as the servant of technology, that is, as serving to change the environment, including other human beings. Correspondingly, science is defined by Anglo-American scientists as largely consisting of the use of the experimental method, which in turn requires prediction, control, and measurement. Under this definition of science, technology stands in a dialectic relationship to science: technology not only results from science but also provides it with ever new tools for control and measurement.

In line with the definition of science in terms of a specific method, 'psychology' is defined as 'the study of behaviour.' Since, however, any 'scientist must ... be concerned to solve problems about the behavior of nature' (Kuhn 1970a, p. 168), this definition does not distinguish the subject matter of psychology from that of other sciences. What seems usually to be meant by that definition is 'the study of the observable movements of animals and of other human beings and the results thereof.'

3.2.1   Technical science claims to be value-free. Since values, interests, and relevance are not observable in others but can only be inferred, questions concerning these issues cannot be investigated by a psychology restricting itself to the control and measurement of observable movements. Such a psychology cannot be critical. It cannot reflect upon itself. It considers critique and self-reflection to be 'armchair psychology'[5] and rejects hermeneutic and emancipatory psychologies as unscientific.

Technical psychology reached its extreme form in behaviour modification, which according to one of its prime defenders 'lacks theory' and is, therefore, 'reduced to a technology rather than a science' which is as 'it should be' (London 1972, p. 916). London wants psychologists to devote themselves merely 'to building treatment methods that work' (p. 913). He exhorts 'the remedial branch of this business to stop worrying about its scientific pretentions ... and to devise a kind of engineering subsidiary' (p. 919).

Any critique of technical psychology must be made from the perspective of a hermeneutic science, be it epistemology, hermeneutic psychology, or sociology of science. Even London's prescriptions, which contain unreflected value judgments, interests, and issues of relevance, cannot be made within a technical psychological frame of reference.

3.3   HERMENEUTIC PSYCHOLOGY Einstein wrote: 'The object of all science, whether natural science or psychology, is to co-ordinate our

---

5   This expression has no German equivalent and appears in English in various German psychological dictionaries. While those by Dorsch (1976) and by Arnold, Eysenck, and Meili (1972) merely explain the meaning of the term, the dialectic-materialist *Wörterbuch der Psychologie* by Clauss (1976) adds that 'the Behaviourist arm-chair-taboo ... contained the positivist fallacy that psychological research can or ought to be pursued without theoretical assumptions.'

---

experiences and to bring them into a logical system' (1923, p. 1). Charles Singer writes in the *Encyclopaedia Britannica* (1961) article on 'Science': '...Science is one of the major activities of our minds... Science may perhaps be regarded as a mood in which we consider our world.' Holzkamp (1964, 1968) considers science as a human activity aiming at the greatest clarity of definitions and greatest communicability. These definitions of science clearly differentiate it from technology: the latter relies on doing, the former on thinking (cf. chapter 9).

Psychologists who consider science to be an activity of the mind usually define psychology by clearly distinguishing it from all other sciences. Thus, Metzger (1966) describes psychology as the only science in which the investigator and the object of his investigation can exchange roles – as, for instance, the Gestalt psychologists frequently did. Similarly, Bischoff (1966) discusses psychology as the science in which the human being is simultaneously subject and object – as, for instance, in psychoanalysis – and can therefore take two 'standpoints': the prototype of the human being can be either the other or the investigator himself. Holzkamp (1964) names as the 'three-fold subject matter of psychology: experiences as such, other people, and the phenomenal world.' Also a psychology whose 'true destination is to understand human beings and to make them complete' (Rubinstein 1973, p. 341) is both hermeneutic and emancipatory.

3.3.1   A hermeneutic psychology thus makes it possible to pursue a psychology of psychologists and a psychology of psychology, namely, a critical, self-reflective psychology, and thereby a discussion of what is relevant to whom and for what. Such a critical, self-reflective psychology is even a requirement in line with Kaminski's statement: 'Any psychology ought to ask itself at least also this: whether its homo psychologicus be capable of living, whether he could develop society, whether he be able to bring about and apply psychology' (1970, p. 5).

From the perspective of a psychology in the service of hermeneutic and emancipatory interests, 'psychoanalysis is relevant to us as the only tangible example of a science which methodically engages in self-reflection' (Habermas 1968, p. 262), whereas the work done in psychological laboratories under experimental procedures appears largely as irrelevant and meaningless 'busy-work.' It seems unrelated to real life and done merely to promote a self-perpetuating profession. It 'reveals very little about the psychology of animals let alone of men' (Peters 1969, p. 136).

3.4 PROBLEMS CONCERNING THE ANALYSIS OF RELEVANCE To reca-pitulate: cognitive interests are values which together with other values, with one's language, culture, emotional needs, etc., determine what is considered to be relevant. The historical origin of these values will be discussed in chapter 9. I shall now reflect upon the values of psychologists in terms of the concept of relevance.

I have presented two conceptualizations of science and of psychology which are largely incommensurable as they belong to two different models of the world (Reese and Overton 1970; Overton and Reese 1973; cf. chapter 4). It will, therefore, be necessary to discuss the relevance of psychology separately for each of the two psychologies. The earlier questions must now be reformulated as: (1) to whom and for what is technical psychology relevant? and (2) to whom and for what is herme-neutic psychology relevant?

However, as demonstrated in section 3.2.1, neither the relevance of technical psychology nor the relevance of hermeneutic psychology can be discussed within the scientific framework of technical psychology. Hence, the relevances of both psychologies must be examined from the perspective of hermeneutic psychology.

In addition to distinguishing between the relevance of technical psychology and that of hermeneutic psychology, the analysis must be further broken down into the relevance of either psychology to techni-cal psychologists, to hermeneutic psychologists, and to human beings in general.

The discussion of 'relevant for what?' could lead to the consideration of an infinity of purposes. I shall, therefore, limit my analysis to some of the common goals of people in a competitive capitalist society and to some individual goals which I believe many human beings to have in common. Specifically, I shall deal with the relevance of the two psychologies to different human beings for the achievement of (1) survival, (2) power, and (3) bringing their experiences into a logical system.[6]

It must have become obvious to the reader by now that the analysis of the issue of the relevance of scientific psychology is extremely com-plex. The question 'Which psychology is relevant to whom for what?' has at least as many answers as result from the considerations of

---

6 These ends can be further problematized. I assume them here to be basic human strivings as proposed by Darwin, Nietzsche, and Einstein respectively.

---

different psychologies, different people, and different goals. A systematic analysis of this problem would go far beyond what can be discussed in a single chapter. I shall, therefore, limit myself to a discussion of some salient aspects of the problem and not even attempt an exhaustive and systematic analysis. Rather than following the earlier schema of psychologies – people – goals in that order, I shall discuss the psychologies and the people under the headings of different goals.

3.4.1 *The relevance of psychology for survival* The motto at the beginning of this chapter stems from the Hanseatic League, which may be considered the precursor of the modern multinational corporation. Translated into our language the motto means: 'The increase of the GNP is relevant, an individual's survival is not.' That view leads easily to a discussion of the relative cost and pay-off of psychological research with complete disregard for the relative cost and pay-off for the individuals labelled 'subjects.'

For all psychologists their respective psychology is relevant in terms of assuring their survival. Psychology is a means of making a living. As Holzkamp (1972) and Kvale (1973) have shown, experimental psychology fits in with a capitalist society. Technical psychology does not have the same relevance in terms of survival for the 'subjects' as for the psychologists, since psychological experiments do not provide steady employment for 'subjects.'

3.4.1.1 The monetary costs for psychological experiments are usually borne by the taxpayer and in some instances by funding organizations, all of whom are non-participants. The costs in terms of anxiety, physical discomfort, decrease in self-worth, time, and other aspects which cannot be expressed in dollars and cents, are borne by the participants, largely by students and other non-psychologists. As in any other capitalist enterprise, the pay-off goes in the first place to the employer, the experimental psychologist who, on the basis of his research, receives a salary increase or a new grant, while the pay-off for the 'subjects' consists merely in grades for a course or some token payment. Technical psychology thus seems relevant in terms of survival to technical psychologists but not to other people.[7]

---

7 Since hermeneutic psychology makes no categorical distinction between psychologists and other people (cf. section 6.1), the above conflict between costs and pay-offs does not arise in the same manner.

In order to achieve the greatest possible pay-off with the least possible cost, technical psychologists will produce whatever is most easily marketable in their society. It is thus relevant for their survival as psychologists that they work within accepted paradigms (Kuhn 1970a) rather than develop 'revolutionary' science (Popper 1970). They consequently attempt to verify rather than falsify and criticize established theories.

In terms of cost and pay-off, falsification of a theory to which one once adhered means loss of one's investment. Lichtenberg wrote during the Age of Enlightenment: 'Most professors defend their statements not because they are convinced of the truth of their statements but because they once claimed such truth' (p. 49). In our own time, Kuhn (1970a) presented evidence from the history of science that once a scientist has committed himself to a given paradigm it is well-nigh impossible for him to extricate himself from that paradigm. There are a few notable exceptions, like Niels Bohr who discarded his own model of the atom, P.W. Bridgman who hesitatingly acknowledged that 'neither does use of the tool of operational analysis put agreement on an almost automatic basis, as I had hoped' (1959, p. 245), and Freud who rejected his own topological theory. But such exceptions are rare. How many psychoanalysts who have invested tens of thousands of dollars in their own psychoanalysis, psychoanalytic supervision, and training at psychoanalytic institutes, in addition to obtaining a PhD in psychology or an MD plus specialization in psychiatry, can even consider abandoning the 'dear' psychoanalytic theory? Such investment is part of the cost in terms of which pay-offs are calculated. That financial and emotional investment frequently go together seems clearly illustrated by this example.

3.4.2   *The relevance of psychology for power: the technical interest* Just as something can be simultaneously financially and emotionally relevant, relevance for survival and for power frequently overlap. Particularly in a competitive capitalist society, survival and power are closely intertwined. Having power increases the chances for survival.

3.4.2.1   Being in control means having power over that which one controls. In the controlled psychological experiment, the psychologist has power over the other participants, his assistants, and 'subjects.' The English word 'subject' clearly expresses the power relationship in the psychological experiment (cf. 2.2.5). The experiment is thus relevant to the technical psychologist for the achievement of power. It is not relevant for that purpose to the other participants.

3.4.2.2   Power over 'subjects' is not the explicit and not even necessarily the technical psychologist's primary reason for conducting experiments. One of the expressed purposes of experimentation in all sciences which use that method is to gain power over events outside the experimental situation, that is, outside the laboratory. In other words, the 'research-motivating and research-guiding interests' or 'cognitive interests' (*Erkenntnisinteressen*) of experimental psychology are technical. The use of experimental methods is paradigmatic for technical psychology.

3.4.2.3   As Holzkamp discussed in detail in his provocative address on the 'Problem der Relevanz psychologischer Forschung für die Praxis' (1970) (Problem of relevance of psychological research for practice), technology can make use of experimental results only to the extent to which technology can duplicate outside the laboratory the controls which were set up in the laboratory. Making use of the laboratory findings of physics and chemistry, technology controls events in the outside world in correspondence with the controls which the scientist sets up. In so far as such duplications of controls are impossible outside the laboratory, the experimental results are useless for technology and give the latter no power over events in the world.

Controls in the psychological experiment with human beings consist of keeping the participants largely in the dark about consequential events, giving the participants orders concerning what to do and what not to do, disqualifying those who do not obey the orders, and frequently even deliberately misleading the participants with respect to significant aspects of the events. In order to make use of the findings from such experiments outside the laboratory one must then, just as in physics and chemistry, duplicate the experimental controls in the outside world. For psychology, this means that one must keep people in the dark about what is going on or even mislead them and one must be able to make them obey one's orders. Otherwise they are beyond one's power just like those people who are disqualified as experimental 'subjects,' namely those who refuse to subject themselves to the power of the experimenter. That the experimenter cannot predict the actions of others and has no power over them when they are fully aware of what is going on and are not forced to obey was demonstrated in an interesting piece of research by Resnick and Schwartz (1973; cf.

3.4.3.3). This fact explains also why psychologists are no more successful than other people in their interpersonal relations and why the nationwide attitude change in China in recent years was not based on the results of controlled experiments (Zellinger 1970).

Thus, the results of experimental psychology are relevant for the achievement of power only over those people who can be kept unaware of certain aspects of the world and who can be made to obey, that is, over whom one already has power. This limits the power of technical psychology to power over children, prison and hospital inmates, and those who wish to be controlled by others, namely those who do not wish to assume responsibility for their own actions. If one wants to extend one's power over people to other groups than the ones just mentioned, one must attempt to create for those others as well conditions which closely resemble the controlled conditions of the experiment. If technical psychologists want to achieve the widest applications of their findings outside the laboratory, they must work for ever greater controls over people's lives, which, in the final analysis, means a totalitarian society.

Technical psychology is thus relevant for staying in power to those who already have power over others. Those who have no power cannot be emancipated on the basis of the findings of technical psychology. They cannot learn from technical psychology how to free themselves from those who have power over them. Furthermore, for all those human transactions which consist mainly of dialogue, cooperation, and compromise, the results of controlled experiments are completely irrelevant (cf. Argyris 1975).

Since hermeneutic psychology is a *Geisteswissenschaft* it is not concerned with gaining and/or preserving power over others. Its relevance for power to people in general consists in showing ways in which one can free oneself from the power others seem to have over one.

3.4.3   *The relevance of psychology for making sense out of one's experiences: the hermeneutic interest* Without making some kind of sense out of one's experiences one would live in chaos and could probably not survive. All human beings can be assumed to try to make, in one way or another, sense out of their experiences, past and present, and to predict, at least to some extent, what their future experiences may be like. It seems, therefore, justified to ask whether and, if so, to what extent psychology is relevant for making sense out of one's experiences. Though making sense out of one's experiences is not completely independent of either survival or power, the issue can be dealt with separately from the other two.

Making sense out of one's experiences is an activity of the mind. It leads to theories in the widest meaning of that word. One of the purposes of controlled experiments is to test theories or to implement them (Holzkamp 1964). Psychology is thus relevant to people to the extent to which their experiences can be, in Einstein's words, 'co-ordinated' and brought 'into a logical system.'

3.4.3.1 Much of what technical psychologists investigate in the laboratory, like rats finding their ways through mazes or pressing levers in a box, is far removed from the kind of experiences most people have most of the time in everyday life. Even most of the experiences of psychologists, including those they have as experimenters, cannot be understood on the basis of technical psychology. The theories tested in laboratories cannot even explain how a psychologist designs an experiment and carries it out or how he writes it up for publication. At best can some of the theories of experimental psychology be relevant for making sense out of some aspects of perception and of motility. For making sense out of interpersonal relations, technical psychology is relevant only when such relations are taking place under highly controlled conditions and not when they are symmetrical and mutual and based on understanding and compromise.

It may be countered that lots of people 'explain' many of their own actions and those of others as due to 'habit' or 'conditioning.' Such people usually know nothing about theories of habit formation or about the difference between classical and instrumental conditioning theories. These theories can, therefore, hardly be considered relevant to those people for making sense out of their experiences.

3.4.3.2 Hermeneutic psychology aims directly and expressly at being relevant to both psychologists and others – between whom it explicitly makes no distinction – for making sense out of human experiences. This is the purpose of the theory of personal constructs (Kelly 1955), of Thomae's (1968) personality theory, of the various psychodynamic theories,[8] of

---

8 Kohut (1977) writes: 'Freud's values were not primarily health values. He believed in the intrinsic desirability of knowing as much as possible: he was ... intransigently committed to the task of knowing the truth, facing the truth, seeing reality clearly' (p. 64).

---

the double-bind theory of schizophrenia (Bateson et al. 1956), of dialectic-materialist psychology, of Piaget's genetic epistemology which aims at understanding the development of the structure of thought, and of all other truly cognitive psychologies.

As stated before, technical and hermeneutic sciences use different methods. Hermeneutic psychologists conduct their research in situations in which all participants have a large amount of freedom, in which there is dialogue, cooperation, and compromise. The results of such research are, therefore, not limited to making sense out of highly controlled conditions. They are relevant to making sense out of a large variety of experiences which people commonly have in their everyday lives.

3.4.3.3 The difference between technical and hermeneutic psychology in terms of methods and of relevance for making sense out of one's experiences can be illustrated by the research reported by Resnick and Schwartz (1973). They conducted two experiments in which undergraduates were presented with cards with six personal pronouns and a verb and were told to construct a sentence beginning with one of the pronouns followed by the verb. Whenever the student made up a sentence beginning with either 'I' or 'We' the experimenter said 'good' or 'mmm-hmmm' or 'okay.' Half the students were told that this was an experiment to study how college students construct sentences. The other half were informed that the researchers wanted to investigate the effects of full disclosure in a verbal conditioning experiment. The entire procedure was explained to the students in full detail.

The findings from the first group which had gone through a standard verbal conditioning experiment without having been told so were not only irrelevant with respect to the way people act in unmanipulated situations, but also did not contribute any new knowledge about people's actions in highly controlled situations. The findings from the non-manipulated group, however, contributed some interesting facts about people who are invited to participate in a psychological experiment with full knowledge of the procedure and of what the researchers want to find out.

Unfortunately, Resnick and Schwartz seem not to have appreciated their own contribution to making sense out of the ways in which others make sense out of their own experiences. From Resnick's and Schwartz's own way of making sense out of their own experiences they considered 'ethical standards as an independent variable.' (Why ethical standards and not the methods derived from ethical standards?)

Consequently, the researchers discussed their findings merely in terms of ethics and of the effects different methods derived from different ethics have on controlled experiments. Their highest value, which is incorporated in their concept of science, is 'rigour.' Resnick and Schwartz thus deplore 'that full disclosure permits the subject alternatives of either resistance or conformity which may not have been available to him without disclosure, roles which essentially are functions of a subject's past history' (p. 138).

Had Resnick and Schwartz been guided in their research by hermeneutic cognitive interests, they would have recognized their findings as highly relevant to human beings who, from the time of toilet training on, have 'alternatives of either resistance or conformity' in most situations in their lives, and whose actions are always 'functions of [their] past history.'

The analysis of the relevance of psychology for survival led to the conclusion that psychologists, like other scientists, usually refrain from falsification attempts with respect to theories in which they have made a considerable investment in terms of effort, time, and money. The same applies also – and perhaps particularly with hermeneutic psychologists – to investments in a given way of making sense out of one's experiences. By giving up a theory formerly adhered to one acknowledges that one's earlier way of interpreting one's experiences was erroneous and thus creates, in some way, chaos of one's earlier life. Most people, including both technical and hermeneutic scientists, are not 'ready to accept a qualitatively different ordering of reality which may result from changing our methods of investigating it' (Resnick and Schwartz, p. 138). Thus, to the extent to which psychology is relevant to psychologists for their survival and for co-ordinating their experiences, to that extent it can interfere with its own progress as a science. On the other hand, the tenaciousness with which some psychologists cling to a theory they once proclaimed may push that position to extremes and thereby increase the possibility of testing it further.

3.5   πάντα ῥεῖ Survival, power, and meaning (co-ordinating one's experiences) are interrelated frames of reference. Human beings can hardly survive without meaningful experiences and, by giving some kind of meaning to their experiences, human beings exert some power over these experiences. As the meaning of one's experiences changes, those experiences change as far as the experiencer is concerned. Thomae (1968) expressed this in the title of his book *Das Individuum und seine Welt*, indicating that each of us lives in his/her own world which is similar to but not identical with the worlds of others. Hence hermeneutic psychology too changes one's world (cf. Popper's [1973] 'World 2' and Brandt and Metzger's [1969] 'reality$_2$'). But whereas technical psychology attempts to change others by interfering with their 'observable behavior,' hermeneutic psychology attempts to bring about change through new conceptualizations, through new ways of making sense out of one's experiences, through new meanings resulting from different perspectives and different reference systems. Whereas technical psychology aims at power through controlling others, hermeneutic psychology aims at power through questioning the taken-for-granted and through self-control, including control of what I want from others to whom I confer power over me by wanting something from them. Such self-control, which gives me greater power by my conferring less power to others, can result only from greater self-understanding. Thus, through hermeneutics psychology becomes emancipatory.[9]

While survival, power, and meaning are thus interrelated, different value systems place different emphasis on each of them. Survival was until recently the highest value in Anglo-America. It has even frequently been used as a coverall explanation by technical psychologists (Skinner 1971). It is now being questioned: In Canada, the churches are debating whether or not to keep severely mentally deficient babies artificially alive, and the medical profession is reconsidering the application of artificial life-sustaining procedures to terminally ill patients. Similarly, the value of power is being questioned: the Canadian prime minister has rejected the use of force to keep Quebec in Confederation should its population democratically decide to separate from the rest of Canada.

As there are shifts in values in other areas, there are indications that such shifts are also slowly taking place within psychology. More and more psychologists in Anglo-America seem to be attracted by psychologies with hermeneutic and emancipatory interests. At the same time, a considerable number of European psychologists have in recent decades pursued a psychology with technical interests which seemed to provide them with more power.

---

9 'It must be honestly admitted that here lies a new limit for the effect of analysis which is not intended to make pathological reactions impossible but to create for the ego of the patient the *freedom* to decide thus or otherwise' (Freud 1923, p. 280n.).

---

4 Psychologists Caught in Different Physics Frameworks

Psychologists Caught in
Different Physics Frameworks
After the fall of the apple

4.0   In the preceding chapter, I discussed how psychological research is influenced by the psychologist's values, which function as a reference system of cognitive interests, and how these are related to various issues of relevance. In that context, I distinguished between two definitions of science and two corresponding definitions of psychology. Since many technical psychologists assert that they use physics as a reference system for their psychology, for instance, by using 'the scientific method,' I shall now examine the justification of that claim.

For technical psychologists the criteria for calling research 'scientific' are 'prediction, measurement, and control.' Technical psychologists frequently think of an empirical science as one in which one conducts experiments. They confuse 'empirical,' which means merely 'based on experience,' with 'experimental.' (They disregard the fact that the oldest natural science, astronomy, has been empirical for millennia without performing experiments.)

Since technical psychologists use experimental laboratory physics (as opposed to theoretical physics) largely as their model of science, it seems pertinent to reflect upon what physics consists of and to investigate whether the image technical psychologists have of physics actually corresponds to the practices of physicists. Stating it differently: Is physics actually the exact science which technical psychologists believe it to be?

4.1   CLASSICAL PHYSICS 'Classical physics assumed essentially the existence of an objective reality which could be described entirely independently of the "subjects" who observe it. This is, as Bohr subtly remarked, the reason for which classical physics could claim the epithet of exact science' (de Broglie 1937, pp. 279-80). It further assumed with Aristotle the continuity of natural phenomena, which implied homology of events on all scales from the infinitely small to the infinitely large (Heisenberg 1971a). It espoused metaphysical monism. Another assumption of classical physics was the, at least theoretical, possibility of the exact specification of both space-time variables and dynamic states, from which followed that complete knowledge at a given moment in time of all natural forces and of the respective positions of all components of the universe would eliminate all uncertainty and make both complete reconstruction of the past and complete prediction of all future events possible. This possibility arose from the axiom of causality that all events are caused by and are thus the effects of other events.[1] Furthermore, events could be investigated separately in terms of their spatial and temporal aspects, and the latter were not considered to have any historical features, that is, the historical time at which they were studied was considered not to affect them.

4.2   REVOLUTION IN PHYSICS In contrast to classical physics, modern physicists question the meaningfulness of speaking of 'an objective reality.' They no longer believe that the world can 'be described entirely independently of the "subjects" who observe it.' In Heisenberg's words 'quantum mechanics could not satisfy the requirements [of] ... a complete separation of the world into an objective and a subjective area and ... that one must be able to speak about the objective side in an unambiguous manner ... It does not look as if natural science could ever find its way back to [these] postulates' (Born 1969, p. 12). To Pauli 'and also to other representatives of quantum mechanics the experimental

---

1 Piaget's (1930) genetic psychological investigation of the axiom of causality uncovered its origin in animism. The concept of physical causality develops out of one's subjective experience that one can cause events through one's actions. Paradoxically, the concept of causality is thus founded on the subjective experience of freedom to act. Hence, it is also related to the psychoanalytic concept of infantile omnipotence feelings. The infantile idea that 'n'importe quoi produit n'importe quoi' (anything causes anything; (Piaget 1925, quote in Flavell 1963, p. 142) reappears as the basis for associationism and stimulus-response psychology (cf. Metzger 1963).

---

and theoretical evidence against the implementability of the ideal of the "detached observer" seems sufficient' (ibid., p. 291). Viewing the issue of the objective observer of objective facts from a different angle, Pauli wrote that the *'state of a system is defined only through indication of an experimental set-up.'* To which Born added: 'Einstein says instead of "indication of an experimental set-up," that "the state of a system depends on how one looks at it." But that's the same' (ibid., p. 290, original emphasis).[2]

The continuity of natural phenomena is questioned today by those physicists who consider the laws of microphysics as inapplicable to macrophysics, while all agree that the laws of macrophysics do not apply to microphysics. Within microphysics events are not assumed to be continuous but discontinuous in terms of quantum jumps. Thus monism is replaced by pluralism.

It has further been recognized that exact specification of the spatio-temporal location and the speed or momentum of a particle is impossible. It is not even considered meaningful to say that a particle 'has' an exact position and momentum just as 'we have. ... reached the point at which the term splitting ceases to mean anything' (Heisenberg 1971b, p. 101). In Einstein's words: 'The particle has in reality neither a definite momentum nor a definite position. ... The rigorous localization which comes to the fore during the measurement is brought about only through the unavoidable (not negligible) measurement-interference ... The foregoing applies mutatis mutandis equally to the description of systems' (Born 1969, p. 230). As Heisenberg has demonstrated, any set-up enabling us to measure the position of a particle has the effect of upsetting its speed in an unknown manner, and this to an increasing degree as the measurement of its position becomes more exact. And the reverse is equally true. In other words, complete knowledge of the momentum of a particle implies absolute uncertainty about its position. Exact prediction is therefore impossible. Only probabilistic statements can be made.

In line with the impossibility of precise measurements, modern physics 'is very largely qualitative, consisting in an effort to comprehend,

---

2 This idea is expressed by phenomenologists by stating that all facts are 'co-constituted' by the observer and external events.

---

even in a very rough way, some facts of nature that are entirely new to us at present' and 'errors of 50 per cent are tolerated if they cannot be improved upon' (Park 1964, p. 78).

According to Einstein's theory of relativity, we can reach a universally valid understanding of events only by considering the four-dimensional universe as consisting of space-time and by no longer regarding events separately in terms of *either* space *or* time. Thus, time is not identical across different systems and the concept of 'absolute simultaneity of two events at different places in space' is consequently meaningless. Furthermore, we say that particles decay and that new ones can be formed out of energy, that they undergo transformations, have life spans and thus have histories. It is, therefore, not irrelevant at which point in space-time they are observed.

A further characteristic of modern physics is the attempt to understand many events in terms of cooperative phenomena, namely, of transactions between particles. Such cooperative phenomena cannot be reduced to characteristics of their component parts. For instance, the boiling temperature of water cannot be derived from the characteristics of the hydrogen and oxygen atoms. It is particularly in connection with these cooperative phenomena that physicists frequently resort to analogies with gestalt psychology.

The distance modern physics has travelled from the mechanical model of the nineteenth century is further illustrated by its field theories. An electromagnetic wave field has, and needs, no mechanical explanation that we know of. Its waves cannot be localized in space as particles can. At the same time, there are other fields, for instance, meson fields, gravitational fields, etc. One kind of field cannot be reduced to a field of another kind. As Park (1964) states: 'To live in a world composed of fields seems to be a very different thing from living in a world that operates like a mechanism. Most of our language and our philosophic viewpoints are still based on a mechanistic conception of the universe, to the extent that they are based on anything scientific at all' (p. 44).

It is thus evident that modern physics has abandoned many of the basic assumptions of nineteenth-century natural science. Lest the reader assume that the new views apply only to the physics of elementary particles I quote once more from Pauli: 'It is clear that quantum mechanics must claim to be valid in principle also for *macroscopic* pellets ... If one could measure with sufficient precision, this would naturally be as true for macroscopic pellets as for electrons. Naturally, this can be demonstrated by ... thought experiments' (Born 1969, p. 290).[3]

4.3   THE PHYSICS OF PSYCHOLOGISTS

4.3.1   *Objectivity* Technical psychologists still basically follow the mechanical model of classical physics. The belief in a knowable objective reality which is independent of the observer and the method of observation and measurement is well documented by the much larger number of supporting references in the psychological literature to the 1927 operationism of Bridgman than to his 1959 statement that '"proof" ... is entirely an affair of the individual and is therefore private' (p. v). In spite of the fact that operational definitions were exactly what demonstrated the relativity of data with respect of their measurement (e.g., [$hunger_1$ = hours of food deprivation] $\neq$ [$hunger_2$ = number of food pellets consumed] $\neq$ [$hunger_3$ = voltage of grid crossed] $\supset$ $hunger_1$ $\neq$ $hunger_2$ $\neq$ $hunger_3$), technical psychologists continue to define experiences operationally in the belief that objectivity can thereby be achieved.

4.3.2   *The uncertainty principle* The human acts of observation and measurement are largely disregarded in macrophysics because they are of

---

3 To those not familiar with microphysics, the uncertainty or indeterminacy principle can be illustrated by the following thought experiment which I owe to Professor G. Papini of the Department of Physics of the University of Regina. Let us assume we want to determine the exact temperature of the water contained in a glass. In order to measure the temperature of the water we need a thermometer. The thermometer has, of course, also a given temperature which we can read off before placing it into the water. Since we do not know the water temperature before measuring it, we do not know the difference in temperature between the thermometer and the water. As we put the thermometer into the water, the thermometer will either raise or lower the water temperature, unless the thermometer had exactly the same temperature as the water had before the thermometer was dipped into it. The temperature which we read off the thermometer after having it put into the water and stirred the water is thus the temperature of the water after the thermometer has been put into it. We can, therefore, never know what the water temperature was before we placed the thermometer into the glass of water.

---

different kinds and magnitudes from what is being observed and measured. In microphysics, the tools for observation (e.g., photons) are, however, of the same order as the objects of observation (particles). The interference in the observation by the tools is, therefore, no longer negligible. As Bohr remarked – and one could easily think that he was referring to psychology – 'The situations in physics have emphatically reminded us of the old truth that we are both spectators and actors in the great drama of existence' (quoted in Zimmer 1940, p. 287). That this view does not apply merely to microphysics is clearly expressed by Pauli: 'Since I cannot see any difference in principle between microbodies and macrobodies, I consider it *untrue* that a "macrobody" has always a quasi-sharply determined position' (Born 1969, p. 295, original emphasis).

Now, the reason for indeterminacy can be seen to lie in two facts: (1) the similarity in structure and magnitude of the tool and the object of observation and (2) the movement of the object whose exact pre-observational position and momentum cannot be known. Both these facts are evident in psychology just as they are in physics: (1) The tools for scientific observation are in the last analysis always human perceptions guided by human conceptualizations and human emotions. Thus, the tools of observation and the objects of observation are similar both in kind and in magnitude. (2) The objects of psychology are changing actions and experiences. Their pre-observational development is as incompletely known as the pre-observational position and momentum of a moving particle and 'the repetition of the ... measurement at consecutive moments in time with the same exactness Δx_0 *is of no* use *at all* for the predictability of later ... measurements' (Pauli in Born 1969, p. 297).

Furthermore, the frequently found differences between the results from different experiments investigating the 'same' psychological concepts on the basis of different operational definitions (e.g., 'hunger' defined by hours of food deprivation vs. 'hunger' defined by amount of food consumed) seem to indicate that, as in quantum mechanics, in psychology 'the state of a system is defined only through indications of an experimental set-up.'

Some awareness of the influence of the experimental set-up upon the observed activities is shown by psychologists studying the ecology of human development as recently reported by Bronfenbrenner (1977). While these researchers seem to neglect to consider themselves as part of the ecology of those whom they study, others have shown a beginning awareness of the influence of the experimenter on experimental findings. That the interaction between observer and observed is, however, not yet fully understood by the investigators of experimenter-bias-effects is evidenced by the methods with which these effects have so far been approached (cf. 7.1.6). The goal of experimenter-bias-effect research seems to be the elimination of the effects of the observer on the observed. The fact that observer-effects and observational effects are, in psychology as in physics, not avoidable side-effects and 'that our ability to know things has absolute limits that seem to correspond exactly to limits inherent in quantum mechanics' (Park 1964, p. 45) is still unacknowledged by most psychologists. They continue their naïve attempts to nullify the observer/observation effects instead of defining them as specifically as possible and accepting the limitations of science.

A detailed description and definition of the observer-effects requires an investigation of the observer. Since further observer-effects must occur in the investigation of the observer by another observer, the question arises whether the usual 'allopsychological' study, in the sense of Max F. Meyer's *The Psychology of the Other One* (1921), cannot profitably be combined with an 'autopsychological' (Keiler 1970), namely, self-observational, investigation. The observer and observation characteristics can be further specified through the joint reciprocal exploration of all participants in a psychological investigation.

The only approach in psychology in which the systematic investigation of the observer by both himself and another observer is a requirement for the observation of others is psychoanalysis. In psychoanalysis the awareness of the observer-effect was recognized and acknowledged even before Heisenberg's declaration of the uncertainty principle in physics, and led to the requirement that every psychoanalyst must be analysed. The purpose of the psychoanalyst's analysis cannot be to help him avoid having effects upon his analysands, but only to be aware of these effects. Just as in quantum mechanics, knowledge in psychoanalysis is never absolute or unequivocal. The description of the analysand, like that of the particle in physics, is never complete. A psychoanalysis is always incomplete (Freud 1937b) like all science (Heisenberg 1971b).

The uncertainty principle applies particularly to such areas as personality, social psychology, and psychopathology. Like position and momentum of a particle, the motivations and attitudes of an individual are not objective characteristics but depend on where, when, how, and by whom they are observed. They depend to a large extent on the observer's values as discussed in the previous chapter. That different researchers in psychology obtain different results is thus not always due to inexactness in measurement, oversight, interferences, or other 'uncontrolled' variables, but largely to the fact that the different results were obtained by different researchers and at different points in space-time. *Your motivations and attitudes observed by me are my conceptualizations of my perceptions of your actions in relation to your hypotheses about my intentions in relation to you within a certain situation at a specific space-time point.* Thus, there is in psychology a similar arbitrariness of the distinction between object and subject or 's' and 'E' as there is in physics. It therefore becomes questionable whether it is any more meaningful to say that an individual 'has' certain motives and attitudes than it is to say that a particle 'has' an exact position and momentum.

Monism vs. pluralism Following the model of classical physics, technical psychology is based on metaphysical monism. Modern physics has largely abandoned monism: different rules are applied on different levels, for instance, in macrophysics and in microphysics. In mircophysics events are described in both wave and material terms which cannot be reduced to each other; the behaviour of magnetic, gravitational, and meson fields cannot be translated into the same terms.[4]

It seems that just as the description of the behaviour of an elementary particle in either wave or material terms does not give a complete picture of the particle, the description of man in either physiological or psychological (or sociological or economic) terms alone does not give a complete picture of him. Just as the description of the particle in wave terms cannot be reduced to a description in terms of matter or vice versa, so a description of man in psychological terms cannot be reduced to one in physiological terms or vice versa. 'If [the neurophysiologist] should state that nerve impulses moving in certain patterns are one and the same thing as mind, he accomplishes little for his future work except to deprive himself of a useful working terminology' (Penfield and Roberts 1959, p. 8). Just as position and momentum are never co-present for an observer in physics, so physiological and psychological data are never co-present for *one* observer of man. When a neurosurgeon touches a spot on a patient's brain and the patient hears music, the music is not heard by the neurosurgeon and the touching of the brain is not felt by the patient. The two events, touching of brain and hearing music, thus

---

4 More familiar with contemporary physics than most psychologists, neurosurgeons like Penfield (1959) and Pribram (1976) and psychopharmacologists like Kety (1969) reject monism too.

---

are not co-present in either the surgeon's or the patient's observation-experience.

In further analogy to modern physics, it seems useful to take a dualistic – or rather, pluralistic – approach in psychology, not only in terms of psyche and soma – and society – but also in other respects. Thus, 'tacit' and 'articulate' knowledge (Polanyi 1958) may require different methodologies for their investigation, as well as different explanatory principles. That animal and human functioning require different explanations was recognized by Pavlov in his distinction between 'the single signalling system of animals' underlying condi-tioned reflexes and the 'second signalling system,' consisting of 'the totality of all signal relations of the verbal type peculiar to man' (Pickenhain 1970, p. 127), whose underlying 'first signalling system' is assumed to be different from the single signalling system of animals. Different levels of consciousness may follow different rules, as assumed in Freud's distinction between primary and secondary processes. Per-ception and 'formal operations' may be better understood in terms of distinctive properties as suggested by Piaget (1969).

The need for methodological pluralism is recognized by dialectical-materialist psychologists. Since 'one and the same action can be carried out both through an impulsive motive and as the result of a conscious decision,' and since 'the empirical fact has in this connection no unam-biguous meaning but proves to be psychologically equivocal,' psycho-logical research needs its own methods, each of which 'is usually adequate only with respect to a corresponding stage in the research, a specific area of psychic phenomena or certain special aspects of the object of research' (Iwanowa and Assejew 1974, pp. 182 and 199).

The inadequacy of a monistic approach becomes particularly clear in communication and information theories. Events investigated within these frameworks can be conceptualized in terms of both energy and information. Depending on the concepts used entirely different princi-ples apply. Within a closed system energy follows the law of conserva-tion but information does not. The transmission of a message requires energy which the source or sender loses and the receiver gains. However, the sender does not lose any information while the receiver gains some. (I am not decreasing the amount of information I have by writing this book, and the information contained in this book does not decrease with every reading of its contents though the reader may gain information). The mathematics of energy thus differ from those of information since the latter is not fractioned or diminished by being distributed.

4.3.4 *Measurement* Unforeseen problems have arisen in modern physics with respect to measurement, which used to be considered the A and Ω of science. But since physicists have become aware of the dialectical relationship between measuring instruments and what is being measured, measuring has been called into question. Bridgman, who, to his later regret, was credited with the idea of 'operationalizing' definitions like 'length' by describing what the scientist did when taking a measure, concluded that 'the concept of "true length" would seem to be a survival from pre-quantum days, and is perhaps a projection of the fact that we have always been able to improve our best instrument ... But our experience with quantum phenomena shows that we have concealed here an assumption about the behaviour of matter which is not justified. For there is ... no scale, no matter how rigid the material, which does not itself fluctuate in length' (1959, p. 140).

Yet, technical psychologists continue to 'measure' indiscriminately 'abilities,' 'attitudes,' 'personality traits,' and other not even observable, but merely hypothesized characteristics. They are blissfully unaware that 'a measurement and the reading of a measuring instrument have no meaning – are no data – if one does not know how they were formed. In other words, one needs a *theory (map) about data-producing "systems" – before* one can obtain data ... The "map" must also represent *how processes of the investigated "strata" ... causally necessitate the processes in the measuring instrument*' (Radnitzky 1971, p. 159). However, psychologists almost never know how their measuring instruments were formed (Holzkamp 1964). Precise information about the construction of psychological scales is almost never available as those who have tried to obtain such information have discovered. But most technical psychologists do not even make the attempt to obtain such information and to understand a theory about data-producing systems. They blithely and blindly 'measure' hypothetical constructs and members of fuzzy sets. Accordingly, they disparage hermeneutic psychologists like gestalt-phenomenologists and psychoanalysts who do not attempt to measure what cannot be quantified.

Piaget has shown a true understanding of measurement. When studying geometrical-optical illusions in his work on perceptual development (1969), he measured the length of lines perceived as equal and counted the number of eye-movements. In contrast, in his research on the development of thinking, he categorized qualitative differences of concepts by using content analysis, a basic hermeneutic method.

4.3.5   *Probability* While some physicists interpret Heisenberg's principle of indeterminacy as requiring the abandonment of strict determinism, others interpret it to mean merely that individual events cannot be predicted but are strictly determined. The difference is a philosophical and not a scientific one. Causality is a metaphysical concept. However, physicists of both persuasions agree that only probabilistic statements are possible in science, that is, statements about large numbers of and not about individual events. When probabilistic statements are formulated with respect to individual events or systems, they become scientifically meaningless. 'That [the probability] Ψ describes the "state" of *one* system is only a manner of speaking as in every day life: "My life expectancy (as a human being of 67 years of age) is 4.3 years." Also this is a statement about a single system, but meaningless in the empirical sense. For, what is meant, naturally, is: Take a totality of individuals, each 67 years old, and count what percentage lives for a given period' (Born 1969, p. 250).

In psychology the use of statistics gives the semblance of making probability statements. However, psychologists commonly do not use statistics to make truly probabilistic statements. They do not report the percentage of individuals in whom a given phenomenon occurred. Instead, they give a 'level of confidence' with which they think they can claim 'certainty' or can 'prove' the 'general' occurrence of the phenomenon. Even more frequently they delude themselves in 'proving' the existence of a 'hypothetical construct' by the use of statistics. Contrary to the views held by contemporary philosophers of science (Polanyi 1958; Popper 1959) as well as by modern physicists, many technical psychologists use 'verification' on the basis of statistics and 'evade falsifications with impertinence through linguistic games' (Metzger, personal communication). Such use of probability is not in line with modern physics, as those who insist on that use and on teaching it seem to believe. Nor does it correspond to the basic rules of mathematics, which are completely ignored whenever unequal units are treated as equal and when ordinal numbers (ranks) are treated like cardinal numbers.[5]

---

5   Applied statisticians, like technical psychologists, usually disregard the fact that the third, the fifth, and the twelfth of a collection are three items and not the twentieth. In addition, they usually ignore such non-arithmetic areas of mathematics as topology and set-theory. When at all

---

The application of the probability concept of physics to psychology would have far-reaching socio-political implications: Are decisions affecting individuals to be made on the basis of predictions about large numbers of people? How is this going to affect thinking in terms of the interests of individuals and those of organizations (cf. Krauch 1969; Krauch, Feger, and Opgenoorth 1970)? How is this going to affect individual choice and freedom?

4.3.6   *The relativity of time* Classical physics could largely disregard time. With the advent of the theory of relativity and the discovery of radioactive elements time began to become a factor in physics too: in terms of the theory of relativity, the concept of simultaneity became meaningless; each radioactive element turned out to have its own individual clock; different particles were found to have various lifespans.

The relativity of time is known to psychologists in connection with studies on subjective time, as well as from such concepts as mental age and emotional maturity. It is, however, widely ignored in experimental research, as I recently pointed out for the area of decision-making (Brandt 1971b). While Piaget, Freud, Sullivan, and their followers take the relativity of time into account in their discussions of developmental stages by not assigning specific chronological ages to them, behaviourists like Cattell and Eysenck disregard time in their works on personality. In contrast to this 'classical' approach to personality, Thomae (1968) developed a theory based on individual histories and individual differences in the apportioning of time.

Behaviouristic studies in learning and memory do not usually take subjective time into account but treat time as absolute. By comparing, for example, the clock-time of learning or of memory span of different individuals, one applies the time of one system to another system. An application of the relativity concept to learning and memory would require the prior empirical investigation of a given individual's subjective clock, for instance, the way in which s/he divides her/his time among different activities.

The connection between Einstein's theory of relativity and psychological time is made explicit by the dialectical-materialist psychologist Rubinstein (1974), who points out that 'the objective logic of this

---

applying the theory of fuzzy sets they destroy its purpose by again assigning numbers and forgetting that by definition numbers are never fuzzy.

---

thought [theory of relativity] leads with an inner necessity to the acknowledgment of qualitative particularities of the time of the history of society and of the time of the human life which depend on structural particularities of these processes. Time shifts in experiencing the past, present, and future. [There is a] Differential perception of the temporal extension of an interval (e.g., a year) in youth and in old age' (p. 284f.). Rubinstein refers in this context to Lewin's gestalt-psychological experiments 'about the objective influence of the organization of time upon the life of a human being' (p. 285).

4.3.7   *Cooperative phenomena* By 'cooperative phenomena' modern physics refers to events which cannot be understood in terms of their components. Such 'emergent' qualities have 'whole' characteristics which cannot be derived from or reduced to characteristics of their parts. They are *Gestalten*, as Goethe called them in his work on comparative anatomy (1795), and as they were described in Köhler's work on the physical [sic] gestalten (1920). As Goethe showed in his discovery of the *os intermaxillare*, the parts can be understood in terms of the whole but not the whole in terms of its parts. As various physicists (de Broglie 1937; Born 1969) have stated, the gestalt approach is at least as useful in psychology as it is in physics and biology. Concerning the cross-fertilization between psychology and physics, Born (1969) wrote to Einstein: 'I am truly sorry that you do not like my "observational invariants." They are an inheritance, in a new form, of Wertheimer's *"Gestalten."* And I value them. But I am angry at you for accusing me of having positivist ideas; that is exactly the last thing I am striving for. I can't stand those guys' (p. 225).

Technical psychologists acknowledge cooperative phenomena and emergent qualities to some extent in the area of perception. In other areas of psychology (Metzger 1963) these concepts are still widely ignored by English-speaking psychologists. Those few psychiatrists who work truly in 'psychosomatic' medicine are, as even the word 'psychosomatic' indicates, aware of cooperative phenomena. Both those psychiatrists and gestalt psychologists relate these phenomena to the concept of fields.

4.3.8   *Fields* Another difference between classical physics and modern physics lies in the mechanistic and atomistic world-view of the former and the field theories of the latter. Here, too, technical psychology follows the model of classical physics. While this model may have some usefullness for reflexology, the field model seems more adequate for a description of the mind, namely, of purely psychological phenomena. Whereas the older applications of field theory to psychology by Köhler and Lewin are known in North America but have been little pursued, the more recent steps taken in that direction in West Germany (Katz 1969; Keiler 1970) are still awaiting further development.

One particular characteristic of fields is that they have no clearly defined spatial limits and can coexist in the same space with objects. They transcend the material objects which constitute their 'carriers.' 'Carrier' and 'field' stand in certain dynamic interactions. For instance, changes in the carrier lead to changes in the field which may bring about changes in some other material objects. Thus, field theory seems particularly appropriate for the understanding of *the transactions taking place between body and mind*, and between a mind and other minds and bodies (Keiler 1970). The role played by the field approach in psychiatry is illustrated by Mitscherlich's (1970) statement that 'psychosomatic medicine is never medicine of the isolated individual but always, when the term psychosomatic medicine is properly used, diagnosis and therapy in the *field* of interpersonal relations, beginning with the doctor-patient relationship' (p. 348, emphasis added).

4.4   EMANCIPATORY PSYCHOLOGY AND PHYSICS: PSYCHOANALYSIS The basic concepts of modern physics were developed in Europe. Bohr, Born, de Broglie, Einstein, Heisenberg, Pauli, and Planck were Europeans educated in Europe, as were Freud, Köhler, and Wertheimer, who had close personal contacts with some of the physicists. It is, therefore, not astounding that some of the European schools of psychology are closer to the concepts of modern physics than are most Anglo-American schools.

What may seem astounding to technical psychologists is that psychoanalysis, which by their criteria seems unscientific, has as much in common with contemporary physics as I have mentioned in this chapter. I shall now draw those commonalities between modern physics and psychoanalysis together.

By 'psychoanalysis' I refer to a body of closely interrelated dynamic theories about both normal and abnormal personality and its development, and corresponding research methods (cf. 5.1.1). Psychoanalysis is emancipatory because of 'the turning of observation upon our own being [*Wesen*] and using thinking for its own critique' (Freud 1927, p. 356f.), for uncovering rationalizations and ideologies.

Contrary to the 'Copenhagen school,' but in line with many other contemporary physicists, psychoanalysts assume strict determinism.

Freud started the development of his theory with the idea that all psychological events have causes, just as all other events are assumed to have. It was on the basis of this assumption that he introduced the concept of unconscious motivation. At the same time, the uncertainty principle is acknowledged in psychoanalysis in the sense that individual events and events of individuals cannot be predicted because of the necessary interference by the observer and the observation with what is being observed. Both psychoanalysis and quantum mechanics are theories based not on the ability to predict future events exactly, but on the possibility of explaining past events meaningfully in causal terms. This may require '*ad hoc* approximations' to which technical psychologists object on principle, but which 'abound in modern mathematical physics [and] play a very important part in the quantum theory of fields' (Feyerabend 1975, p. 63). Like modern physicists, psychoanalysts recognize that 'verification ... is an unusually fuzzy concept' (Bridgman 1959, p. 56) and that all scientific theories are, as even Popper finally realized, immune to falsification so that 'none could simply be described as "falsifiable" ' (1976, p. 42).[6]

Interpretation, which plays a central role in psychoanalysis, has been recognized by modern physicists as being an important factor in their science too. This can be seen in such statements as: 'Often, as in his studies of atomic phenomena, [the physicist] finds that he is not able to observe directly either the structure or the function of what he is studying and that he must subsist entirely on indirect hints derived from *measurements whose very interpretation often poses the most severe problems*' (Park 1964, p. 3).

Presenting an analysand with an interpretation is an empirical test of a hypothesis derived from psychoanalytic theory. As I have shown on the basis of an actual instance (Brandt 1974), giving an interpretation fulfils the requirements for a scientific experiment, if one applies the criteria for acceptance or rejection of one's hypothesis which Freud clearly stated in his paper on 'Constructions in Analysis' (1937a).

Like modern physics, psychoanalysis has renounced metaphysical monism for a pluralist approach, as indicated by the requirement that

---

6 With this acknowledgment Popper destroys his own critique of psychoanalysis as well as that of dialectical materialism and unmasks his critique as irrational.

---

all psychological events be explained from a structural, a dynamic, an economic, a genetic, and an adaptive perspective (cf. Rapaport 1960).

Also like modern physics, psychoanalysis 'is very largely qualitative, consisting in an effort to comprehend, even in a very rough way, some facts of nature that are entirely new to us at present' (Park 1964, p. 78).

Since individual development plays a central part in psychoanalysis, time is never ignored. By not assigning developmental stages to chronological age groups the importance of subjective time is recognized, as it is also by the emphasis on the timing of interpretations with respect to the analysand's individual clock. In these ways, the relativity of time is accounted for in psychoanalysis.

The concept of 'cooperative phenomena' enters into psychoanalysis through the idea of 'multideterminism.' An action and an experience are not conceptualized as having a single cause or reason. There are always a multitude of motives present which contribute to a given psychological event which might not have occurred on the basis of any one of those motives alone.

To the fields of modern physics correspond processes and systems in psychoanalysis. The frequent emphasis by critics of psychoanalysis on Freud's occasional analogies with a hydraulic model disregard the fact that Freud conceptualized the mind from the beginning in systems terms (1895), and what are usually referred to as 'structures' ought to be conceptualized as processes or fields (cf. Brandt 1966a).

Finally, Freud's concept of science was very close to Heisenberg's, as a comparison of the following two statements indicates:

The task of science is fully circumscribed, if we limit it to showing how the world must appear to us as a consequence of the uniqueness [*Eigenart*] of our organisation ... The problem of the characteristics of the world [*einer Weltbeschaffenheit*] without accounting for our perceiving psychic apparatus is an empty abstraction without practical interest. (Freud 1927, p. 380)

and

Thus the aim of research is no longer an understanding of atoms and their movements 'in themselves', i.e., independently of the formulation of experimental problems ... The common division of the world into subject and object, inner world and outer world, body and soul, is no longer adequate and leads us into difficulties. Thus even in science *the object of research is no longer nature itself, but man's investigation of nature*. Here, again, man confronts himself alone ... The new mathematical formulae no longer describe nature itself but *our knowledge* of nature. (Heisenberg 1958, p. 24f.; original emphasis)

4.5   TOWARDS PSYCHOLOGICAL PSYCHOLOGY In this chapter I tried to show that different psychologies have affinities to different reference systems in physics. I presented these comparisons because those who have adopted the views of Anglo-Saxon schools of metascience (Radnitzky 1973) expect all sciences to conform to the same model and to use the same methods. As I have shown, there exist different models of the world within physics even at the same period in time, since, whenever new ideas appear, some people hold on to the old ones. Thus, 'opinions still differ, and occasionally we may hear the view that this new form of natural description is still unsatisfactory, since it fails to satisfy earlier ideals of what scientific truth ought to be and must thus be considered itself a symptom of the crisis of our times, and as by no means final' (Heisenberg 1958, p. 25). To resort to physics can therefore bring no unity into psychology.

Furthermore, I regard psychology not as a *Naturwissenschaft* (natural science) like physics, but as a *Geisteswissenschaft* (human science) – though the quote from Heisenberg in the preceding section may make this distinction more problematic than ever. Psychology cannot afford to disregard history: the history of the individual (ontogeny), the history of the species (phylogeny), or the history of the society in which ontogeny takes place (which I chose to call 'poligeny'). Consequently, psychology must largely rely – like archaeology, one of Freud's great interests – on uncovering what is hidden and on hermeneutically interpreting its finds.

In order to investigate to what extent different psychological frames of reference are helpful in gaining a better understanding of human activities and experiences, I shall discuss in the next chapter what light different psychological theories throw on the functioning of psychologists.

5 Psychologists Caught in Different Theoretical Frameworks

Psychologists Caught in Different Theoretical Frameworks
Of rats and men

5.0   Having shown some problems arising from attempting to place psychology into frameworks of physics, I shall now reflect upon various schools of psychology from their own and from each other's perspective. In the first part of this chapter, I shall follow the suggestions by Kaminski (cf. 3.3.1), Bannister (1968), Criswell (1958), Riecken (1962), Lyons (1963), Grinker (1967), Neisser (1967), Rychlak (1968), and Schultz (1971) – all unheeded to my knowledge – for applying psychological theories to their defenders. I shall deal with the question 'What conclusions can be drawn from psychology X about psychologists X and how a psychologist X invented psychology X.'

In the second part of this chapter, I shall discuss how those different psychologies fare when applied to each other. The questions I shall try to answer are: 'How can the construction of psychology X be explained on the basis of psychology Y?' and 'How can psychology X be evaluated and compared to psychology Y from the perspective of psychology Y?'

5.1   THE MIRROR

5.1.1   *The psychologist within a psychoanalytic framework* The term 'psychoanalysis' stands for (a) a complex theory of normal and abnormal personality development and (b) 'a special technique for the investigation of human motivation' (English and English 1958) which is closely connected with the theory and also serves as a method of dealing with emotional problems. According to the theory, much of human motivation is the result of unconscious drives and unconscious defences against those drives. Human actions are further considered to be frequently re-enactments of childhood situations which the actor no longer remembers and which thus cause conflicts which may also remain unconscious.

One frequent source of problems in adulthood is assumed to have its origin in unsatisfied narcissistic needs, that is, the individual did not receive sufficient recognition in early childhood (cf. Kohut 1971).

5.1.1.1 In terms of psychoanalytic theory, psychoanalysts are human beings who have over many years applied to themselves, with the help of colleagues, 'a special technique for the investigation of human motivation' and attempted to solve some of the emotional problems they had. Otherwise, they function like other people. Qua psychoanalysts they are more on the look-out for indications of unconscious, infantile motives and defences in themselves than most people are.

It follows from psychoanalytic theory that psychoanalytic work, the investigation of human motivation through listening to other people's verbalizations of their most private experiences, their most intimate thoughts, fantasies, and dreams, is probably a sublimated form of voyeurism, of peeping into other people's bedrooms and bathrooms. Psychoanalysts do so, however, only figuratively and not as an end in itself, and are moreover aware of the vicarious sexual pleasure they may derive from this aspect of their work.

According to their theory, psychoanalysts satisfy also their aggressive drives by frustrating their analysands when the latter ask directly or indirectly for, but receive 'No "reaction." No advice. No explanation. No solution. No help. No love' (Menninger 1958, p. 55). Another source of aggressive gratifications for the analyst is his interpretations to the analysand, since according to psychoanalytic theory 'such an "interpretation" is always a "blow" (to one part of the ego ...) even when it is enlightening and freeing. It seems to the patient like a stone, when he asked – or hoped – for bread ... It often seems critical, and it is not comforting' (p. 137).

The psychoanalyst's narcissistic needs are partially fulfilled from the analysand's recognition of him/her as a prospective helper, a confidant, someone with knowledge and insight, and, frequently, someone to be emulated. The choice of becoming and being a psychoanalyst can, in psychoanalytic terms, be determined by some identification with an idealized parent imago, that is, with the kind of parent the psychoanalyst unconsciously wished to have in early childhood. But also, in accordance with psychoanalytic theory and techniques, psychoanalysts have, when they are practising analysts, become aware of these drives (sexual and aggressive), of their narcissistic needs, and of the defences they habitually use, and can take them into account in their work.

According to psychoanalytic theory, voyeurism is merely the reverse of exhibitionism and one may be a defence against the other. The writings of psychoanalysts who are required by their theory and technique to remain as anonymous to their analysands as possible can then be understood as resulting from psychoanalysts' needs to exhibit themselves and to be admired by others. Since psychoanalytic theory states that all human functioning is overdetermined, that is, has more than one reason for its occurrence, psychoanalytic publications can additionally be explained as determined by otherwise unsatisfied narcissistic needs of the analyst.

5.1.1.2 Psychoanalytic theorizing too must, in terms of its theory, be explained as resulting from unconscious sexual and/or aggressive drives and unconscious defences against those drives. The construction of a theory is a thought process. Freud wrote about the latter: 'If we include thought processes in the wider sense among these displacements, then the activity of thinking [*Denkarbeit*] is supplied by the sublimation of erotic drive energy' (1923, p. 274). Other defence mechanisms directly related to thinking are intellectualization and rationalization. The first consists of the pursuit of intellectual activities in order not to become conscious of unconscious wishes which would be unacceptable to the adult personality. In rationalizing, the individual invents reasons for his/her actions and believes them to be the actual motives because the true motives conflict with his/her standards and self-concept. Again, by the use of a defence mechanism, these motives are prevented from reaching consciousness. What reaches consciousness are 'often ideational-representations of repressed drives ... When their emergence subserves the defense against a still more forbidding striving ... the liberation of the energies used formerly ... against those drives which now come to consciousness ... are accompanied by relief, elation, exultation, and so forth ... similar to the experiences attending another form of thought-organisation, namely, wit and humor' (Rapaport 1951, p. 719f.).

That the psychoanalytic theory of creative thought and theory construction applies to psychoanalysts themselves is clearly demonstrated by Freud himself, who repeatedly called his own theoretical formulations 'speculations' and 'fantasies' and who wrote with respect to his theory about destructive drives: 'I remember my own defensiveness when the idea of the destructive drive first emerged in the psychoanalytic literature, and how long it took until I became receptive to it. For, the little children do not like to hear it when the inborn human inclination toward "evil," toward aggression, destruction, and thus also to cruelty is mentioned' (Freud 1930, p. 479). Here Freud recognized his own previous defence and its childhood origin which were related to his theorizing.

5.1.1.3   The psychoanalytic evaluation of psychoanalysis qua science is difficult. Although Freud and his followers have insisted that psychoanalysis is a science, I have found no criteria by which they distinguish science fron non-science. In his posthumously published last presentation of psychoanalysis Freud wrote that all sciences 'make it possible to determine the laws which [unknowable processes] obey, and to pursue their mutual relations and dependencies over long uninterrupted stretches, in short, [to pursue] what one calls the understanding of the respective area of natural phenomena' (1940, p. 80f.). In the same work one finds stated that 'the task [of all sciences] consists in discovering behind the qualities of the research object which are directly given to our perception something else which is less dependent on the particular receptive capacity of our sense organs and which approximates more closely the assumed real state of affairs ... Reality will always remain "unknowable" [*unerkennbar*]. The gain which scientific work ... unearths will consist in the insight into connections and dependencies which exist in the external world, [which] can be somehow reliably reproduced or mirrored in the internal world of our thinking, and the knowledge of which enables us to "understand" something in the external world, to foresee it, and possibly to change it' (p. 126f.). A few years earlier Freud had written in his letter to Einstein on the subject 'Why War?': 'Perhaps you have the impression that our theories are some kind of mythology ... But does not all natural science in the end amount to such mythology? Is that different for you today in physics?' (1932, p. 22).

5.1.2   *The psychologist within a gestalt-phenomenological framework* According to English and English (1958) gestalt psychology or theory is 'the systematic position that psychological phenomena are organized, undivided, articulated wholes [whose properties] are properties of the whole as such and are not derived by summation of its parts ... The notion of "parts" with attributes of their own, independent of the whole, is held to be misleading'; while 'phenomenology advocates the study of *phenomena* or direct experience taken naively or at face value; ... behavior is determined by the phenomena of experience rather than by external, objective, physically described reality ... Data are necessarily the product of the methods used in observing.'

At the symposium on 'Behaviorism and Phenomenology' MacLeod (1964) stated: 'The phenomenologist begins his observation of phenomena by ... a deliberate attempt to identify bias and temporarily suspend it or at least to shift observation systematically from one bias to another ... For the phenomenologist, meaning is central and inescapable. To try to abstract or extract meaning from the phenomenal world is futile; all we achieve is a change of meaning ... To build a science of psychology one must begin with the phenomenal world, but then one must transcend it' (pp. 52ff.).[1]

What MacLeod refers to as 'bias' corresponds to what I discussed in my Introduction as 'frame of reference' and 'perspectivity' (cf. 0.3). By using different frameworks and approaching basic psychological issues from different perspectives I am making, throughout this book, 'a deliberate attempt to identify bias and ... at least to shift ... systematically from one bias to another.'

5.1.2.1   The application of gestalt-phenomenological conceptualizations of human activities[2] to gestalt-phenomenologists leads to the conclusion

---

1   Some Anglo-American readers may wish a justification for my hyphenating gestalt and phenomenological psychology and discussing them in one breath. First, the gestalt psychologists have been widely recognized as phenomenologists, as evidenced by MacLeod's many examples drawn from the works of gestalt psychologists in his above quoted paper entitled 'Phenomenology: A Challenge to Experimental Psychology,' and by Michael Wertheimer, who refers to 'a phenomenological approach like that of the gestalt psychologists' (1972, p. 103). Second, phenomenology is, among Anglo-Americans, frequently linked to existentialism and I definitely want to avoid that association. Gestalt-phenomenology confronts, as the reader will find in my final chapter, problems, while existentialism (or 'existential phenomenonology') 'has the earmarks of the least fruitful kind of escape from a set of traditional constraints – an escape to an *Answer* rather than a *problem* ... There are woolly revivalist overtones – a disposition to accept in advance an intellectual object the properties of which have hardly been cognized.' (Koch 1964, pp. 35f.; original emphasis).

2   In order to avoid the kind of *behaviourization* mentioned in 2.5.2, I shall not use the word 'behaviour' in relation to gestalt-phenomenologists. In-

---

that their activities consist of meaningful acts which are wholes that cannot be further broken down and which relate to a total situation as it is experienced by each gestalt-phenomenologist individually. That situation is meaningful. At the same time, the meaning it has for any given gestalt-phenomenologist is, in terms of his approach, only one among many aspects of that situation. From the perspective of another gestalt-phenomenologist the situation may have quite a different meaning. However, each gestalt-phenomenologist can, to some extent, change positions and thus experience different aspects of that situation.

The activities of gestalt-phenomenological psychologists qua gestalt-phenomenologists consist of the phenomenal analysis of experiences-as-such, the comparison of phenomena in the naïve perceptual world to phenomena in the measured perceptual world, and the study of actions and experiences [*Erlebnisse*] of others through dialogue, observations, and experiments. The phenomenal analysis of experiences-as-such consists of detailed descriptions of experiences like feeling anxious, feeling cold, sensing something else as cold, etc. The comparison of the naïve perceptual world to the measured perceptual world is the subject matter of the study of perception and of psychophysics. In the study of the actions and experiences of others, their life-space, namely, the meaning these actions and experiences and their environments have to those others, must first be determined (Holzkamp 1964).

Gestalt-phenomenological research, whether experimental, observational, or consisting of dialogues, leads only to the meanings which such observations have for the investigator. Consequently, published reports by gestalt-phenomenological psychologists are expressions of their individual experiences which they have made from their always limited perspectives, though they may have shifted from one perspective to others. The meaning any given gestalt-phenomenologist obtains from reading the reports by another gestalt-phenomenologist depends, in terms of this approach, on the perspective or perspectives taken by the former and contains only aspects of what the writer experienced.

---

stead, I shall use the words 'action' and 'activity' when referring to what a human being deliberately does and what presupposes the presence of a mind (cf. chapter 3, footnote 1).

5.1.2.2 The theories developed by gestalt-phenomenological psychologists, in so far as they engender theories at all, result from taking new perspectives which lead to new questions and further research. However, gestalt-phenomenologists are usually less interested in inventing theories which necessarily attempt to explain experiences by means of hypothetical constructs, than in discovering lawful, that is, invariant, relationships between phenomena (gestalt laws). Being concerned with meanings, gestalt-phenomenologists are cognitive psychologists who conceptualize relations rather in terms of reasons than in terms of causes (cf. Toulmin 1970). Their discoveries of laws and even their inventions of theories result from their own experiences and the meanings these experiences have to them. The discovering of laws and the inventing of theories, qua cognitive activities of the gestalt-phenomenological psychologists themselves, can be accounted for in terms of their own approach as resulting from an active cognitive search for further meaning.

5.1.2.3 In line with the relationism expressed by the concept of perspectivity, gestalt-phenomenologists differ as to the criteria for what they consider to be scientific. Thus, Kelly (1955) makes no categorical difference between scientists and non-scientists and considers all constructions of one's world as science. On the other hand, Laucken (1973), who analysed in great detail the theories each of us develops to explain people's actions in everyday life, seems to indicate by the title of his book *Naive Verhaltenstheorie* that he distinguishes between naïve and scientific theories. Others explicitly differentiate 'pre-scientific' from 'scientific' theories and research (cf. chapter 8, footnote 3).

When such a distinction is made by gestalt-phenomenologists, it is made on the basis of the degree of the explication of viewpoints, of the number of different perspectives taken and aspects considered, and of the clarity of definitions. There can thus be no claim made for clear-cut decisions as to what is and what is not scientific. 'Science' is considered to be a 'fuzzy set' (Gaines 1976). Research as well as theories may be more or less scientific.

Since gestalt-phenomenologists study the meanings events have to human beings, they do not consider the meanings events have for them as different from the meanings events have for others. They may, therefore, just as well describe their own experiences, as Kohler (1961) did after wearing prism lenses for extended periods of time, or participate as partners in each other's experiment (cf. 6.1.2). They do not need 'naïve subjects' for their experiments. They rather need sophisticated partners who can discover bias and propose alternative perspectives.

The apparent paradox in the gestalt-phenomenological position lies in the fact that laws are established where only aspects of relationships can be known and that gestalt-phenomenologists need collaborators who draw each other's attention to ever new aspects of events while sharing the basic approach to psychology, namely that it always suffers from some kind of perspectivity and is never complete.[3]

5.1.3　*The psychologist within a Piagetian framework*　Since English and English (1958) list neither 'genetic psychology' nor 'Geneva school' nor 'Piaget' or 'Piagetian psychology,' I shall, for a description of his approach, let Piaget speak for himself in my own English translation. He states: 'Whatever we do, whether acting overtly or thinking internally, what we do presents itself as an adaptation or rather as a re-adaptation. The individual acts only when s/he experiences a need, i.e., when the equilibrium is temporarily interrupted between the environment and the organism. Then, the action strives to re-establish the equilibrium, namely to re-adapt the organism' (1947, p. 10). After puberty the individual is capable of performing such re-adaptations through 'formal operations,' namely, through hypothetico-deductive reasoning which is fully reversible because it can always return to its point of departure, its premises, and seek alternative detours. The adult is, according to genetic psychology, less egocentric and more objective, that is, relativistic, than the child because the adult can consider an event from various perspectives.

The research of the Geneva school has consisted of the recording of the spontaneous verbal productions of children, of observations of their doings at various ages, of experiments in natural settings, and of the recording of children's answers to open-ended questions. The application of Piaget's theory to himself, his followers, and his research leads to the conclusion that observations made by the genetic psychologists

---

3　For an extremely detailed and sophisticated phenomenal analysis of the psychologist, particularly in his role as diagnostician, see Kaminski's (1970) 'micropsychological analysis.' Kaminski points out the impossibility of explaining the behaviour therapist's diagnosis of a client's problems in behaviourist terms.

---

established disequilibria in them by raising questions and presenting problems, and that the genetic psychologists proceeded 'to re-establish the equilibrium' through their research and through the invention of their theories. The latter were developed by means of formal operations leading to new disequilibria (questions) and further research using different perspectives and thereby becoming more and more objective without ever eliminating all egocentrism. 'Moreover, as an equilibrium is never achieved entirely in reality' (1947, p. 177), research and theory construction always continue.

Thus, Piagetian psychology seems entirely applicable to itself and its adherents. Their writings can also be conceptualized as resulting from experienced needs and the use of formal operations for re-adaptation. Like the verbalizations of thoughts which these writings contain, the latter are themselves verbalizations of thoughts and can be understood and analysed in their own terms without leading to logical or psychological paradoxes. The publications of Piaget and his students are scientific because they use hypothetico-deductive reasoning, that is, formal operations.

5.1.4   *The Psychologist within a dialectic-materialist (diamat) framework*
Neither English and English (1958), Eysenck, Arnold, and Meili (1972), nor a number of German-language psychological dictionaries that I consulted list dialectical-materialist psychology. Cole and Maltzman (1969) also do not give any description of the principles of diamat psychology in their *Contemporary Soviet Psychology*, though they at least point out in their introduction that even 'before 1950 ... Pavlovian theory was not a conspicuous part of their [the Soviet psychologists'] conceptual framework' (p. 8) and that 'a common misinterpretation of Soviet psychology is that it employs, almost exclusively, classical Pavlovian conditioning methods and that all phenomena are forced into a common theoretical framework which views behavior as the sum of atomistic, elementaristic reflexes. Psychology in the USSR was never like this, was never restricted to Pavlovian conditioning, and certainly it is not today ... Relatively little classical conditioning is being conducted, much less than in the United States' (p. 11f.). What then is the diamat concept of man?

For an answer to this question, I turn to Sergej L. Rubinstein, who was the leading diamat theoretical psychologist between 1940 and his death in 1960, who is still widely quoted by present-day diamat as well as non-diamat German-language psychologists, and whose works have been translated into twelve languages – but not into English. According

to Rubinstein, the main characteristics of human beings are consciousness, which may be used reflectively, and practical and theoretical
activity, which stands in a dialectic interaction with consciousness. Consciousness is itself an activity. It reflects the objective world in correspondence to one's personality. In society, activity takes on the form of
work. In work human beings interact, and this interaction has led to the
development of language. Work is related to consciousness because the
former *requires that the result of the work becomes conscous as its goal*
(1973, p. 296; emphasis in original).

The meaning of 'materialist' in 'dialectical-materialist' is much misunderstood by empirical positivists. 'Consciousness is no "lesser" reality than matter' (1974, p. 281), but 'in rejecting the reduction of
everything that exists to inorganic matter the diamat preserves the
qualitative characteristics of matter and overcomes the homogeniza-
tion and the complete reduction to quantitative data' (p. 280). This is no
materialism in the sense of Anglo-American philosophers. 'Objective
reality is not only matter – the consciousness of a human being for
another human being is also objective reality' (p. 282). Rubinstein
objects again and again to the elimination of consciousness from psychology: 'First one separates man's consciousness from life, from his
actions, from everything external, material, real, and then one is aston-
ished that one finds no access to it' (p. 286).

Since consciousness is central to diamat psychology, it deals – like
other non-positivist psychologies – with meaning: 'The "meaning" of
the things, the phenomena (ideas, etc.) determines behaviour ... [and is]
objectively determined by the subject, his characteristics, demands,
needs' (p. 289).

In the Anglo-American sense, diamat psychology is a humanistic
psychology. As the study of 'the lawfulness and conditions ... of the
reflection [*Widerspiegelung*] of the characteristics of the environment,
of the ability to change it and finally to form it in cooperation [with
others]' (Clauss 1976) it also does not avoid such subjects as 'love,'
'hate,' and 'creativity.' Thus, Rubinstein (1974) wrote that 'love [is] the
confirmation of the human existence of one concrete human being for
another. To be loved means to be the most existing of everything.' On
the other hand, 'hate [is] the ideational form of annihilation, of the
moral murder of a human being' (p. 288).

The application of such a psychology to psychologists presents no
problem to me. (In his empirical study of thinking and problem solving,
Rubinstein [1977] points out that 'problems' exist always only for the
individual who reflects an event as problematic. There are no problems

in themselves.) Since the world is reflected in the consciousness and in the activity of human beings, it is also reflected in the consciousness and in the activity of psychologists. Psychology as a science thus consists of 'an ever more encompassing and more adequate reflection of the objects of scientific knowledge' (Budilowa 1974, p. 133). This reflection depends on 'the particularities, the general characteristics of human thinking and of the human psyche in general. They encompass the individual qualities of the creative thought of the scientists as well as the typical peculiarities of the consciousness of a society at a given historical epoch. As representatives of the societal consciousness and the ideology of their time, the creators of science depend, with regard to both their general world-view and their scientific concepts, on the developmental conditions of the scientific epistemological process' (p. 132). (Budilowa points out that this subjective aspect of science has so far not received the attention it deserves.) Thus even the creation of psychological theories like Rubinstein's reflection or mirroring theory can be explained on the basis of diamat theory itself. The latter does not cause a paradox. Only when diamat psychologists, as they usually do, write about 'objective knowledge' without specifying what they mean by that expression do they introduce a paradox into their framework.

5.1.5   *The psychologist within a behaviourist framework* English and English stated in their *Comprehensive Dictionary of Psychological and Psychoanalytic Terms* (1957) under 'behaviorism,' after referring to 'the difficulties of defining *behavior*': 'Today it is almost true that no one is a bahaviorist, or that nearly everyone is, and the term has lost most of its distinctive reference.' The situation has hardly changed since 1957. Under these circumstances a discussion of 'behaviourists' in their own terms becomes well-nigh impossible. Nevertheless, I shall stake out the area I intend to cover by speaking about 'behaviourism.'

I shall make use here of the definition by English and English (1957) of 'behavior theory' as 'a general point of view, rather than a particular theory, that conceives of the task of psychology as the determination of the relation of stimulus to response, both of these as measured in physical units.' In addition, I shall follow Koch's (1961) definition of 'behaviourism' as 'a conception of psychology ... which holds its subject matter to be the objectively observable actions of organisms ... seen as "responding" to conditions (stimuli) set out by the outer environment and inner biological processes.'

'Cognitive behaviourism' or 'cognitive psychology' of the last decade does not represent any essential departure from this definition of 'behaviourism' as Hein (1979) clearly demonstrated. The new 'cognitive psychologists' assume cognitions to be 'intervening' or 'mediational variables' which can be inferred from observable behaviour. Contrary to the previously discussed psychologists, cognitive behaviourists do not consider experiences – either their own or those reported by others – to be the primary data of psychology.

5.1.5.1   The application of the behaviourist conceptualizations of organisms to behaviourists leads to the conclusion that the behaviour of behaviourists consists of measurable and objectively observable responses to environmental and biological stimuli. These responses are, as far as behaviourists qua behaviourists are concerned, experimental behaviour. Unfortunately, contrary to the behaviour of psychotherapists like Rosen (English 1961, Scheflen 1961), which has frequently been directly observed by other scientists and made public through tape-recordings, films, and video-tapes and their transcriptions, the behaviour of experimental psychologists is hardly ever observable by other experimental or non-experimental psychologists. In spite of the rejection by behaviourists of introspection, all that is observable are usually self-reports by experimental psychologists about their expectations (hypotheses), their experimental behaviour, and their observation of the behaviour of others (assistants, confederates, 'ss'). In the few instances where films of experiments have been made (e.g., Milgram 1965) these contain only selected excerpts from an experiment and show little or nothing of the behaviour of the experimenter.

The self-reports (articles and books about experiments) by behaviourists are observable by others and supposedly enable others to make the same observations themselves about which the authors of the self-reports report. There are, however, several unanswered problems involved here. First, publications are the results of writing behaviour. But the writing behaviour of behaviourists is usually not made public. Nor would it be of any use if it were made public. For, from observations of someone's writing behaviour no behaviourist can determine what prior observations by the writer have led to his writing behaviour. Since, to my knowledge, no studies have shown any difference between the writing behaviour of writers of experimental research and writers of fiction, the observation of writing behaviour could not determine the fidelity of the self-reports of experimenters.

Nor has behaviourist research reached the point where the content of what someone writes can be gathered from his/her writing behaviour. The implicit assumption that behaviourists' reports about their experiments are valid descriptions about those experiments – and without that assumption no behaviourist would even attempt to replicate another behaviourist's experiment – is hence not experimentally founded in behaviourism. So far behaviourists have determined neither the relationship between experimental events as stimuli and writing about these events as responses, nor the relation between printed words in publications as stimuli and replication of experiments as responses. Second, as I shall discuss in detail in chapter 10, published reports about experiments commonly contain insufficient information for true replication of the experiments. Thus, even if behaviourists had determined the relation between a published report as stimulus and replication of a reported experiment as response, such replication would in practice be almost never possible. Thus, the claim by behaviourists that their experiments consist of objectively (which I take to mean 'intersubjectively') observable behaviour is untenable both on theoretical and practical grounds.

Furthermore, if the behaviourist's experimental behaviour (designing and carrying out an experiment, data collecting and analysing, writing up and discussing the results) is conceptualized within the framework of classical conditioning, then it results from prior conditioning of the behaviourist. If conceptualized in terms of operant/instrumental conditioning, the behaviourist's experimental behaviour is the result of previous reinforcements. In either case, it is difficult to understand how new experiments are ever designed and performed.[4]

5.1.5.2 Now, behaviourists also develop theories which they test through their experiments. These theories too must be conceptualized as the results of either previous classical conditioning or reinforcements of theory-generating behaviour. In either case, the theories result from 'conditions set out by the outer environment and inner biological processes.'

The application of behaviour theory, specifically of classical and operational/instrumental conditioning, to the experimental behaviour and theory construction of behaviourists raises a number of further

---

4 Irle (1975) reports about a West German exchange student who returned from Stanford characterizing the colossal idling of psychological research in the U.S. in the following words: 'The same dogs are again and again entered in the dog-race and no one notices that they have been dead for the longest time' (p. 98).

---

questions.[5] In the first place, how can one distinguish between scientific research and theories, and non-scientific research and theories, if all behaviour, including experimentation and theory construction, consists of responses to environmental stimuli and inner biological processes? In other words, by what criteria are the published verbal responses of behaviourists to be considered scientific and not the published verbal responses of other people? Are all verbal responses by behaviourists to be considered scientific or only some? And if only some, how are the scientific verbal responses of behaviourists to be distinguished form their non-scientific verbal responses on the basis of behaviour theory? Do scientific verbal responses differ from other verbal responses in terms of the environmental stimuli causing them or in terms of inner biological processes or both? Are scientific verbal responses distinguishable from unscientific ones on the basis of prior reinforcements?

Assuming that behaviour theory provides criteria for differentiating between scientific and unscientific verbal behaviour and behaviour in general, the question arises why behaviourists attempt to build a science on the behaviour of 'naïve subjects' instead of building it on the scientific behaviour of other behaviourists. The distinction made by behaviourists between 'naïve subjects' and psychologists raises the additional question whether observations made on the behaviour of one provide any knowledge about the behaviour of the other. If this is not possible, two behaviour theories and corresponding research programs are required: one for the study of the behaviour of psychologists and one for the study of the behaviour of 'naïve subjects,' that is, one for Es and another one for Ss (cf. 6.3).

The experiment by Resnick and Schwartz (1973; cf. 3.4.3.3) was designed to justify research with 'naïve subjects': people who are aware of reinforcements qua reinforcements are not responding to the reinforcements. In other words, stimuli are reinforcing only, if at all, when they are not recognized as reinforcements. However, since it is not clear what 'recognized' means in behaviourist terms, let us make a little 'thought experiment' and imagine that we are watching Greenspoon (1955) on whose experiment the one by Resnick and Schwartz was based. We should then notice two people, of whom one says single

---

5 'Social-learning theory' (Bandura 1969) begs the same questions, plus the one of whom the inventor of new theories like that one imitates.

---

words and the other says occasionally 'unh-hunh.' As the two of them carry on we may first notice that the second individual says 'unh-hunh' more and more frequently. If we are very attentive and good scientific observers, we may also notice after a while that the first individual says more and more plural nouns. We may now develop a hypothesis to the effect that the increase in unh-hunhs and the increase in plural nouns are not mere statistical correlations but that there exists a cause-effect relation. Thus, we may conclude that plural nouns reinforce unh-hunhs or vice versa. There seems no unequivocal criterion for deciding which is the reinforcement for which response.[6]

From observing the behaviour of the two individuals one cannot tell whether the one increasing the number of plural nouns or the one saying 'unh-hunh' more and more often reinforces the other, or whether the increase in the frequency of the occurrence of both is merely accidental. Nor can one tell whether one of the two utterances is a conditioned stimulus for the other and, if so, which of the two for the other.

The puzzle presented by this experiment cannot be solved by behaviour theory. The behaviourist whose position Koch (1964) considers as 'based on thin and shifting rationales, and adopted more to serve needs for comfort and security than a passion for knowledge' (p. 20; i.e., in Habermas's terms, to serve technical rather than hermeneutic interests) tries to wiggle out of this dilemma by calling the one who utters 'unh-hunh' 'experimenter' and the other 'naïve subject.' As we have seen, there is no observational basis for this distinction. If one refers to the 'intentions' of one of the partners, one moves outside the behaviourist framework. There is no basis even outside the behaviourist framework for attributing intentions to one of the two individuals and not to the other. Even post-experimental questioning of the two as to their awareness of what went on during the experiment cannot produce more than mere verbal behaviour, that is, sounds which may be interpreted in many different ways. For instance, Newberry (1973) reports about an experiment in which he found that the results of post-experimental

---

6 The difference between this example and the famous cartoon in which one rat says to another rat 'I have trained this behaviourist experimenter to bring food when I press the lever' lies in the distinction I make between rats and human beings. I attribute, on the basis of my experience, reflections upon their own actions to the latter but have no basis for such attribution to the former.

---

inquiries about what the 'subjects' knew about the experiment and what they intended during it are highly unreliable. To put it plainly, according to Newberry, not only experimenters lie but other people do too.

All of this raises new questions. Are there 'naïve subjects'? If so, how can they be identified? Can valid conclusions be drawn from the behaviour of 'naïve subjects'? What does their behaviour tell us about the behaviour of others and particularly of psychologists?

5.1.5.3 Behaviourists assume that the bonds between stimuli and responses or between behaviour and reinforcement – depending on whether a classical conditioning model or an operant/instrumental one is used – are purer or stronger in some instances than in others. Behaviourists further assume that in 'naïve subjects' stronger bonds can be established than in behaviourists. Since the responses of behaviourists are classified by them as science, it follows that weaker bonds between stimuli and responses or between behaviour and reinforcement are more scientific than stronger ones. Now, weaker bonds are, according to behaviourist theory, the result of intervening variables and/or contamination of conditioning. Hence, it becomes more obscure how the stimuli and the responses or the behaviour and the reinforcements are related. With respect to the behaviourists' theories and research this means that their antecedent conditions are less clearly determinable than the antecedent conditions of the behaviour of their 'naïve subjects.' What then is scientific about behaviour the antecedent conditions of which cannot be determined?

One of the possible responses to this question (stimulus) by behaviourists is that their behaviour is scientific because they perform experiments or, in their own jargon, because they use 'the scientific method.' We must ask what makes their method scientific in behaviourist terms. Their method is, in their own terms, a 'habit' which has resulted from conditioning, for instance, from such positive reinforcers as promotions, salary increases, grants, public recognition by other behaviourists, etc. Thus, behaviourists give positive reinforcement to one another. The more behaviourists there are the more reinforcement each one can get. The status quo is thereby ensured for behaviourists on the basis of their own theory and practice. In the presence of large numbers of behaviourists other psychologists will get much less positive and much more negative reinforcement. This situation promotes the technical interest of the behaviourists but not the hermeneutic or the emancipatory interest of others.

Neither the experimental nor the theory-construction behaviour of behaviourists can be described in behaviour-theoretical terms. Merely the observable power position of behaviourists, the control they exert over psychology in terms of its teaching, research, publications, etc., can possibly be explained in behaviourist jargon: 'By giving positive reinforcement to the behaviour of behaviourists and negative reinforcement to the behaviour of all other psychologists, behaviourists control the behaviour of psychologists and make it largely predictable.'

This is, of course, not the only possible way of presenting the situation. One can, for example, describe the actions of behaviourists in cognitive terms as self-fulfilling prophecies (Merton 1949). Such an interpretation would be more in line than the above one with the views of the much abused physicist P.W. Bridgman who wrote with respect to 'Skinner's solution' that it is not 'the only possible one or ... a solution that takes into account all that we see or is significant. Furthermore, I believe,' Bridgman wrote, 'that at least some psychologists find this solution congenial because they take it for granted that the world has to be public and one. It follows that any solution consistent with this conviction stands a better chance of being adopted without searching analysis of all the implications' (1959, p. 216).

5.2   ONE PSYCHOLOGIST CAUGHT IN ANOTHER'S FRAMEWORK: THE HALL OF MIRRORS The representatives of any psychological theory are more or less critical of competing psychological theories. Their critique is usually expressed from the vantage-point of some metascience (Radnitzky 1973) rather than from the vista of their own psychological theory. Thus, behaviourists criticize the other psychologies discussed here for lack of controlled experimentation to support their claims, for the absence of control groups and of quantified data by means of which the statistical significance of observations can be determined and the correspondence of observed to predicted results can be evaluated. Behaviourists judge the other psychologies to be unscientific when the latter present as supporting evidence of their theories unsystematic observations, phenomenal analyses, interpretations, and reflections. Similar metascientific critiques are raised by other psychologists against psychoanalysis, like the diamat reproach that the generalizations of psychoanalysis are too broad (Clauss 1976). However, I am not dealing here with metascientific evaluations of one psychology by another, but am raising the question as to whether any given *psychological theory* makes it possible to compare various psychological theories in terms of their usefulness, that is, of their explanatory power. In order to discuss such evaluations of psychological theories in terms of one another, one must stay within the framework of what, in psychological terms, a given psychological theory considers a psychological theory to be.

5.2.1   *A psychoanalytic evaluation of psychological theories* Human psychic functions can be evaluated in psychoanalytic terms with respect to the developmental stage of which they seem to be an expression. Hence, any psychology which denies the existence of unconscious motives or drives and of unconscious defence mechanisms gives, from a psychoanalytic standpoint, evidence of the use of the defence mechanism of denial by its proponents. To the extent to which they deny such unconscious dynamic factors, psychological theories are consequently considered to represent irrationality and immaturity.

5.2.1.1   This would apply not only to behaviourism but also to gestalt-phenomenological, genetic, and diamat psychology. However, the three latter rank higher on a scale of maturity than behaviourism because they deal at least with consciousness and are reflective. Gestalt-phenomenological and genetic psychology in particular may be considered to give evidence of the defence mechanism of intellectualization, as their representatives have little to say about emotions. Since this defence mechanism is related to adolescence in psychoanalysis (A. Freud 1937), gestalt-phenomenological and genetic psychology result from a rather advanced level of maturity.

5.2.1.2   The psychoanalytic understanding of behaviourism is quite simple. The behaviourist concern with prediction and control can be related to the training of the child to predict elimination and to control its sphincters. The child is told: 'Control yourself' and 'Behave yourself.' Its thoughts and feelings are disregarded, as they are by the behaviourist model. Like the subjects in a behaviourist experiment, the child is toilet 'trained' in a mechanistic way. As McGuire (1967) stressed, behaviourists must 'do something,' must produce, just as the child is expected to produce when placed on the potty. From a psychoanalytic point of view behaviourism thus has the characteristics of anal fixations. Correspondingly, it uses the defence mechanisms characteristic of that stage of object relations: isolation, reaction formation, and undoing.

'The study of behaviour' independently of thoughts and feelings can be ascribed to isolation. The quantification of non-quantifiable qualities, the 'measurements' of reified hypothetical constructs, and the use of statistics which cannot 'help us to explain the functioning of organisms' (Hayek 1964) can be explained as *metromania*, resulting from reaction formation against the insight that human actions and experiences are 'complex phenomena' which are largely unpredictable and uncontrollable. Undoing (*ungeschehen machen*; literally translated 'to make not to have happened what actually happened') is possible only by means of magic, and magic is commonly performed through rituals and specific words. The 'propensity to imitate as closely as possible the procedures of the brilliantly successful physical sciences – an attempt which in our field may lead to outright error ... [and which] is decidedly unscientific in the true sense of the word, since it involves a mechanical and uncritical application of habits of thought to fields different from those in which they have been formed' (Hayek 1975, p. 433) – this 'scientistic attitude' is clearly a mere ritual. On the other hand, the pretence of explaining 'structures of *essential* complexity, i.e. ... whose characteristic properties can be exhibited only by models made up of relatively large numbers of variables' (p. 435) by means of such ambiguous (English and English 1958) and therefore meaningless terms as 'stimulus,' 'response,' 'behaviour,' and 'conditioning' is, from a psychoanalytic view, pure word magic.

Another example of undoing is what is called 'debriefing.' This is supposed to make the experimenter's deception of the 'subjects' not to have happened. As Orne pointed out, debriefing serves in the first place the purpose of relieving the experimenter's guilt feelings for having lied to the other participants in his/her experiment. This means that it serves as a defence mechanism. Like all defence mechanisms, such debriefing may have quite different results from the consciously intended ones. The participants may feel insulted and/or foolish when they are told that they were lied to, and they may consider behaviourists rather as liars who are not to be trusted than be relieved and grateful for being told the truth after the experiment is over. In believing that s/he debriefs the participants for their good the experimenter is also using the defence mechanism of rationalization.

From the adaptive point of view of psychoanalytic theory (Rapaport 1959) these defences can be seen as enabling behaviourists to continue with minimal anxiety 'acting out' their aggressive drive in experiments with living beings, and to 'happily proceed on the fiction that the factors which they can measure are the only ones that are relevant' (Hayek 1975, p. 434). Equally adaptive, because anxiety reducing, is the behaviourists' refusal to learn other languages and become thereby aware of the mistranslation of the few foreign publications in psychology which have been rendered in English, and of the vast amount of psychological research which conflicts with the claims of behaviourism.

5.2.2   *A gestalt-phenomenological evaluation of psychological theories* The attempt to evaluate different psychological theories from a gestalt-phenomenological point of view was specifically made by Holzkamp in his *Theorie und Experiment in der Psychologie* (1964). The criterion used by Holzkamp which he called 'representativeness' can be related to the gestalt-factor of similarity. Holzkamp proposed a number of dimensions on which to judge the representativeness of an experiment for the theory from which it is derived (cf. Brandt 1967b). In addition, he discussed various kinds of 'liabilities' of theories. These liabilities, which can be compared to lack of closure and to poor *Prägnanz*, decrease the 'empirical value' of a theory. When hypothetical constructs are reified and a 'hidden reality,' a 'second reality' behind our experienced reality, is thus created, the liability of a theory is increased. Consequently its empirical value is diminished.

5.2.2.1 If hypothetical constructs like ego, id, and superego, defence mechanisms, and drives are treated as hidden realities, the empirical value of psychoanalytic theory is reduced. As long as they are treated as mere 'connecting principles' psychoanalytic theory can be considered as a relatively good theory because it has a high 'integration value,' namely, it integrates more aspects of human psychic functioning than any other theory.

5.2.2.2 On the basis of Holzkamp's criteria, genetic psychology can be said to have a high integration value because it uses relatively few connecting principles (equilibrium, accommodation, assimilation), which is, however, reduced by the fact that genetic psychology does not deal with the area of emotions.

    Both psychoanalytic and genetic theories have little empirical value because development plays an important role in them and one can hardly design experiments in which development becomes the independent variable. The same applies to the historical-societal aspect of diamat theory. Neither history nor society nor the means and relations of production can easily be made into independent variables. 'Constructive implementation' (experiments) must, within the framework of these theories, be replaced by 'selective implementation' (field observations).

5.2.2.3 The reader may now think that behaviourism has a high empirical value in Holzkamp's terms. This is not, however, true because behaviourist theories contain statements – and that is what theories consist of anyhow – about human actions and experiences while, at the same time, excluding the individuals' life-space, without which actions and experiences do not exist. Moreover, behaviourists define terms 'operationally' and thereby not only exclude the life-space of the people whom they investigage, but also restrict their theories to lose all generality. For instance, when 'anxiety' is defined as the administration of an electric shock it means something *the experimenter does* and no longer something *the other person has*. It is no longer conceptualized as someone's anxiety, namely, as part of the life-space of the participant. In addition, the experiment is not about the general concept of anxiety but only about 'responses' to electric shocks. Thus, the use of operational definitions introduces an 'irreducible basic liability' into behaviourist theories. No representative experiments can be designed on the basis of such theories, which therefore also have a 'maximal basic liability.' Behaviourist theories have consequently, by Holzkamp's criteria, both a low empirical and a low integration value.

5.2.3 *A genetic psychological evaluation of psychological theories* Genetic psychology and particularly 'genetic epistemology' deals with cognitive development. This development is conceptualized as taking place in cumulative stages. In each stage new cognitive 'operations' are added to previous ones. Each subsequent stage is characterized by less 'egocentrism,' more 'objectivity,' and greater 'reversibility' of the operations compared to the preceding stage. 'Egocentrism' is defined as the inability to take different points of view, 'objectivity' as 'relativism' or the awareness of the existence of many points of view and the ability to take several perspectives into consideration, and 'reversibility' as the possibility of returning to the point of departure. Thus, reversibility makes objectivity possible because it enables one to take a new approach to the same issue.

Genetic epistemology thus contains, like psychoanalytic theory, a series of stages to which different psychologies can be assigned in terms of the operations which are preferred by them. Since these stages refer originally to cognitive operations, genetic epistemology seems a particularly appropriate framework for the evaluation of various psychologies, more so than psychoanalytic theory, whose stages are derived from psychosexual development and from object relations.

5.2.3.1　Psychoanalysis is entirely based on interpretations and thus functions on the level of 'formal operations.' Gestalt-phenomenology takes place on the same level, in view of the consideration of perspectivity and of different frames of reference (Metzger 1963, Witte 1966) and approaches (Giorgi 1970). Diamat psychology too functions on the level of formal operations, since consciousness and reflectivity play a central part in it.

5.2.3.2　To the extent to which behaviourism investigates only 'responses' to 'stimuli,' it deals merely with functions in the sensori-motor stage. However, this does not mean that behaviourists themselves qua behaviourists function on the level of the sensori-motor stage. They can rather be said to function on the level of 'concrete operations [which] are not yet completely dissociated from the concrete data to which they apply. In other words, the operations develop separately field by field, and result in a progressive structuralization of these fields, without complete generality being attained ... Concrete operations fail to constitute a formal logic; they are incompletely formalized since form has not yet been completely divorced from subject-matter ... They are fragmentary. We can, with the aid of concrete operations, classify, order serially, form equalities or set up correspondences between objects, etc., without these operations being combined into a single *structured whole*' (Piaget 1957, p. 15ff.). A psychology which claims to study only 'observable behaviour' by experimentally isolating variables and 'measuring' them functions on the level of concrete operations. It is egocentric by considering the experimenter's point of view as the only one and disregarding the fact that the experimental situation may be conceptualized quite differently from the point of view of the participants. The repeatedly mentioned reification of concepts is, in Piagetian terms, a sign of 'nominal realism,' which is also characteristic of the stage of concrete operations. Finally, behaviourists explicitly reject formal operations as a scientific method by calling them disparagingly 'armchair psychology.'

5.2.4　*A diamat evaluation of psychological theories* Diamat psychology acknowledges explicitly that a developmental theory must include 'the development of processes of knowledge-acquisition [*Erkenntnisprozesse*] themselves' (Kostjuk 1974, p. 114). According to diamat theory, development of human psychic functioning progresses, despite possible momentary regressions, 'from lower (simpler) to higher (more complicated) forms of the total system and its dialectic with the environment, its structural and functional perfection, and the increase of its organization and stability' (ibid.). Human consciousness was first 'directly interwoven with material activity' and develops later into 'cognitive actions, actions "in the head" [which] enable human beings to plan their practical actions and foresee the results of the latter. Different kinds of intellectual [*geistige*], theoretical activities originated enabling human beings to penetrate more deeply into the essence [*Wesen*] of the phenomena of the objective [*gegenständliche*] world in which they were intereted' (p. 102f.). Individual development also progresses from being taught by one's elders to learning through interaction with others, namely through co-operation in work. Through working together human beings create themselves. They develop further through self-regulation, self-correction, and self-improvement. For the evaluation of different psychologies, the historical-social position of the psychologies may also be taken into consideration.

From this last point of view all the other psychologies mentioned here are bourgeois because they were invented in bourgeois capitalist societies. One can, however, discern differences between them in terms of the developmental concepts of diamat psychology sketched in the last paragraph.

5.2.4.1 Psychoanalytic theory is derived from and continuously being revised on the basis of psychoanalytic work, the cooperation between analyst and analysand. Their work consists of mental activities and the communication of these through language. 'Practical action' is explicitly excluded from their work. The goal of psychoanalytic work is, specifically for the analysand, to create him/herself through this work, but also for the analyst, to gain new insights and understanding of human psychic functioning. Self-regulation, self-correction, and self-improvement play a central role in psychoanalytic work, which thus combines theory and practice.

5.2.4.2 In so far as gestalt-phenomenologists cooperate in their experiments with the other participants, take their own perspectives into account and reflect upon them, and study intellectual activities and the resulting meanings, they function on an advanced level of development in diamat terms. Because they disregard both individual histories and the histories of the societies in which they and their participants live and work, they have not reached the highest level of development from a diamat standpoint.

5.2.4.3 From that approach, the neglect of the history of society is also a shortcoming in genetic psychology. This psychology has, however, reached an advanced level because of its emphasis on activity and consciousness and their dialectic, as expressed in the interaction between schemata and aliments and by the concepts of accommodation and assimilation. Genetic epistemologists too are reflective and apply their theoretical activities to themselves and their theory. As the studies by Piaget and his co-workers demonstrate, they cooperate with the children whom they study and enter into dialogues with them whenever possible.

5.2.4.4 Behaviourists do not enter into dialogues with their 'subjects,' who merely receive instructions about what to do, if they are human, and who most of the time are rats and other animals with whom dialogues and cooperation are not even possible. In behaviourist experiments, the experimenters are preferably also merely following instructions and are ignorant of the hypotheses which are being tested (cf. 7.1.6). Intellectual activities are considered to interfere with the acquisition of knowledge. Neither the experimenters nor the 'subjects' are expected 'to plan their practical actions and foresee the results.' In its attempt to copy an outdated model of the physical sciences, behaviourism disregards not only the individual histories but also the histories of the societies of both the researchers and those who are being studied. From a diamat viewpoint, behaviourists thus function on a low, primitive level of development in every respect.

5.2.5 *A behaviourist evaluation of psychological theories* What was said in the preceding section about behaviourism as a psychological theory from a behaviourist approach (5.1.5.3) applies equally to a behaviourist evaluation of other psychological theories. All of them must be considered as epiphenomena of responses to stimuli, particularly of reinforced responses. Differences between various theories can be the results only of different stimuli which impinged on the respective theorists and/or of different reinforcements received by those psychologists. As far as the evaluation of competing psychological theories is concerned, behaviourism thus leads to

5.2.5.1 *The evaluation of theories paradox:* No psychological theory is any better than any other because all of them are mere verbal behaviour resulting from stimuli having impinged upon and reinforcements having been received by different psychologists.

Consequently, without resorting to some metascience behaviourists cannot rank various psychological theories by any criteria offered by their own theory. For such a ranking there would have to exist some rank order of stimuli and/or reinforcements enabling behaviourists to test experimentally the hypothesis that stimuli A, B, C and/or reinforcements X, Y, Z result in the verbal behaviour through which theory T has been stated. First it would, however, be necessary to demonstrate experimentally that those stimuli and reinforcements are 'better' than other stimuli and reinforcements which have produced different verbal behaviour leading to other theories. 'Better' would have to be operationally defined and made measurable. The result of such an attempt at evaluating various psychological theories within a behaviourist framework would always remain mere verbal behaviour.

The above-mentioned paradox and the impossibility of evaluating different psychological theories, including behaviourism, within the framework of behaviourism must be seen in the light (or darkness?) of the behaviourist claim to be a 'value-free' science. A 'value-free' science has no criteria for e-valu-ation. From the behaviourist point of view a theory must 'prove itself.' This view is consistent with behaviourism's technical interest.

5.3   THROUGH THE LOOKING GLASS Non-positivist readers will agree with me that theories cannot be evaluated without values and without theories. They will accept my relationism, namely that any given theory is better or worse than other theories only in relation to some frame of reference.[7] However, positivist readers will insist that there exist 'objective' standards by which a theory can be 'proved' to be either 'true' or 'false.' But theories do not 'prove themselves' nor can people 'prove' them (cf. footnote 9 of this chapter).

One problem with 'objective' is that the word has different meanings to different people. To some it means 'unemotional,' 'without bias,' or 'absolutely true.' I cannot conceptualize a psychologist who works

---

7 For example, Hall and Lindzey (1957) state that theories are 'only *useful or not useful*' (p. 11; their emphasis). This brings us back to my chapter 3: Useful to whom for what? (3.4). When I was twelve years old we had a gardener who explained to me that a rose in a potato field is a weed and that a potato plant in a rose garden is also a weed. I do not think he had ever heard about 'relationism,' but he had the concept.

---

without any 'emotional' involvement in his/her work,[8] without some point of view from which s/he starts, or who makes no assailable assumptions.

Others, by 'objective,' mean: taking several perspectives and becoming aware of relativity (Piaget); 'situations in which there is more than one, and perhaps many, methods of getting to the same terminus' (Bridgman 1959, p. 46); 'arguable, which can be exposed to rational criticism ... which does not merely appeal to our subjective intuitions' (Popper 1976, p. 138); intersubjective, or 'concordant' (Traxel 1968).

In view of this multiplicity of uses of the word 'objective,' I cannot but side with Feyerabend (1970) that 'it seems to me that an enterprise whose human character can be seen by all is preferable to one that looks "objective," and impervious to human wishes.* The sciences, after all, are our own creation, including all the severe standards they seem to impose on us. It is good to be constantly reminded of this fact' (p. 228).

5.4   REFLECTION: OUR FURRED AND FEATHERED BROTHERS AND SISTERS The theoretical systems of psychoanalysis and genetic psychology do not apply to animals. Though some gestalt-psychologists like Köhler (1925) did research on the problem-solving of primates and on the perception of chickens, gestalt-phenomenologists have done their investigations with human beings rather than generalized from amoebae to homo sapiens. Only the behaviourists do not believe that any relevant differences exist between rats and people. In spite of the classical behaviourists' frequent references to Pavlov and his work on conditioning, behaviourists commonly ignore that, with the introduction of the idea of the second signalling system, Pavlov made a categorical distinction between human and animal learning – a distinction which has pervaded diamat psychology ever since.

In the context of this chapter on psychologists caught in different theoretical frameworks, the question of the applicability of findings

---

8 My inability to conceptualize an 'unemotional' psychologist seems shared even by Rosenthal (1969), who believes that 'no scientist would select intentionally a procedure likely to show his hypothesis in error' (p. 195), i.e., that no scientist would ever do what Popper (1934) stipulated under the name of 'falsificationism' as the basic requirement of science.

* For this problem of 'alienation' cf. Marx (1844a, 1844b). – Footnote by Feyerabend

---

from animal research to psychologists arises only with respect to behaviourists. Since the most popular toy in their game of science is still the Skinner-box, which is the model for programmed learning, whether with computers or through 'token economies,' I shall briefly investigate the parallel between rats and humans by means of an example involving the most eminent ratologist himself (Koestler 1967).

Which human 'behaviour' resembles most closely the lever-pressing of rats? Most likely the operation of a one-armed bandit. Money is generally considered as a reinforcer for the human animal according to behaviourists. Losing money to a slot-machine is considered by them as negative reinforcement and hitting the jackpot as the ultimate positive reinforcement.

It is well known that the frequency of lever-pressing by the rat increases when it leads to the release of food-pellets and decreases when no food-pellets are dropped by the machine as a result of lever-pressing. Does lever-pressing by humans at the one-armed bandit increase and decrease in frequency correspondingly? According to Professor B.F. Skinner's report in a telephone interview broadcast by the Canadian Broadcasting Corporation in its program 'As It Happens' in August 1977, Skinner, like many other gamblers, put coins into a slot-machine and pressed the lever as long as he did not win, but collected the loot and ran when he hit the jackpot. In other words, being deprived of his money and receiving negative reinforcement led to the continuation of lever-pressing, whereas positive reinforcement led to its extinction. My own observations of people at slot-machines corroborate this first-hand report right from the horse's mouth. This is surely empirical evidence falsifying the assumption that all human beings are rats. As to Skinner's experiments with pigeons, they are clearly for the birds.[9]

---

9 Readers may argue that what Hofstätter (1956) called 'dubious anthropomorphizing of the rat [and subsequent] bizarre myomorphizing of the human being' (p. 364) has led to such successful technologies as programmed learning and token economies. I am concerned here with theories. The issue is therefore whether those technologies cannot be more meaningfully described by other theories than by behaviourism. The Phoenicians travelled very successfully from the eastern Mediterranean to Scandinavia and possibly to North America on the basis of a cosmology which has been widely rejected. Their successes can now be explained by what is considered to be a better theory of the universe (cf. Klein et al. 1969).

6 Psychologists Caught in Different Interpersonal Frameworks

Psychologists Caught in Different Interpersonal Frameworks
U & I

6.0 Human psychology is the only science besides medicine pursued for the ultimate benefit of both the researcher and the objects under investigation. (Ratology is not pursued for the benefits of rats.) In human psychology members of the same species interact. I mentioned these interactions before. Following the discussion of several psychological theories in the last chapter I want now to reflect on the relationships between various kinds of psychologists and their respective partners as these relationships result from the theories and methodologies. The problems which are specific to the psychologist-object relationship in experiments and in personicating (impression formation) will be dealt with in detail in special chapters (cf. chapters 7 and 8). The theme which is central to this book will reappear in connection with the issue of the alienation of psychologists (cf. chapter 10).

6.1 PSYCHOLOGIES WITH A HERMENEUTIC INTEREST: $E \equiv S$ Hermeneutic psychologists aim at understanding human actions and experiences. They make no distinction in principle between themselves and others. I express this fundamental equality between hermeneutic psychologists as investigators and other people as investigatees by the formula $E \equiv S$, in which E stands for any investigator and S for any investagatee. $\equiv$ represents equivalence but not identity.

In a hermeneutic psychology, whatever can be stated about S as a human being applies also to E qua human being. The difference between E qua E and S qua S is one of roles. In addition, there exist individual differences not only between any given E and any given S but also between any two Es and between any two Ss. Each individual interprets his/her own actions and experiences and the actions of others. There exist no uninterpreted 'facts.' Other people's interpretations of events are of as much interest to the hermeneutic psychologist as his own. Hermeneutic psychologists, therefore, cooperate with others in research and consider the others as partners; perhaps as junior partners who have less knowledge and experience in research, yet as human beings capable of reflection and self-reflection and whose interpretations of psychological events are themselves relevant psychological events.

6.1.1   *Psychoanalytic relationships* I discuss psychoanalysis here as a research method to investigate the psychology of analysands, about whose role Menninger (1958) wrote: 'In theory, it *might* be possible to defend the thesis, that, other factors being equal, the passive contributions of the therapist are sufficient ... It is helpful to discuss the possibility of a psychoanalytic therapy proceeding from beginning to end without the analyst ever having said a word. Of course, he would contribute to it by his consistency of appearance, attention, interest, and audience. But would not the patient, by virtue of the experience itself, gradually overcome his resistances enough to learn what the deeper meaning of his behavior was and decide how much of it he could relinquish, how much he could alter, and how much better off he would be to do so?' (p. 127f.) By silently listening, the analyst could both collect his data and minimize the contamination of the data through his expectations (hypotheses). Recognizing that data can, however, never be completely independent of the collector, Menninger (1958) wrote: ' ... The analyst is also a person ... He, too, is a party to the contract ... He, too, is reacting, even though his predominate, overt reaction is one of silent listening ... It is never accurate to say that a certain reaction is that of person A to person B ... A's reaction is modified by the way B reacts to the way A reacts to the way B reacts, and so on' (p. 86).

Not only in theory but also in practice are the same principles applied to both analyst and analysand. Every psychoanalyst must not only undergo his or her own analysis but continues to analyse his/her counter-resistances and counter-transferences with the help of another psychoanalyst, and ought to continue his or her analysis every five years according to Freud's (1937b) suggestion. The basic psychoanalytic assumptions that resistances interfere with people's functioning and self-understanding, and that transferences interfere with their relations with one another, are thus fully applied to psychoanalysts themselves:

It is incontestable that, in their own personality, analysts have not entirely achieved the measure of psychic normalcy to which they want to educate their patients ... Analysts are persons who have learnt to perform a specific art and are besides permitted to be human beings like others too ... As a result of the special conditions of analytic work, the analyst is by his own defects truly handicapped in correctly grasping the circumstances of the patients and in reacting to them appropriately. Hence it is reasonable to require of the analyst as part of his credentials a higher measure of psychic normalcy and correctness; in addition, he also needs a certain superior quality in order to act toward the patients in certain situations as a model, in other situations as a teacher. And finally, it must not be forgotten that the analytic relationship is built on love for truth, that is, on the recognition of reality, and excludes all pretence and deception ...

... But where and how ought the poor guy to acquire that ideal qualification which he will need in his profession? The answer will be: in his own analysis with which his preparation for his future activity begins ... Its work is fulfilled when it gives the apprentice the firm conviction of the existence of the unconscious, when it brings about the resurgence of repressed material and the otherwise unbelievable self-perceptions, and when it shows him through a first sample the technique which alone proved itself in the psychoanalytic activity. This alone would not be sufficient as instruction. However, one reckons that the stimulation received during the self-analysis will not end with the [didactic] analysis, that processes of ego-transformation continue spontaneously within the analysed person, and that all further experiences will be utilized in the newly acquired sense. This actually happens and in as far as it happens it makes the analysed individual fit to be an analyst.

It is regrettable that something else also happens. (Freud 1937b, pp. 93ff.)

Concerning the relationships between psychoanalysts and their analysands it is further relevant to note that analysands participate in the relationship always voluntarily because nobody can undergo psychoanalysis involuntarily. Even in this respect, the relationship is one of equals.

Psychoanalysts and analysands are unequal in a number of obvious ways. The former have been previously analysed, are experts, are being paid. The analysands pay for the analysis, need not 'be polite ... considerate ... fair ... practical ... realistic,' in exchange for which the analyst 'promises there will be no retaliation, no passing of judgment, not even a definite conclusion' (Menninger 1958, p. 52). This is part of the contract which analysand and analyst freely enter. The common purpose of that contract is the joint investigation of the analysand and not the analyst. The difference between hermeneutic research and technical experiments lies in the fact that in the *joint* investigation of psychoanalysis one of the participants is simultaneously subject and object, whereas the 'subject' in the experiment is mere object. Experimental 'subjects' do not investigate. For that reason, one can experiment just as well with flatworms, rats, or pigeons as with other human beings. Whereas in psychoanalysis cooperation between investigator and investigatee is a *sine qua non*, cooperation in experiments is undesirable, as discussed in the literature on 'demand characteristics,' 'suspiciousness of experimenter's intent,' 'evaluation apprehensions,' etc. (cf. Rosenthal and Rosnow 1969).

$E \equiv S$ is recognized in psychoanalysis as applying also to individual differences. Just as psychoanalysis deals with individual differences among people in general, it takes into account individual differences among psychoanalysts: 'I must say explicitly that this technique [free floating attention] has resulted as the only effective one for my individuality; I dare not dispute that a differently constituted medical personality may be urged to prefer a different position (attitude) toward the patient and toward the task to be solved' (Freud 1912, p. 376).

6.1.2   *Gestalt-phenomenological relationships*   When the gestalt-phenomenologist Wolfgang Metzger (1966) defined psychology as the only science in which the investigator and the object of his investigation can exchange places, he meant what I designate by $E \equiv S$. Such exchange of places was actually the rule in the experiments of the gestalt psychologists, as well as in those by Bühler and others at Würzburg who investigated the psychology of thinking. Their participants frequently operated the equipment or presented the questions to the principal investigators, who thus served as 'subjects.'

Particularly in the study of various kinds of experiences, be they perceptual, conceptual, affective, or conative, the experimenter has an additional check on the reports received from others and on his/her interpretation of those reports, if s/he has placed her/himself into the same environment and observed her/his own experiences under those conditions. If the experimenter takes Lewin's concept of 'life-space' seriously, the experimenter recognizes that his/her life-space is not identical with that of the experimental partners, that their perspectives differ, and that the experimental results must be interpreted in terms of possible differences between their respective life-spaces.

The relationship between the researcher and his/her partners in gestalt-phenomenological investigations is stated quite unambiguously by Giorgi (1970): 'Man as subject of research can in no way have assumptions attributed to him that one would deny to man as research-er ... The investigator and the subject are equals with respect to basic assumptions about their humanity' (p. 203). From this statement follows that 'the relationship between experimenter and subject will have to be based upon appeal and cooperation and understood in that sense as well. However, research designs will always have to be open-ended so that the final closure can be made by the subject himself. When the closure is accomplished, data are obtained, but now they are obtained from a perspective that includes the subject's more spontaneous participation' (p. 203f.).

The interaction between E and S is a social action to which social action theories must apply. For example, qua human beings, both E and S may try to deceive the other. Either of them may at one point during their interaction suspect the other of lying. Such suspicion leads to conflict in their interaction and may interfere with the aims of the investigation. In order to avoid such disruption as much as possible, a group of gestalt-phenomenological social psychologists involved in the development and testing of a social action theory set up the following ground rules:

6.1.2.1 1 All participants are informed about the goals and interests guiding the experiment.
2 Participation in the experiment must be entirely voluntary, even to the extent that any participant may stop participating at any time during the experiment.
3 No form of deception whatsoever is permitted in the experiments.
4 At the beginning of the experiment, the experimenter teaches the participants ways of testing his statements so that he can conclude later during the experiment that participants trust him whenever they do not test his statements.
5 Experimenter and participants agree that the latter openly express any doubts they have about any aspects of the experiment and that the former dispel those doubts to the satisfaction of the participants.
6 The experimenter promises to make the results of the experiment available to all participants in an easily understandable form. (Werbik 1976)

6.1.3   *Piagetian relationships* Piaget's, Inhelder's, and their many co-worker's research method is basically phenomenological. Genetic epis-temology is based on other people's conceptualizations. In the numerous publications by the Geneva school the verbalizations of those conceptualizations are faithfully reported. The researchers did not use questionnaires on which Ss had to fit checkmarks into E's concepts. Piaget was one of the first psychologists to use content analysis for the categorization and classification of the spontaneous utterances of others (Piaget 1923). In that sense, E ≡ S applies also to his work and that of the Geneva school as a whole. Where it cannot apply is in their analysis of the thought processes and structures of children. The latter, being on an intellectual level preceding that of formal operations, can, therefore, not make the same analyses of their thought processes which the investigators performed. The difference between Es and Ss in genetic psychological research must be seen as referring to different levels of development but not to 'basic assumptions about their humanity.'

6.1.4 *Dialectical-materialist relationships* E ≡ S is perhaps most strongly contained in a psychology according to which 'the human being is a human being only in his reciprocal relation to other human beings – "the human being" – that are human beings in their relations to one another. "The human being" as something absolute, as "thing in itself," as something isolated and separate by itself is no human being, rather is no being at all, is nothing … In reality we have always two relations: human being and existence as well as human being and other human beings … We shall also investigate [these relations] thus, for only if one takes them in this reciprocal relation and determinedness, can one correctly uncover both the gnoseologic relation to the human being to existence and the human being's moral relation to the other human being' (Rubinstein 1974, p. 272).

This statement stems from the most frequently quoted dialectical-materialist (diamat) psychologist. A distinction, except in terms of roles, cannot be made between E and S in diamat psychology. There is no place for research with animals in a psychology which considers as its main subject-matter the 'complex dialectics of consciousness and activity [and] their relation to the external world' (Schorochowa 1974, p. 18). The basic similarity between human beings in the role of Es and others in the role of Ss is also expressed in diamat concepts of psychological research methods: 'On the one hand the subjectivity of data derived from self-observation and interviews does not at all mean that those data are false. On the other hand such methods as observation, experiments, and tests which are usually considered to be objective, do not in themselves protect us from some kind of subjectivism … The subjectivity of facts does not consist in their being derived directly from the "subject," the investigatee, but results from a subjective selection in perception and evaluation of reality whereby they may receive an inadequate, wrong meaning ... be it [through] the biased observation by the scientist or the mistaken interpretation of facts based on erroneous theoretical assumptions' (Iwanowa and Assejew 1974, p. 183).

6.2   PSYCHOLOGIES WITH A TECHNICAL INTEREST: E ≠ S

6.2.1   Technical psychology is *The Psychology of the Other One* (Meyer 1921) and the study of *The Fundamental Laws of Human Behavior* (Meyer 1911). According to this approach, 'psychology ... makes explicit the distinction between the experimenter and the thing observed' (Stevens 1935, p. 517). It is this distinction which I express by the formula E ≠ S. The 'thing' observed may be a flatworm, a rat, or a human being. The explicit distinction indicates that the experimenter is not considered to be a 'thing' which is observed by others. Since others are 'things,' the faculty of observation cannot be attributed to them. They merely 'respond' to 'stimuli' – among which the experimenter is not counted.

As a consequence of considering S a thing, E assumes that what E decides to be a stimulus, a reinforcement, a reward, or a punishment for S will be just that for S, that is, will stimulate, reinforce, reward, or punish S. It will not affect S in ways which E did not intend or in ways which E cannot observe. What S does and E registers is considered to be S's response to what E decided to be the 'independent variable.'

Technical psychologists do not consider themselves or the instructions they give Ss to function as stimuli or independent variables. The instructions given to S in an experiment are always reported separate from the stimuli.

E ≠ S is also illustrated by Rokeach's (1968) definition of 'the task for psychology,' namely 'to learn enough about the structure of belief systems to know how to form them, and how to modify them so that they will best increase the happiness and freedom of the individual and his society' (p. 21). In other words, psychologists 'know,' whereas individuals and society, that is, Stevens's 'things,' have merely 'belief systems' and, consequently, do not 'know' what will best increase their happiness and freedom.

Scientists with technical interests commonly believe that the technological changes which may result from their science will benefit all mankind. Hence, *ad maiorem scientiae gloriam = ad maiorem humanitatis gloriam.*[1] Technical psychologists may, therefore, treat 'the thing observed' in ways which their 'subjects have learned from childhood [to be] a fundamental breach of moral conduct [such as] to hurt another person against his will' (Milgram 1963, p. 376). Thus, 'experimental psychologists ... almost without exception, have at times gathered data involving pain, anxiety, or deprivation of their subjects' (Kaufmann 1967, p. 322). The *Ethical Standards of Psychologists* (American Psychological Association 1963) state correspondingly that 'when a problem is of scientific significance ... the psychologist is justified in exposing research subjects, whether children or adults, to physical or emotional stress as part of an investigation.' Throughout their code of ethics, technical psychologists make it clear that they are the ones who decide whether a problem is of scientific significance and what methods to use for its investigation. Kaufmann (1967) makes E ≢ S particularly clear by stating that the hurting of others by Ss exposes the latter's 'moral flaws,' while the hurting of others by Es is beyond criticism, as such criticism represents 'arguments *contra* [sic!] *hominem*, even more unworthy of fellow scientists and colleagues than outsiders.'

E ≢ S is further indicated by the use of 'deception' by technical psychologists and their use of 'lie'-scales to detect 'cheating' by Ss. In other words, Es 'deceive' and Ss 'lie' and 'cheat.' Moreover, Es are permitted to deceive Ss but Ss are not permitted to deceive Es. E deceives S and gives a lie-test to S only to obtain 'hard data,' 'facts' to solve problems of scientific significance.

The 'explicit distinction between the experimenter and the thing observed,' that is E ≢ S, is further characterized by E's use of reflection and the rejection of reflection on the part of Ss. In order to design an experiment, carry it out, analyse the findings, and write a report, E reflects upon earlier research in the field and the data gathered in E's own experiment. Ss are considered to be 'naïve' and are told, for example when instructed to place checkmarks on a questionnaire, to give their 'first reaction, not a long drawn-out thought process' (Eysenck Personality Inventory).

---

1 The assumption that what is good for science is good for mankind is questioned by Feyerabend (1970): 'It is good to be constantly reminded of the fact that science as we know it today is not inescapable and that we may construct a world in which it plays no role whatever (such a world, I venture to suggest, would be more pleasant than the world we live in today)' (p. 228).

6.2.2   As a result of their own reflections and introspections, technical psychologists construct 'operational definitions' which they use to describe the Ss' behaviour. However, at the conventions at which they present their research reports Es do not operationally define their desire to go to the bar or to be with a member of the opposite sex. (Sex distinctions among Ss are referred to as 'males and females' whereas Es are addressed as 'ladies and gentlemen.')

6.2.3   Operational definitions are usually used to make concepts quantifiable and measurable. Technical psychologists measure only Ss' behaviour and not their own. They are capable of determining the strength of their desire for a drink or for sexual intercourse without measuring either. Es may measure their own temperature to determine whether they *are* sick but not to determine whether they *feel* sick. They determine the latter by introspection. To determine an S's anxiety Es use the Taylor Manifest Anxiety Scale, but to determine one another's or their own anxiety they require no measuring instrument. S's hunger is measured in hours of food deprivation, amount of food consumed, or voltage in a grid S crosses to reach the food. E's hunger is not measured in either hours between meals, dollars spent on a meal, or density of traffic E is willing to cross to reach a restaurant.

    Some technical psychologists take physiological measurements of Ss to determine the Ss' psychological state. But Es do not measure the amount of secretion from their Skene's and Bartholin's or Cowper's glands, as the case may be, to measure their sexual attraction to another convention participant. Nor do they measure their galvanic skin responses to measure their own anxiety. They do not use lie-detectors to determine whether or not they are deceiving Ss.

    Technical psychologists convert idiographic data obtained from Ss, but not those obtained from Es, into nomothetic data. They do not pool the data gathered by different individual Es and perform various statistical analyses on those group data. When different Es obtain different results in similar experiments the Es form *ad hoc* hypotheses about the possible causes for the differences rather than pool their findings.

6.2.4   When performing conditioning experiments, technical psychologists assume that Es condition Ss but not vice versa. Responses by Ss which support E's hypothesis do not reinforce E positively and responses by Ss which contradict E's hypothesis are not assumed to be negative reinforcements for E. (Otherwise these psychologists would have to assume that, in the course of an experiment, those of E's responses increase

PSYCHOLOGISTS CAUGHT 122

which lead to an increase in hypothesis-supporting behaviour by S, and those of E's responses decrease which lead to hypothesis-falsifying responses by the Ss. Without the assumption of E ≠ S, conditioning experiments would necessarily be self-fulfilling prophecies.)

Since much of what is called 'behaviour modification' or 'behaviour therapy' is based on results from conditioning experiments, what applies to the latter applies equally to the former. In this interpersonal framework which explicitly serves technical interests, E's behaviour is assumed to change S's behaviour without reciprocity. Changes in the behaviour of S ('client') do not modify E's behaviour. According to the underlying theory, E but not S can make intelligent decisions on the basis of some freedom of choice.

6.2.5   Another theory which stands and falls with the assumption E ≠ S is cognitive dissonance theory, according to which people attempt to eliminate contradictions in their behaviour. In the corresponding experiments, only the Ss are assumed to defend against dissonance-provoking perceptions and information. E's perception and interpretation of S's behaviour cannot be subject to dissonance theory. Otherwise E's findings would have to be explained as resulting from E's defence against data which conflict with E's hypothesis. This would mean that cognitive dissonance theory was not testable by psychological experiments. The same reasoning applies to attribution theory which, if applied to Es, would make its findings into attributions by Es and, therefore, scientifically worthless.[2]

6.3   CRITIQUE OF THE E ≠ S ASSUMPTION The assumption that E ≡ S, which hermeneutic psychologists make explicitly, is often implicit in what technical psychologists do. When the latter speak of 'voluntary' Ss, they assume that those Ss have a 'free will' by means of which the Ss can decide whether or not to participate in E's experiment. When Es try to 'deceive' Ss – not by classical or instrumental conditioning, but by

---

2 Since attributions play a central role in psychology, particularly in personality theory construction and diagnostics, I shall discuss them separately in chapter 8. The problems of experimenter-effect research, which may have come to the reader's mind, will be dealt with in detail in section 7.1.6.

---

misinforming the Ss about the purpose and procedure of the experiment – the Es assume that the Ss are reasoning and feeling human beings capable of reflection, hypothesis-testing, problem-solving, decision-making, and intentional actions. When Es include 'lie-scales' in their research, the Es consider the Ss capable of lying which means of making intentional choices between various alternative answers to inventory questions. Finally, when Es disregard the development and personality of one another by considering mention of an E's idiosyncrasies despicable *ad hominem* arguments, thus disregarding individual differences among Es just as they disregard individual differences among Ss, $E \equiv S$ is the logical implication.

This combination of two contradictory assumptions, namely $E \equiv S$ and $E \neq S$, is not explained by technical psychologists. They do not seem even aware of the contradiction, which is understandable since they usually do not make either of the contradicting assumptions explicit. I shall, therefore, now critically analyse some of the consequences of assuming $E \neq S$, using as a paradigm

6.3.1   *Milgram's 'obedience' experiments*[3] In order to study 'a determinant of behavior' which he called 'obedience,' Milgram (1963) invited people 'to participate in a study of memory and learning at Yale University' (p. 372). The volunteers were instructed that they had to teach one of them – who was actually a confederate of Milgram – a word-list and 'punish' him with an electric shock whenever the 'learner' did not recall

---

3   I select Milgram's experiments for a detailed critical analysis because they (1) illustrate some consequences of the implicit assumption $E \neq S$; (2) are uncritically reported in most psychology textbooks and promoted by a film, despite serious critiques by Orne and Holland (1968) and myself (Brandt 1971a); (3) are presented as investigating 'obedience' without questioning this concept; (4) offer an opportunity to demonstrate that much of the experimental psychological research to which non-psychologists object on ethical grounds contributes nothing to scientific knowledge. (A much more extensive discussion of these experiments can be found in my paper 'Science, Fallacies, and Ethics' [Brandt 1971].) Please remember that I do *not* analyse this experiment in terms of its ethical, but strictly for its scientific problems related to the assumption $E \neq S$!

---

the correct word from the list. The task was presented to the volunteers as one of paired associate learning , to investigate the effect of punishment as positive reinforcement for memorization. To this end, the 'teacher' and 'learner' were placed in separate rooms. The 'learner' was attached to some wires and the 'teacher' was seated in front of a panel with switches. The 'teacher' had to read the list of word-pairs to the 'learner' once over a microphone, and then test the 'learner's' memory by presenting him with four choices. The 'learner' was to indicate the correct one by pressing a button which lit up a number on a panel in front of the 'teacher.' Whenever the wrong number lit up, the 'teacher' was told to pull down a switch in order to administer to the 'learner' in the next room, *whom the 'teacher' could not see*, a painful but 'no permanent tissue damage' producing shock.[4] Milgram reported that *E saw* most of the Ss 'sweat, tremble, stutter, bite their lips, groan, and dig their fingernails into their flesh,' and several of them to have 'full-blown uncontrollable seizures' (p. 375) and 'a businessman ... reduced to a twitching, stuttering wreck, who was rapidly approaching a point of nervous collapse' (p. 377). Nevertheless, Milgram continued his experiments for over a decade, except for 'one occasion [when] we observed a seizure so violently convulsive that it was necessary to call a halt to the experiment' (p. 375).[5] However, Milgram was not obeying orders.

Both Milgram (E) and other people (Ss) were participating in an experiment. In line with Sherif, Sherif, and Nebergall's (1965) statement 'that subjects have favorable attitudes about the importance of research before they enter the research situation [and] are in some degree personally involved in contributing to scientific research' (p. 70), Milgram (1964) reported that 'the subjects themselves strongly endorsed the experiment' (p. 849). Both E and Ss 'hurt another person

---

4 Actually Milgram's assistant in the adjoining room received no shock. I agree with Orne and Holland (1968) that it is hard to believe that most Ss did not doubt that they were hurting someone and that this was a learning experiment. However, many Ss, like subsequent readers of Milgram's reports and viewers of his film, clearly did not question the set-up.

5 I repeat: I do not wish to arouse moral indignation and am not dealing with the ethics of the experiment, but merely with its internal logic and psycho-logic.

---

against his will[6] [though they had] learned from childhood that it is a fundamental breach of moral conduct' (Milgram 1963, p. 376).

From the perspective of an outsider, Milgram's experiment consisted of two experiments: a pseudo-experiment on 'memory and learning' and a meta-experiment on 'obedience.' In Milgram's set-up, the pseudo-experiment was embedded in his meta-experiment in such a way that he and some of his assistants were Es in the meta-experiment (the obedience experiment), some of his assistants were Ss (learners' or 'victims') in the pseudo-experiment, and the volunteers were Ss in the meta-experiment (without being told so) and, at the same time, Es in the pseudo-experiment.[7] The Es in both the meta-experiment and the pseudo-experiment considered themselves to be serving the advancement of science and, in this name, 'hurt another person against his will' – which is exactly Hilke and Kempf's (1973) definition of aggression. From this perspective – which does not assume $E \neq S$ – both the pseudo-experiment and the meta-experiment can be considered studies on aggression. The 'determinant of [aggressive] behavior' cannot be decided on from Milgram's set-up.

Milgram justified his attribution of 'obedience' to the volunteers (Ss in the meta-experiment and Es in the pseudo-experiment) – and not to himself and his Es in the meta-experiment, whose 'determinant of behavior' he never questioned – by 'the tendency to obey those whom we perceive to be legitimate authorities' (1963 p. 378).[8] He seems to confuse (a) 'authority' with respect to information (e.g., an authoritative source) and (b) 'authority' in the sense of authorized to give orders which must be executed. The two kinds of authority need not coincide.

---

6 The argument that E was hurting voluntary Ss applies equally to the Ss who had been told that the 'learner' in the adjoining room had volunteered to receive electric shocks for the purpose of the experiment.

7 Cf. figure 3 in 7.1.6, where I analyse a different problem arising from embedding one experiment in another, and the ensuing complexities.

8 Milgram committed here what I called elsewhere (Brandt 1970a) 'The Behaviorist's Leap.' He first defines 'obedience' operationally as 'behavior prior to ... rupture [of the administration of shocks]' (p. 372) and then jumps to 'a determinant of behavior' which cannot be observed and which he relates to 'authority.' In neither sense was Milgram 'obeying,' but his assistants may well have been 'obeying' him by considering him an 'authority' in both senses discussed in the text above.

The volunteers may have considered Milgram and his assistants author-ities (in the first sense) on experimental procedures, and consequently followed the experimental instructions. This does not imply that the volunteers considered Milgram and his assistants as authorities (in the second sense) whose orders they had to obey. Unless one assumes $E \not\equiv S$ (which can also be expressed by considering E an authority in the second sense and the volunteers 'subjects' in the dictionary sense of that word) there exists no basis for considering the volunteers' but not Milgram's aggressive actions 'obedience.'[9]

If, then, instead of assuming $E \not\equiv S$ one assumes $E \equiv S$, Milgram's study consists of two nested experiments, in each of which the respec-tive Es act aggressively towards the respective Ss. (The main difference between the two situations is that the Es in the meta-experiment are really hurting the respective Ss but are unaware of their aggression, whereas the Es in the pseudo-experiment erroneously believe they are hurting their Ss and being aggressive.) Under the assumption $E \equiv S$, the entire study (which has been carried on for over a decade) was entirely unnecessary. All that would have been required was self-reflection. Had

---

9 Further arguments against conceptualizing Milgram's study as dealing
   with 'obedience' are: (1) the principle of parsimony, which requires that
   E's and S's expressions of aggression be explained by the same concept
   and (2) Bateson's (1951) demonstration that 'obedience' can never be
   'determined' because 'there are certainly many instances in which [E's
   action] can be regarded as either a plea for help or as a command; similarly [S's action] can often be regarded either as a helping act or as an act
   of obedience ... It is up to [E] and [S] each to weigh his own interpretation
   of the events, to determine whether [E] was dominant or dependent.
   Finally it is important to note that [E] and [S] need not be in agreement in
   their perceptions on this level' (p. 220). Both these arguments assume E
   $\equiv$ S. (I like to add 'meddling' as a third alternative to Bateson's two.) Once
   'obedience' is recognized as an inadequate explanation for the cruelty of
   man against man – only one example of which is 'that from 1933-45 millions of innocent persons were systematically slaughtered on command'
   (Milgram 1963, p. 371) – many different 'determinants of behavior' can
   be imagined. Cf. Koestler (1967) and Brandt (1971a), where I suggest
   rationalization and displacement as defences involved in the aggression
   expressed by Milgram, his assistants, the volunteers, and people in general who mistreat others *ad maiorem dei, scientiae,* or *nationis gloriam.*

Milgram recognized that he was willing to hurt the participants in his experiment in the name of science, he could have logically deduced from $E \equiv S$ that others whom he placed into the role of Es in one experiment while simultaneously studying them as Ss in another experiment might also be willing to hurt participants in an experiment in the name of science.

I have tried to show in this critique that any ethical problem one may see in the Milgram-type social psychological experiment results from the unanalysed implicit assumption about the E – S relationship. The problem lies in the interpersonal framework used by technical psychologists which I have expressed by the formula $E \neq S$, and which Hofstätter (1956) expressed much more brilliantly and poignantly by the formula 'rat: psychologist = human: god – a formula which need no longer be thought of in its nasty grotesqueness because one has become secularized' (p. 363).

7 Psychologists Caught in Different Research Frameworks

Psychologists Caught in Different Research Frameworks
Hide and seek

7.0   In chapter 5 I dealt with the question of to what extent the theorizing by psychologists can be explained on the basis of their own theories. In the next chapter I analysed the psychologist-investigatee relationships resulting from those theories and their respective research-methods, namely, practice. I shall now analyse that practice further. I shall reflect upon the consequences for research of either including or excluding the psychologist in one's conceptualizations. More concretely, it follows psycho-logically, if not deductive-logically, from $E \equiv S$ that the psychologist is considered to be an intrinsic part of research and from $E \not\equiv S$ that E is disregarded and discounted as a factor[1] in psychological investigations.

7.1   RESEARCH METHODS As any textbook on psychological research states, there are several possible methods available to psychologists: observation without intentional interference with what is being observed as practised by ethologists, unstructured or structured interviews, open-ended or closed mail questionnaires, relatively loose field experiments, and highly controlled experiments can be used for the collection of data. It is with the collection of data that I am concerned in this chapter. Since most textbooks on research methodology in psychology stress controlled experiments I shall also pay attention mainly to the latter.

---

1 Since 'factor' means literally 'one who makes,' the psychologist is *the* factor in the research which produces 'facts,' i.e., what is 'made' by the researcher. When Hanson (1969) wrote 'Hypotheses facta fingunt' he realized that the scientists form the facts.

7.1.1   *Psychoanalytic research* Though some psychoanalysts like to make a distinction between therapeutic and research analyses, I cannot visualize any such difference except in terms of goals. If one accepts with Habermas (1971) that hermeneutic research interests have practical implications (cf. 3.1.1), the distinction between a therapeutic and a didactic or research analysis becomes a minor one.

The only research method used in psychoanalysis consists of unstructured interviews and observations. As is evident from the quote by Menninger (cf. 5.1.1.1), the analyst interferes minimally with the data production.[2] Analysts are specially trained to pay attention to their interferences, and their own 'didactic' analyses serve the purpose of making them aware of their own personalities and how these may influence their collection of data in psychoanalysing others (cf. 6.1.1). Continued counter-transference analysis with another psychoanalyst or in small groups of colleagues (cf. 1.7.1) is directed at further analysing the researcher's contributions to his/her observations. The complete elimination of effects by the psychoanalyst on the collection of data and on their interpretation is not considered possible.

7.1.2   *Gestalt-phenomenological research* Gestalt-phenomenologists use a variety of methods to collect their data. The particular method used in a given investigation is determined by the kind of data sought. For example, in a large-scale study on personality, Thomae (1968) used 'explorations,' unstructured interviews of several hours, to obtain autobiographies and descriptions of a typical day from rising to going to bed. In a study on decision-making, Thomae (1960, 1974) asked several hundred individuals to describe the most important decision in their lives and how they went about making it. In research on thinking and problem-solving, Duncker (1945) and Wertheimer (1959) presented individuals with specific geometric, medical, and other problems, and asked the participants to think aloud while trying to solve the problems. When Köhler (1917) studied *The Mentality of Apes* he set up situations in which the animals could obtain food only by solving some problems. Köhler then observed how the animals went about reaching the food.

---

2 The idea of the psychoanalyst as a pure mirror was given up early in the history of psychoanalysis. Freud and his early followers recognized that a science without any 'experimenter-effect,' without uncertainty, is a myth.

In studies of perception, gestalt-phenomenologists usually set up controlled experiments. Often the investigator lets an assistant operate the equipment and makes the observations him/herself. In other instances, participants are asked to report what they perceive in the specifically set up laboratory experiment.

The gestalt-phenomenological axiom of the perspectivity of all knowledge implicitly includes the psychologist as a factor in all psychological research. Though experimenter-effects are not often explicitly discussed in gestalt-phenomenological studies, it is understood that they are always present and can be reduced only by investigating more and more aspects of a phenomenon from different perspectives.

7.1.3   *Genetic epistemological (Piagetian) research* Like the gestalt-phenomenologists, Piagetian psychologists use the method which they consider most appropriate for the investigation of a particular problem. In their studies of the development of intellect and its structure they used pure observations, listening to and recording of spontaneous speech, experiments with few controlled variables, and open-ended questions depending on the age group and the problems under investigation. Research on perception was largely conducted through controlled laboratory experiments.

The Piagetian concept of egocentrism and the assumption that egocentrism may give way to increasing objectivity/relativism, but can never be completely overcome, imply that the investigators too can never leave their frameworks and therefore are factors in their research. I have, however, not seen any explicit discussion of experimenter-effects in Piagetian publications.

7.1.4   *Diamat psychological research* As Cole and Maltzman (1969) state, diamat psychologists' research is deemed 'overly informal' by their Anglo-American counterparts because 'reliance is often placed on individual subjects or small groups whose performance illustrates the conclusions the author is interested in' (p. x). Diamat research is in most respects similar to that of gestalt-phenomenologists and genetic psychologists. For example, Rubinstein (1977) investigated problem-solving by taking verbatim records of the verbalized thoughts of individuals during their attempts at finding solutions to various mathematical and geometrical problems. In cognitive research with objects like the Tower of Hanoi, the steps individuals go through can be observed and recorded in addition to verbalizations. More formal experiments are also not uncommon in areas where they are presumed appropriate.

From the quotes from Soviet psychologists in the last chapter (cf. 6.1.4) it is evident that they are aware of their role in the collection of data. They exhibit, however, some ambivalence when they write about the ability of scientists, including psychologists, to discover 'objective reality.' This would indicate that they do not acknowledge the ever-presence of experimenter-effects.

7.1.5   *Behaviourist research* The paradigm of behaviourist research is the controlled experiment which, as mentioned above, is also used by various hermeneutic, cognitive psychologists whenever they consider it appropriate to the kind of problem they want to investigate. I shall, therefore, analyse in some detail the part played by the psychologist (E) in an experiment.

7.1.5.1   Let us imagine the following situation. You have never heard about the autokinetic effect. I take you into a dark room and close the door behind us. Somewhere in that room is a pinpoint light which does not illuminate any of the surroundings. What are you going to do? I venture to guess that you will try to find a light-switch or the door, or ask me why I took you into the dark room; if you notice the pinpoint light, you may ask me what it is for, or try to inspect that light-source. What I do *not* expect you to do is to say 'two inches.' In order for you to say that I must, most likely, ask you first, 'How much do you see that light over there move?'

7.1.5.2   In other words, one basic requirement for a controlled experiment with human beings is some communication between E and S. I express this graphically in figure 1. If figure 1 is translated into the language of experimental psychology, one obtains the schema presented in figure 2.

   'Apparatus' (A) refers in both figures very broadly to anything E sets up as and/or in connection with the 'stimulus' or the 'reinforcement.' It may be a picture flashed on a screen, a Skinner-box, a maze, a questionnaire, or Milgram's make-believe shock-machine. The 'measuring instrument' in figure 2 may be a mechanical recording device or the same questionnaire which serves also as A. It may also consist merely of E's notes taken during or even after the experiment.

7.1.5.3   Ideally, complete 'invariance under transformation' (Pasztor Brandt 1960) would prevail, that is, no 'noise' would be introduced and no distortion would take place at any of the codings. Since this ideal situation can never be achieved because all transformations in this 'open system' (Bertalanffy 1956) are made by living organisms (human in the

FIGURE 1

Experimental situation schematized in communication terms

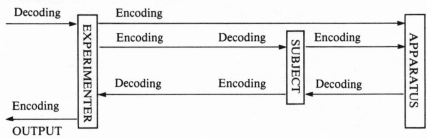

FIGURE 2

Communication flow chart for psychological experiment.
Note that communications in brackets can be eliminated.

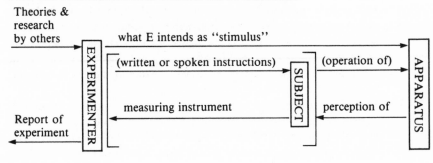

case of E, and human or animal in the case of S), there must be checks on the intrapersonal variables (perception, memory, evaluation, and decision) which may produce distortions, or the variables must be eliminated.

Checks on all codings by E consist of his/her professional training, enforcement of ethical standards with respect to the reporting of experimental results, and the critical evaluation of experimental reports on the basis of decodings by peers. The loopholes left by these checks are too numerous to be listed. They range from sloppy recording and analysing of observations to outright fudging of 'data.' Moreover, these checks themselves require further codings which introduce additional sources of possible 'noise,' as they depend on intrapersonal variables involving human beings. And so do all replications of experiments.

Any elimination of communciations and thus of codings reduces the number of uncontrollable (only 'checkable') variables. Obviously, the E-input in terms of theory and research used by E in designing the experiment cannot be controlled or eliminated but only checked according to the extent to which E makes his underlying assumptions explicit and defines his terms. Nor can A be eliminated. This would lead to ethological or clinical observations. A's encoding by E as 'stimulus' can be checked by E himself against S's 'operation' of A, if such occurs, by repeating the experiment, and by theoretical evaluations by theoreticians (introducing new coding variables). S's decoding of A is checked by E's decoding of S's report via the measuring instrument.

Because of the number of codings involved, the loop E-A-S-E represents a very weak link in the experiment. It contains the 'well-known problem in psychological research that what the experimenter denotes as the stimulus may not be what the subject defines as the stimulus' (Bieri et al. 1966, p. 8). The attempt to improve the communciation from S to E by means of less ambiguous reports obtained through more refined measuring instruments leads to loss of information (Hastorf, Richardson, and Dornbusch 1958). This report by S as decoded by E serves as check against S's decoding of E's instruction, S's possible 'operation' of A, and S's decoding of A.

In order to report the experimental findings, E must first decode and then again encode at least three (four, if S 'operates' A) codings by S. These three or four codings by S and the related possible noise can be eliminated by E serving as his/her own S as Ebbinghaus did in his famous experiments on memorizing non-sense syllables.

Many psychological problems, like those related to individual and group differences, can, for obvious reasons, not be investigated by E qua

s. Yet, many more issues than are at present can be experimentally studied through 'autopsychology.' Hence Es ought to ask themselves when they design an experiment whether the gain from eliminating three or four S-codings plus two E-codings can outweigh possible information losses due to having only a single S, namely E. As Holzkamp (1964) elucidates, a single event is of equal scientific significance to a frequently occurring one and a single S can be more truly – though not statistically – representative of a given population than a large number of randomly selected Ss.

Two E-codings, namely those of the final S-encoding, can always be eliminated by presentation of the raw data (S-encoding) in the report about the experiment. But even the raw data and the report about how they were obtained still contain codings by E which cannot be fully known without fully knowing E's internal functioning. In other words, E's contribution to the production of the events called 'data' can never be fully known.

7.1.5.4 Since behaviourists will not accept my 'armchair psychology,' I conducted with some of my graduate students a number of controlled experiments in which nothing but the instructions were systematically changed. In other words, the instructions became the independent variables. In one set of experiments (Brandt and Maier 1976) we presented two groups of people with one of the most widely used 'personality tests,' the Eysenck Personality Inventory (EPI) which its inventors, Eysenck and Eysenck (1963), claim to 'measure' 'neuroticism' and 'extraversion.' The members of one of our groups were asked to complete the questionnaires, first as if they were applying for a job and then as if they were seeking help for some emotional problem at a mental health clinic. On the basis of their checkmarks on the EPI the same individuals appeared to be extremely normal and extremely neurotic respectively. Another group of participants were given the EPI one time with instructions to imagine that they were seeking a sales position and another time as if they were applying for a research position on a secret defence project. This time, the same individuals obtained extremely high and extremely low extraversion scores respectively – and appeared less neurotic than they had when they completed the EPI with the standard instructions. All participants had assured us before the experiments that they had never seen or heard of the EPI before and we had good reasons to believe them.

Ritter (1972) demonstrated the role of instructions by variation of a study by Anderson (1971), in which the latter had shown that 'the scope, nature, and content of Wundt's approach is not widely recognized' (p. 590). Instead of selecting, as Anderson had done, twelve poorly translated statements from Wundt's German works, Ritter selected twelve statements from Skinner together with the same list of eighteen 'prominent psychologists' whom Anderson had chosen, and with Anderson's instructions to 'designate by the appropriate letter, who might be the actual author of each statement.' Only twenty per cent of the assignments of the statements by thirty-nine graduate students were made to Skinner. When nothing but the instructions was changed, attribution of the statements to Skinner more than doubled, and when the students were told that all twelve statements came from the same author twenty-seven students named Skinner correctly.

In a third investigation I varied the approach to what Rokeach (1960) had called 'a similarity-dissimilarity continuum' of religions, which he used as one of the corner-stones for his widely applied Dogmatism Scale and as foundation for his theory of belief systems. Instead of asking students of various denominations – as Rokeach had done – to indicate their agreement or disagreement with statements of the kind 'I would not hesitate to make friends with a Catholic [Lutheran, Baptist, etc.],' I asked over 300 students at two very different universities to list their five closest friends and the five people whom they would most like to have as friends. Subsequently the students were asked to indicate or guess the church-affiliations of those friends and prospective friends as well as their own. The results conflicted almost entirely with those reported by Rokeach. Whereas he concluded, for example, that 'all six Christian groups are unanimous in ranking as least similar to themselves Jews, then Mohammedans, then atheists' (p. 296), all six Christian groups in my study listed more actual Jewish friends than friends of at least one Christian church, and Roman Catholic students in New Jersey listed more Jewish, atheist, and non-denominational friends than Episcopal, Methodist, or Baptist friends.

The results from our various studies indicate that many psychological findings are not 'objective' by Bridgman's (1959) criterion of getting via 'different routes to the same terminus.' Since, in behaviourist terms, the 'responses' of the 'subjects' were entirely different in Eysenck and Eysenck's (1963) and Rokeach's (1960) experiments from those obtained by myself, the 'stimuli' must have been different ones. Since, however, what distinguished my investigation from theirs was the method, and specifically the instructions given to the participants ('ss'), the instructions must be considered as the 'stimulus.'

If one considers the instructions in an experiment with human Ss the 'stimulus,' one draws the one who gives the instructions into the framework of the experiment, that is, the experimenter becomes part of the experiment.[3]

7.1.6   *Meta-experiments: Rosenthal's dilemma*   In the middle 1960s, it dawned on Rosenthal that experimenters might, in some subtle, unintended ways, influence their Ss and thereby the outcome of their research. After all, even gods are assumed to influence the behaviour of mortals. It was not clear to Rosenthal that experiments are always, as Holzkamp (1964) pointed out, attempts to implement a hypothesis in the face of physical reality, which alone can prevent the outcome which the researcher intended. So Rosenthal sought to investigate 'experimenter-effects' and did so as a good methodological behaviourist. He set up numerous experiments which he himself designed and in which others functioned as 'experimenters' so that Rosenthal could study their effects on the experiments.

The model presented in figures 1 and 2 implies that experimenters design their own experiments and that the 'theories and research by others' represent those aspects of their prior training on which they base their hypotheses. But, as it stands, this model does not apply to experimenter-effect research. Nevertheless, experimenter-effect is commonly presented as if it were based on the same model as standard human experiments.

The actual design of experimenter-effect experiments (EEE) is shown in figure 3. As indicated in that diagram, the EEE consists of a meta-experiment which encompasses a pseudo-experiment. The transactions between 'experimenter' and 'subject' (figure 3) constitute a 'pseudo-experiment' because the researcher is not interested in its results per se, but only in so far as they pertain to the hypotheses to be tested in the experimenter-effect experiment, namely, the meta-experiment. It is the latter with which the experimenter-effect researcher is concerned. The meta-experiment is the experiment which the researcher has designed for the purpose of hypothesis testing. The pseudo-experiment is merely part of the meta-experiment and can be replaced by any number of other

---

3 Since rats are not given instructions, my findings raise further questions about the generalizability from animal experiments to human psychology.

FIGURE 3

Communication flow chart for experimenter-effect experiment

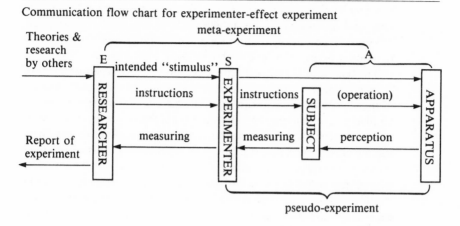

pseudo-experiments without affecting the testing of the hypotheses underlying the meta-experiment (Rosenthal 1966). The 'researcher' is, therefore, the experimenter in the meta-experiment. The true subjects of *her/his* experiment, namely, those individuals whom *s/he* uses to test *her/his* hypothesis, are referred to as 'experimenters,' while those referred to as 'subjects' are 'apparatus' in terms of the model. The so-called 'subjects' serve the same function in experimenter-effect experiments as 'stimulus persons' do in personication research and the 'learners' in Milgram's experiments.

The true positions of 'experimenter' and 'subject' in experimenter-effect experiments are evidenced by their respective actions and status. Contrary to the standard experiment as shown in figure 2, the 'experimenter' in the experimenter-effect experiment does not design the experiment in which he plays the role of experimenter, that is, he does not design the pseudo-experiment, but he merely follows instructions given by someone else (the researcher). Contrary to the standard experimenter, the experimenter-effect 'experimenter' is usually being manipulated and deceived. (One of the basic assumptions in scientific research is that the experimenter is not being deceived, for instance, by his subjects.) Contrary to the standard experiment the 'experimenter's' actions are investigated in the experimenter-effect experiment. However, in the standard experiment the subject merely follows instructions which are part of someone else's experimental design, the subject is frequently manipulated and deceived, and the subject's actions are usually investigated. Thus, the 'experimenter' of the experimenter-effect experiment is clearly the subject of that experiment (the meta-experiment in figure 3).

The actions of the 'subjects' in experimenter-effect experiments are of interest to the true experimenter (the 'researcher') usually only in terms of their being possible results from the actions of the 'experimenters.' Similarly, in the standard psychological experiment the experimenter is interested in changes in the apparatus only in so far as such changes may result from actions by the subjects. For instance, the extinction of a light on some apparatus is of interest to the experimenter when brought about by a subject within the design of the experiment, but not when brought about by some power failure. The 'subjects' in the experimenter-effect experiment are thus clearly part of the apparatus of the meta-experiment.

The experimenter-effect experiment is thus not just another experiment in psychology. As indicated by figure 3, and evident from comparison of it with figure 2, the experimenter-effect experiment is considerably more complex than the standard psychological experiment – as some readers may have realized when trying to keep the respective experimenters and subjects of the meta-experiment and the pseudo-experiment apart. Because of the inclusion of one experiment in another, each participant plays two roles. This dual position is particularly evident for the 'experimenters,' who are experimenters in one experiment (the pseudo-experiment) and simultaneously subjects in another (the meta-experiment). This dual position and the consequent complexity of the situation is veiled by the terms commonly used to refer to the various participants in experimenter-effect experiments.[4]

---

4 In several of his works Rosenthal (1966, 1969) discusses 'investigators' who gave instructions to 'experimenters.' As Rosenthal does not clearly identify those 'investigators' the issue becomes further complicated without becoming clearer. From Rosenthal's reports I get the impression that at least some of those 'investigators' were subjects in some meta-experiment. 'Each principal investigator *was* then *to* employ two research assistants' (Rosenthal 1969, p. 193; italics added) seems to imply that the 'principal investigators' had been told by someone else what they *were to* do. The true experimenter who again is not identified is merely removed

Are we dealing here merely with a semantic problem which could easily be solved by speaking about, for instance, 'research-experimenter,' 'experimenter-subjects,' and 'sub-subjects' or using some other designations? I do not think so. I rather think that experimenter-effect research, as it is being conducted by behaviourists using common experimental designs, represents another futile attempt at solving the liar-paradox. What results from these efforts is

7.1.6.1 *The experimenter-effect experiment paradox* If one hypothesizes that experimenters subtly and without their own awareness bias the results of their experiments by influencing their participants to produce the desired findings, then experimenters ('researchers') in experimenter-effect experiments (the meta-experiment in figure 3) must also be hypothesized to bias their participants ('experimenters') to produce the desired findings. As a consequence, experimenters ('researchers') like Rosenthal who want to demonstrate the existence of experimenter-bias-effects must obtain such effects in their pseudo-experiments as a result of experimenter-bias-effect in their meta-experiment – and experimenters ('researchers') like Barber and Silver (1968) who want to disprove the existence of experimenter-bias-effects must *not* obtain such effects in their pseudo-experiments as a result of experimenter-bias-effect in *their* meta-experiment. In other words, if experimenter-bias-effects are operative in all experiments with Ss, then these effects must operate in such a way that they support their existence for experimenters who believe in their existence *and* falsify their existence for experimenters who are out to disprove their existence: both positive and negative results from experimenter-bias-effect experiments can be attributed to experimenter-bias-effect. This is Rosenthal's dilemma.

One might want to resolve Rosenthal's dilemma by claiming that experimenter-effects occur only when the experimenter is not a fully trained psychologist and do not happen in research conducted by fully trained psychologists. Such a claim would be metaphysical, because it could not be experimentally investigated owing to Rosenthal's dilemma (Popper 1935). Moreover, such a claim would raise the question of the relevance of much up-to-date experimenter-effect research, at least some

---

one further step. The insertion of 'principal investigators' between the researcher who is the true experimenter and his 'experimenter'-subjects illustrates the infinite regress to which this kind of design leads.

---

of which seems to be directed at experimentation by full-fledged psychologists. Though Rosenthal (1969) sets himself occasionally apart from 'experimenters' (for instance, 'the experimenter, who very likely knows no more than we' [p. 254]), his research is designed to 'learn about those effects which *the behavioral scientist* unwittingly may have on the results of his research' (p. 182; emphasis added). Thus, Rosenthal's dilemma cannot be resolved, following Russell's solution of the liar-paradox, by assigning 'researchers' and 'experimenters' to two different levels in the hierarchy, namely $E \equiv S$ but $R \not\equiv E$ (researcher $\neq$ experimenter).

7.1.6.2 The additional question then arises as to the extent to which the 'experimenters' in experimenter-effect experiments are representative of experimenters in psychology in general (Holzkamp 1964).

Usually, experimental psychologists (the researcher in figure 3) have had many years of study and training in psychology and are well versed in the literature of their field. They usually have done work for a PhD or are at least involved in such work. On the basis of their studies and training they design their own experiments in order to test their own hypotheses and expectations. They are responsible for the experiments they carry out and for the welfare of the participants in their experiments. They are expected to publish the results of their experiments and to stand up with their name for the work they have completed. Their professional status is involved in their work. This status gives them furthermore a rather elevated position in the social hierarchy of their place of work. Consequently they have a great deal of personal involvement in their experiments and the outcome, particularly if they do not 'select intentionally a procedure likely to show [their] hypothesis in error' (Rosenthal 1969, p. 195).

The 'experimenters' in experimenter-effect experiments have so far been mostly non-psychologists. Some of them were undergraduates, others graduate students in the natural sciences or in law school, and some psychiatric aids (Rosenthal 1969). They did not design the experiments in which they acted as 'experimenters,' and the hypotheses they were testing were not their own. They were '[mis]led to expect' a certain outcome, instead of acting in terms of their own expectations. The responsibility for the various aspects of the experiment in which they acted as 'experimenters' was in the hands of others. They remained anonymous and their status among their peers was in no way involved in their experimental work. The 'experimenters' were in a correspondingly low position within the social hierarchy, a position in which they were carrying out instructions and were expected to be cooperative and execute those instructions as best they could. They were filling the positions of 'foremen.' Consequently they cannot be expected to have a personal involvement in the outcome of the experiment in which they 'serve' as 'experimenter.' Their motivation may rather be to earn a good grade in a course or to please the 'researcher.'

Earlier in this chapter (7.1.6), I discussed the fact that the 'experimenter' is an 'experimenter' only in a pseudo-experiment and that the 'researcher' is not interested in the results of that experiment per se. The question thus arises whether this lack of interest in the outcome of the pseudo-experiment is not subtly conveyed to the 'experimenters' by the 'researcher' and gives the 'experimenters' some cues as to how they can most please the 'researcher.' If the main motivation of the 'experimenters' is to please the researcher, they may be particularly well tuned in to notice those cues.

The above comparison between experimental psychologists and those individuals who most commonly served as 'experimenters' in experimenter-effect research indicates that most 'experimenters' used to date in experimenter-effect experiments are not representative of the scientists on whose activities the experiments were intended to throw some new light.

7.2   ARIADNE'S THREAD Can we get out of the labyrinth of experiments in experiments without embedding them in further experiments? In my original paper in which I presented Rosenthal's dilemma (Brandt 1975), I suggested that some decrease in experimenter-bias-effects could be brought about by having psychologists with different theoretical backgrounds observe the total procedure of an experiment. However, Watzlawick, who has analysed many psychological paradoxes (Watzlawick, Beavin, and Jackson 1967), expressed his doubts even about my partial solution: 'With respect to your solution I have my doubts. They rest on earlier work by our institute in which we tried in vain to come to an objective determination about what a specific behaviour 'really' communicates. For example, to say: "The corners of his mouth rose temporarily by about 5mm," left it nevertheless completely indeterminable whether the respective individual smiled sarcastically, cordially, or embarassedly. The hair-splitters among us found always new, deeper, yet more hidden meanings behind the meanings' (personal letter written in German, dated 6/11/76).

I agree with Watzlawick. We may not reach consensus, and when we reach it, it may be superseded later by a new consensus. Final answers can thus come neither from experiments nor from experiments about experiments. That experimenter effects can be discovered without an infinite regress, and without further experiments, is illustrated by the following episode.

7.2.1   In a graduate research seminar, a student reported on an experiment by one of the professors in which the student was participating as a research assistant. The experiment was supposed to test the hypothesis that a communicator's attire affects the credibility of his/her message. My colleague had carefully produced a video-tape on which an identical message is presented twice by the same individual, who is well-dressed on one occasion and sloppily on the other. Each of two groups of Ss was shown only one delivery of the message and rated it on semantic differential scales. The Ss were university students whom the graduate student from my seminar contacted at the university cafeteria and asked to volunteer for a psychological experiment. As I looked at the graduate student while listening to his report, I noticed that he was the only student in my seminar who was wearing a tie and a jacket, and I remembered that I had never seen him dressed otherwise. When I asked him whether he had discussed his own attire with the professor to whom he was a research assistant, he said he had not but he had noticed that only students who were dressed similarly to himself ever volunteered for the experiment, while more casually dressed and hippy-type students refused to participate. My colleague, who was investigating the effects of attire on the credibility of a communication, did not consider the effect the attire of his research assistant might have on the credibility of the communication of the latter to the prospective Ss. The researcher did not realize that the experiment was already completed before it – in his conceptualization – began. This conclusion was reached by my having my eyes open and using my mind, and did not require any experimenter-effect-experiment. My colleague could have come to the same conclusion himself.

As this episode illustrates, the experimenter-effect problem – not the effect itself though – derives from the lack of a systems approach, namely from the experimenter's neglect to include him/herself *and* his/her research assistants in the research framework. This omission results logically from the axiom $E \not\equiv S$.

7.3   AM I DREAMING? Even $E \equiv S$ does not solve the problems of psychological research. More than 2000 years ago, Chuang Tzu told the Butterfly Dream: 'Once Chuang Tzu dreamt he was a butterfly, a fluttering butterfly which felt good and happy and knew nothing of Chuang Tzu.

Suddenly it awoke: now it was really and truly again Chuang Tzu. Now I do not know whether Chuang Tzu dreamt he was a butterfly or whether the butterfly dreamt that it was Chuang Tzu although there is certainly a difference between Chuang Tzu and the butterfly. Such is the change of all things.' (Dschuang Dsi, II, 12).

Not only have I had dreams during which I was not aware of dreaming, but I have also had what I considered waking memories about non-dream events which did not fit in with other such memories, and which I therefore classified later on as memories of dreamt events. Consequently no experimental, psychoanalytic, phenomenological, or any other dream research can ever solve Chuang Tzu's problem. The researcher may be dreaming while doing the research. Kekulé reported having discovered the formula for benzol, Poincaré an important mathematical formula, while dreaming. Did they? Schrödinger (1960) drew the only conclusion which makes it possible to continue doing research: it does not matter whether he be awake or dream as long as he believes he does research in a common, shared world. Though he accepted in 1933 the Nobel prize for his contributions to physics, Schrödinger did not claim to have made any statements about a material world beyond his consciousness, a material world which he considered to be a 'mystical and metaphysical idea,' to which he referred by the Hindu term *maya*.

The existence of a material world beyond my consciousness cannot be empirically demonstrated any more by reasoning, self-observation, the phenomenological method, or free association than by means of controlled experiments. At least the following problems always remain.

7.3.1   *The problem of observation* Feelings, thoughts, and volitions of others are not observable. Behaviourism refused, therefore, to include them in its area of investigation in scientific psychology. Other schools of psychology have assumed that feelings, thoughts, and volitions of oneself can be observed. This kind of observation is commonly referred to as introspection. I do not want to revive the discussion around the old objection to introspection, namely that its results cannot be shared and thus not checked by others. I rather want to question introspection itself as a form of observing.

When I observe a stationary object in order to describe it I can look again and again at the object and check the completeness and correctness of my description against the object, without producing any change in the object under observation. When I observe an animal or a human being, my observing may or may not influence what the other is doing and thereby what I am observing. The possibility of my observational act interfering with what I wish to observe derives from the ability of the other to observe me. This situation is similar to but not an instance of Heisenberg's principle of indeterminacy. My act of observing does not directly influence what I observe but only indirectly through the other's observation of me.

The situation is entirely different when I attempt to observe a feeling or thought of my own. In this case the principle of indeterminacy applies directly. Just as the temperature of the water in a glass is changed by inserting a thermometer into the water, a feeling changes at the moment when I observe it, pay attention to it, or, in phenomenological terms, bring it from marginal awareness into focal consciousness, 'thematize' it. One of the immediate changes a feeling usually undergoes when I try to describe it is that it decreases in intensity. I cannot, therefore, observe twice the same feeling as I may observe twice the same object or even sometimes an animal or another human being during the same action.

When I attempt to observe my thoughts I may have thoughts concerning my observing. These observational thoughts will interfere with the thoughts I want to observe. Since this interference results directly from the act of observing, this is another instance of the indeterminacy principle.

An additional problem concerning the observation of thoughts is that I can usually not hold a thought in my mind for any length of time without other thoughts joining and/or replacing the first one. Thus, for this additional reason, it is not possible to complete or correct my observation of a thought in the way I can do so with a stationary object.

My volitions may or may not be affected by my observing and describing them. The situation here resembles that of observing animals and other human beings. It is, however, different in so far as any change in my volition may be the direct result of my observing and describing it.

7.3.2   *The problem of retrospection* Since we cannot observe our feelings and thoughts, what are we talking about when we speak about them? We all know the difference between looking and seeing, between listening and hearing. By 'observing' I refer to *activities* of the type of looking and listening. Thus, when I claim that feelings and thoughts cannot be observed, I do not mean to say that they cannot be passively perceived like something which is seen or heard without being looked at or listened to.

In the course of the day, including during sleep, we become aware of much to which we do not direct our attention. Much of that can be recalled. Thus, I can also recall thoughts and feelings, particularly those which are quite recent, which belong to the immediate past of the moment. Just as I can recall a tree I saw pass in front of a train window a second ago and which I did not and could not look at, I can recall a feeling or a thought I had a moment ago. I can describe the tree, the feeling, and the thought.

It may be objected that memory is unreliable even in the scientific meaning of reliability: that its results are not identical at different times. Memory is a process: its content undergoes change. However, there is little change in short-term memory and that is what I am concerned with when retrospecting upon a feeling or a thought I just had. When I retrospect upon an immediately past feeling, thought, or volition, I do not change that past feeling, thought, or volition through my reflecting on it, just as I cannot change any other past event by reflecting upon it. Only my memory of a past event can change, not the event itself as it happened in the past.

The argument about the unreliability of memory still holds. It means that any report based on memory is open to question. This applies equally to every report about an experiment when the report contains observational data which were not recorded simultaneously with their occurrence. How much of what we call 'science' would be left if only concurrently registered data were admitted to it?

7.3.3 *The problem of data production* When I ask human beings – including myself – a question which they never asked themselves, the answer may contain new, never previously formed thoughts which were produced at the moment in reply to my question. For example, individual A is asked about his/her impression of individual B or opinion about issue X. A may instantaneously formulate an impression of B or an opinion about X which did not exist in A's mind prior to the question. From A's answer to the question one can usually not derive whether or not it consists of a previously formed and formulated impression or opinion.

If A's answer is produced at the time of answering the question and does not consist of the recall of a memory, we have another instance of Heisenberg's principle, namely a datum produced by our research. The impression or opinion we receive in reply to our question corresponds to the water temperature produced by the insertion of the thermometer into the water (cf. chapter 4, footnote 3). In both instances, the datum we receive is not independent of events preceding our research: A must have met or at least heard about B or issue X previously, just as the water had some temperature before it was measured. Thus, the data are not the result of 'spontaneous generation' but are co-constituted by antecedent events and present research methods.

The researcher's contribution to the production of data can be reduced but not eliminated by using data which were produced prior to the beginning of the research: diaries, correspondence, clinic records (Brandt 1963), which were generated under real-life conditions and not on the researcher's request. But psychology like all other sciences consists of solving problems. Problems are meanings. Someone problematizes a situation in his/her mind. The data on the basis of which problems are dealt with and possibly solved must, therefore, contain meanings. Events in the world must be decoded and re-encoded in order to become 'data.' Events must be interpreted. In research on the thoughts, feelings, volitions, and actions of human beings, interpretations of interpretations – and even interpretations of interpretations of interpretations, etc. – can never be avoided. The number of interpretations may be reduced, but the hermeneutic function of the psychologist can be eliminated entirely neither in 'pure' observations nor in laboratory experiments – as long as psychology remains a human enterprise and is not entirely taken over by computers built, programmed, and analysed by other computers.

7.3.4   *The problem of verbalization* If I describe over the telephone to a painter what I see through my living-room window, the painter will never be able to produce a painting which in all details, in all relationships, proportions, colours, etc., is identical with what I see, though he can ask me always for further details and I can go over the window-view again and again. This is true even if nothing changes outside my window while I am describing the view and the painter attempts to paint it.

When I attempt the same process with a scene in my mind, a memory of a scene I observed, or of a dream, or a fantasy, the 'problem of observation' is added to the problem of verbalization, because the scene in my mind may change while I try to describe it and particularly while the painter is asking me questions about some of its details.

This problem is even more severe when I describe something which is not visual, such as my impression of another individual. There are many facets to my impression of someone, which are better considered to be 'feeling-tones' I have than clear-cut thoughts. These 'feeling-tones' may reflect the way in which I act towards this individual, in distinction to my way of acting towards others, and I may not be able to put these 'feeling-tones' into words.

The problem of verbalization includes further all the issues deriving from the limitations inherent in each individual language (cf. chapter 2). Since no one individual masters the entire vocabulary and expressions of any language, there are individual differences in the ability to verbalize observations, feeling-tones, etc. In order to realize these differences one need not even introduce the concept of defence mechanisms.

All of these problems apply to the verbalizations of psychologists when they report on their research, just as they apply to verbalizations in answer to questions from psychologists – even if the questions are contained in true/false questionnaires. For the questions may have different meanings to different respondents.

7.3.5 *The dialectics of the four problems* The problems of observation, retrospection, data production, and verbalization concern processes of perceiving, thinking, feeling, and speaking. These processes are not independent of one another but 'feed back' into one another. Someone's question leads to further external and/or internal search and observations and verbalizations. As I hear my own verbalizations, these may lead to additional questions in my mind and subsequent search and observations. My original thoughts, feelings, memories, impressions, opinions, etc. may thereby undergo further change. These changes may bring about new verbalizations and/or make me aware of the limits of what I can put into words. I may get confused or say something which is quite different from my original thoughts, feelings, etc. I may get doubts about what I first reported.

Let us take a concrete example. I ask you what a friend of yours is like. The question evokes some aspects of your friend as you conceptualize him. Some of these aspects you can put into words, others not. As you describe your friend to me you think of characteristics which you had never thought of before.

Let us assume that my original question was: 'Please describe one of your friends to me.' You may formulate all your answers by 'my friend' or 'they' – and I may never find out your friend's sex if I do not specifically ask you whether you are describing a man or a woman. In most European languages other than English this particular problem cannot occur (cf. 2.2.3).

I may then ask you whether your friend has a good sense of humour. You may never have asked yourself this question previously. As you think about my question you may come to the conclusion that your friend has no sense of humour. This, in turn, may 'explain' to you a number of experiences you have had with your friend, and thus put other aspects of your friend into a new light for you. You may end up with a largely new impression of your friend – and you may no longer be able to reconstruct your earlier impression of your friend in its entirety. Unless there exists a diary or letters from the past in which you wrote down your impression of your friend, it will be impossible to establish whether or not your impression has changed subsequent to my question and, if it has, how it has changed.

7.4 THE BOUNDARIES OF THE SCIENCE OF PSYCHOLOGY *'Zwar weiss ich viel, doch möcht ich alles wissen'* (Though I know much, I like to know everything). These are the words which Goethe, the great scientist, writer, and poet, put into the mouth of Wagner, the ridiculous student of Faust, at the beginning of the play in which over a century and a half ago the present dilemma of mankind was predicted. At the end of the play, Faust is blind and believes that his workers are clearing a former marsh to prepare it for farming to feed millions of people – when, in reality, they are digging his grave. Instead of heaven on earth, knowledge and technology have led to pollution, overpopulation, and raw material shortage.

I consider the 'progress' in science made in our century to lie in the recognition that we cannot 'know everything.' In physics, the limitations of scientific knowledge were recognized in the theory of relativity and the principle of indeterminacy; in mathematics, they are expressed in Gödel's theorem; and in the philosophy of science, in the acknowledgment that all data are theory-laden, that is, there are no theory-independent facts.

Psychology will be *mündig* (cf. chapter 3, footnote 2), will have matured (cf. 5.2.1, 5.2.3), it will speak with an adult voice, when it too acknowledges its boundaries and limits itself to working within them. I propose that psychology's boundaries are set by the four problems I discussed, the problems of observation, retrospection, data production, and verbalization, and their dialectics. These are some of the boundaries of psychology as a science. There are additional problems, some of which will be discussed in the next chapter.

However, as a first step, I want to delineate the area bounded by the four problems and beyond which the science of psychology cannot possibly go. Additional boundaries may merely restrict this area further but cannot extend it.

In the experiment on the effects of dress on the believability of a message (cf. 7.2.1), both researcher and experimenter can be considered to have been what Holzkamp (1964, 1968) called 'naïve psychologists.' But all psychologists are naïve, differing only in degree of *naïveté*. No human being can escape perspectivity and can take all aspects of an issue into account. This limitation can become merely more obvious in reflecting upon an experiment than in reflecting upon field observations or self-observations, because experiments have a more limited focal point, are more circumscribed, specify more clearly the variables with which they are concerned, and can therefore be critically analysed more easily.

One must not conclude from my critique of psychological experiments that I believe naturalistic research or self-observation to be without problems and to lead to 'truth' and 'certainty.' In some areas of psychology like perception and psychophysics, experiments may be the most useful method. Psychologists from Wundt (cf. Danziger 1979) to Piaget recognized the usefulness of controlled experiments in some areas of psychology and their uselessness in others. It is the indiscriminate application of the experimental method to all questions in psychology which has produced the tremendous amount of published garbage and confusion.

In order to dispel the impression that I believe in the salvation of psychology through contemplation of one's uncut umbilical cord, I shall point out some of the problems resulting from a mere withdrawal from the system of the experiment.

7.4.1   In figure 4, the observable universe is delineated by a solid line as we cannot go beyond it, and need not raise the question here whether or not there exists a non-observable part of the world (cf. Schrödinger 1960). Within this observable world lies the verbalizable universe. Whatever is present or given to any individual at any particular moment consists of verbalizable and non-verbalizable aspects of the universe. When the individual is asked to report about what is given to him/her – and this applies obviously also to a psychologist reporting about an experiment s/he conducted – aspects of the observable universe which were not formerly present, both verbalizable and non-verbalizable ones, are evoked and aspects which were formerly present recede from awareness. What will be reported about is thus that shaded area in figure 4 surrounded by the dotted line which lies within the verbalizable universe.

The report then contains false positives, namely aspects of the universe which were not present to the respondent before being asked to

FIGURE 4

Poppers's (1973) World 2 and Metzger's (Brandt and Metzger 1969) reality$_2$ in terms of the limits of their scientific investigatibility

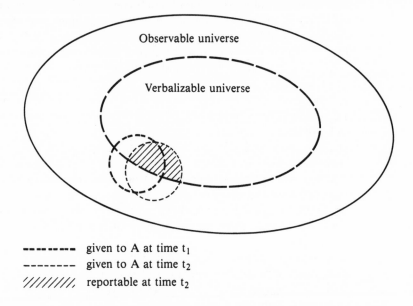

Observable universe

Verbalizable universe

‑ ‑ ‑ ‑ ‑ ‑ ‑ ‑   given to A at time t_1
‑ ‑ ‑ ‑ ‑ ‑ ‑ ‑   given to A at time t_2
////////   reportable at time t_2

report, as well as false negatives, consisting of those aspects of the observable universe which are non-verbalizable and those which are no longer given[5] as a consequence of the question having been asked.

Psychology – like all other sciences – must acknowledge that it can investigate only a limited area of the total observable universe and that even within this limited area the indeterminacy principle holds. This is in part due to the fact that all reports are retrospective and that thoughts, which are processes, change during the interval between observation and report.

---

5 The Latin word *datum* means 'given.'

---

8 Psychologists Caught in Different Personicating Frameworks

Psychologists Caught in Different Personicating Frameworks

'Dr Livingstone, I presume'

8.0   In chapter 5 I caught psychologists at building theories and evaluating the theories of their colleagues. In the last chapter I caught them at their research and reached its boundaries. In the present chapter we[1] shall catch them at the practice of their trade – and encounter further limitations.

8.0.1   Psychologists are *Menschen*, human beings. They bring values, feelings, ideas into their psychological activities – values, feelings, and ideas which they bring into their psychological activities from outside their laboratories, offices, and consulting rooms. The ideas every scientist must bring with him/her into his/her work from the past, from every-day life, are called 'pre-scientific.' They form a pre-scientific framework for scientific work.

Pre-scientific ideas and scientific ideas cannot always be clearly distinguished. Pre-scientific ideas differ from scientific ideas by not having been formed on the basis of *systematic* observations and by not having been *systematically* tested. All beliefs and 'knowledge' which people act on in everyday life and which are not based on systematic investigations are pre-scientific. The language people use, both in every-day life and in science, is, with the exception of some clearly defined scientific terms, pre-scientific. It is acquired before one becomes a

---

[1]   This chapter and chapter 10 are so much the result of close collaboration between L.W. and Elisabeth Pasztor Brandt that we agreed to use 'we' in them. We can no longer tell for sure which ideas are whose.

---

scientist. Pre-scientific 'knowledge' need not be 'wrong.' It is mostly very valuable and useful. People could not act without it.[2]

People act on the basis of expectations.[3] They act in terms of their ideas about the likely effects of their acts. Such ideas form pre-scientific theories. Pre-scientific theories about what-will-happen-if are usually not clearly formulated. Some of them are part of 'tacit knowledge' (Polanyi 1958), that is, they are non-verbalizable. Some pre-scientific theories can be verbalized by others on the basis of their observations of someone. Argyris (1975, 1976) referred to such pre-scientific theories as 'theories-in-use.' They can be derived from analysis of someone's actions, if one assumes that all human actions are guided by some kind of theories.

People hold pre-scientific theories about almost everything. They have theories about human beings in general ('People are selfish'; 'People help one another unless they have been antagonized'; 'All people are basically alike') and about specific individuals ('John will

---

2 Those people whose pre-scientific belief is that people merely 'respond' to 'stimuli' may disagree with that statement. Their pre-scientific belief is, however, not systematically testable.

3 This is a pre-scientific statement. I cannot observe other people's minds. I have no evidence that anyone besides myself feels, thinks, and wills. My wife's contribution to this chapter may be my own imagination, a dream, or a hallucination. Or it may be sounds which she mechanically produced, 'responses' to 'stimuli' which I emitted. However, I carry the assumption which I make in everyday life – namely that other human beings feel, think, and will – from everyday life into my scientific work, just as I do with most of the language I use in science.

  I have also no evidence that anything beyond my mind exists (cf. 7.3). The assumption of the existence of anything outside my mind (Brandt and Metzger's [1969] 'reality₁'; Popper's [1973] 'World 1') is pre-scientific or metaphysical. The way to make pre-scientific, metaphysical assumptions scientific is by what phenomenologists call 'bracketing' their ontology; that is, suspending judgment as to whether the assumptions are true or false. Thus, I bracket the existence of a world outside my mind and I bracket the existence of other people's feelings, thoughts, and volitions. I merely *assume* them to exist, for the purpose of discussion, and I am aware of my metaphysical assumption without repeating all the time that it is merely an assumption. (LWB)

---

always find an excuse for not working'; 'Whatever Mary starts she will finish to perfection').[4] Such pre-scientific theories about human beings are dialectically related to impression formation, that is, they are based on impressions formed of people and they enter into new impressions formed of people.

8.0.2   *A new classificatory framework: personicating*   Before continuing the above theme and applying it to psychologists, we want to introduce a new classification system. Impression formation has been called alternatively 'person perception' and 'social perception.' Both of these terms are incorrect because one does not *per*ceive someone as selfish or helpful, one *con*ceptualizes someone in that way. (One *per*ceives someone to be pale, tall, blond.) Since grammatical constructions with 'impression formation' easily become awkward ('Peter formed an impression of Mary on the basis of what John tells Peter about John's impression of Mary and of Peter's impression of John,' etc.), we decided to introduce new terms also with our new classifications. The reader will probably find these strange at first, as we ourselves did, but will, we hope, find them useful and clear after a little while.

In order to preserve the process character of impression formation we call it 'personicating.' The individual who forms the impression is the 'personicator' and the one of whom the impression is formed is the 'personicatee.' The impression is called "person" and will always appear in double quotation marks to avoid confusion with human individuals. The impression which you, the reader (R), have formed by now of the author (A) of this book is your author-"person," which can be expressed by the formula $R(pA)$ meaning 'the reader's impression of the author.' $R(pA)$ is in part based on the author's self-concept as presented in chapter 1. The formula for the author's self-concept is $A(pA)$, which is to be read as 'the author's author-"person,"' namely, the author's impression of himself, his self-concept. In both formulas, the letter in front of the bracket stands for the personicator and the letter in the bracket for the personicatee. The bracket contains the "person." The bracket may serve as a reminder to 'bracket' A, namely

---

4   We need not here go into theories which explain why Mary acts the way she does. Everyone has such pre-scientific 'implicit theories of personality' or 'naïve behaviour theories.' Laucken (1973) did under Kaminski an excellent detailed analysis of such pre-scientific theories.

---

to suspend judgment as to the extent to which A corresponds to A(pA) or to R(pA).[5]

8.0.2.1 When someone (S) personicates another individual (J) without any intermediary, that is, when S has contact with J without being told about J by a third party, we speak of 'first-hand personicating.' When S personicates J on the basis of a third party's (T) description of J, we speak of 'second-hand personicating.' S then becomes the second-hand personicator who receives a 'report' from T. In that case, we call T the 'reporter' and J the 'reportee.' To the extent to which T met J, T first-hand personicated J. Expressed in a formula, S's second-hand (pJ) then looks as follows: S[pT(pJ)]. As will become clearer when we discuss second-hand personicating in detail, it is actually much more complex than expressed in the last formula.

8.1 PHENOMENAL ANALYSIS OF PSYCHOLOGISTS PERSONICATING FIRST-HAND... Psychologists must personicate (form impressions of people, including of themselves) not only in everyday life but also in many aspects of their field. Personality theories and tests, classifications of psychopathology, and norms of psychological development are, in the last analysis, based on personicating. We shall return to the role of personicating in research and theory construction after having presented how psychologists personicate others in practical psychological work situations. We are aware that we thereby are not following the logical sequence according to which research and theory construction ought to precede the practice of psychology. But the dialectics of theory and practice mean that the two mutually influence each other rather than form a simple causal chain.

8.1.1 *... in counselling*

8.1.1.1 The first contact between a psychologist (M) and a client (W)[6] occurs frequently over the telephone. Like everyone else, the psychologist

---

5 In line with Heisenberg's statement (cf. 4.4), it does not seem meaningful to speak of A, namely the 'true' author, independent of his being personicated at least by himself.
6 Merely to simplify our presentation we shall throughout assume the psychologist to be a man (M) and the client or analysand to be a woman (W).

---

forms immediately some ever so vague first impression of the caller $[M(pW)_1]$.[7]

And also like other people, M feels a certain way when he picks up the phone, expects perhaps a call from someone quite different, is involved in some activity which is interrupted by the ringing of the phone, has, perhaps, just seen a client with whose progress M is very satisfied or, to the contrary, a very difficult client, etc. All of this may colour both M's way of answering the phone and $M(pW)_1$.

$M(pW)_1$ is further based on M's pre-scientific personality theories, that is, on M's past experience with people in his life outside his office and his past experience with clients, particularly with clients whose voice he heard for the first time on the telephone. In addition, there may be something in the way W talks which actualizes[8] some scientific theory in M that M once learnt in his studies and which became part of his psychological thinking.

If not from this moment on, then at least during their first interview, M's scientific theories will play an important part in personicating W. $M(pW)$ will largely depend on whether M actualizes psychoanalytic, behaviourist, existentialist, Rogerian, Sullivanian, or other psychological concepts when he personicates a prospective client.

---

7 The number subscripts refer to time t_1, time t_2, etc. A first impression will thus always be indicated by the subscript 1. In order not to make our formulas too complex we shall later omit the time-subscripts. However, the reader must remember that personicating is a process which changes over time, and that "persons" are not fixed or invariant but change to varying degrees.

8 In this chapter, we lean heavily on the work of Kaminski (1959, 1970), who was also kind enough to comment on a draft of our original paper (Brandt and Brandt 1972). We are using here his term 'to actualize,' by which he means to bring forth from 'storage' (memory). Kaminski distinguishes between storage of different areas of knowledge (knowledge about possible changes in people, about the psychologist's competence, about necessary conditions for change, about what is considered ethical, and about how to compare a given client to other people). Each of these knowledge-area storages is further subdivided into knowledge acquired from everyday life experiences, knowledge acquired at work as a psychologist, and scientific knowledge obtained from lectures, books, and journals.

During the initial telephone conversation, M's silent listening as well as M's answers to W's questions will influence W's pre-scientific theory about psychologists and lead to $W(pM)_1$, which will influence whatever W says next. Thus, $W(pM)_1$ will have some impact on $M(pW)_1$ and possibly change it to $M(pW)_2$ – and so on until the end of the telephone call. Let us assume M and W agreed on a first appointment. We shall refer to their respective impressions of each other at this point as $M(pW)_2$ and $W(pM)_2$ respectively.

8.1.1.2　$M(pW)_2$ and $W(pM)_2$ will influence all further personicating by M and by W. At the first interview, M will personicate W further in terms of $M(pW)_2$. M's personicating will again be coloured by the way M feels in general (M's 'personality') and by how M feels at that particular time (is W the first client in the day after M had a good night or is W the last client after M had already a heavy work-load?); by the amount of time M set aside to 'diagnose,' that is, to formally personicate W; and by M's past experiences with people in general and with clients in particular, and largely by his theoretical framework.

M will also personicate W on the basis of his preferences for dress, perfumes, jewellery, racial features,[9] etc., brought into play by W's appearance. If the client who preceded W was a striking beauty, M will personicate W probably differently from the way he does after just seeing an elderly man. M may have a cold which prevents him from smelling W's breath, which otherwise might give M some cue that W may be a heavy drinker. A ring W is wearing may actualize a long-forgotten memory in M, leading M to conclude that there may be similarities between W and the woman whose ring M suddenly remembers. All such cognitions[10] will play some part in $M(pW)_3$.

9　L W B: I saw a woman for several weeks in analysis without ever giving a thought to her racial background. If I had been asked about it, I would have said that I thought she was Caucasian. Even when she spoke about herself as a 'Bermudan,' this meant nothing to me in racial terms. As it turned out later on, one of her problems was that she and her relatives and friends considered her black, whereas her employer and co-workers considered her white. This was in New York City at a time of strong racial discrimination against blacks.

10　Kaminski (1970) discusses almost exclusively 'cognitions': the psychologist's cognitions of the client, stored cognitions of past experiences and of

---

When she entered M's waiting-room for the first time, W may already have changed $W(pM)_2$ to some extent. It may change further upon meeting the psychologist face to face because of his appearance, his looks, his suit, his office furniture, pictures on the wall or on his desk, etc., as well as in reaction to his probably unconscious, communication of his $M(pW)_3$ to her. She may, for example, cognize M's facial expression as of surprise or disappointment, as tired or as relaxed. In so far as M perceives a change in W's tone of voice or countenance, he will alter his impression of the client.

Thus, much mutual personicating has taken place between the psychologist and the client before the first interview has even begun. The purpose of that interview is some more formal $M(pW)$, namely some kind of diagnosis on the basis of which M can decide whether or not he will treat W. A 'diagnosis' is merely a more formal "person," a diagnostician's impression of someone whom the diagnostician met in a professional capacity.

8.1.1.3   As M begins his formal diagnosis, he ought to be aware of his limitations, of the kind of problems he thinks he can successfully deal with as opposed to those for which he would do better to call on a colleague and make a referral. He will have certain treatment methods in mind, like desensitization, aversive training, hypnosis, relaxation, counselling, psychoanalysis, etc., but most likely not all of these. Those specific treatment methods which M considers useful will shape $M(pW)$ in the course of the interview.

M may base his decision about whether to continue seeing W, to refer her to someone else, or to reassure her that she needs no treatment on psychological tests on W's replies to a number of questions, or on merely listening to what she spontaneously tells him and asking questions only to obtain a clearer idea of what W wants to tell him. Both the

---

his conscience, and cognitions of the client's cognition of self, others, events, and situations as these are communicated verbally and non-verbally to the psychologist. What we call someone's "person" of someone else is, in Kaminski's terms, a cognition. Such a phenomenological approach is basically different from that of one speaking of 'observed behaviour,' independently of someone cognizing it. Behaviourists do not bracket existence and disregard the cognizer and his/her process of cognizing.

---

method used by M to arrive at the M(pW) on which he will base his decision, and the M(pW) resulting from that method, depend largely on the scientific psychological theories M makes use of in his work. They determine whether W is personicated as being reinforced, as responding to stimuli, as not being self-actualized, as having an Oedipus, Electra, or inferiority complex, as concluding she is not O.K., as suffering from vitamin B or orgone energy deficiency, etc. M's past experience as diagnostician and counsellor, psychotherapist, or psychoanalyst, his interest in certain types of problems and clients, and the time he spends on his diagnosis all determine his decision. Kaminski (1970) unfolded many aspects of this diagnostic process, illustrated it with many different examples, and developed large flow-charts with multiple feedback loops. It is impossible to summarize his 600-page book here.

8.1.1.4   If M and W decide to work together in the form of counselling or some form of psychotherapy, W will tell M more and more about herself which will change M(pW) further. That change may consist merely of expansions of M(pW), of new aspects being added to M(pW) as the psychologist learns more about the client, or it may involve some revisions of parts of M(pW) if the psychologist realizes that he had jumped to some unwarranted conclusions about the client. In so far as the counselling is successful, the client will actually change some of her ways of interacting with the psychologist and will report changes in her interactions with her environment outside the counselling situation, and possibly changes in her self-concept, W(pW). All of these changes must lead to alterations in M(pW). These changes are brought about by M's counselling on the basis of M(pW).

8.1.2   ... in psychoanalysis Up to the formation of M(pW), whatever we wrote above applies also if M is a psychoanalyst and if W wishes to undergo an analysis with M. In psychoanalysis too, personicating plays a central role in terms of what is called 'transference.' Transference, which in Piaget's (1947) language can be said to consist of assimilation of the analyst by the analysand with only minimal accommodation, means that the analysand displaces parent 'imagos' onto the analyst. English and English (1958) define 'imago' as 'a representation of a person, most often a parent, formed in the unconscious in early childhood and uncorrected by events in later reality, hence often idealized ... The imago may influence personal relations at the conscious level, esp. by providing a pattern for the kind of person with whom to fall in love.' Thus, the psychoanalytic concept of imago corresponds to what we have called "person" though not all "persons" are imagos.

Psychoanalytic work has two aspects which are interrelated: resistance analysis and transference analysis. The latter is the analysis of the analysand's "person" of the psychoanalyst, to the extent to which that "person" results from insufficient accommodation or, in psychoanalytic terms, from insufficient reality testing. The purpose of transference analysis is to enable the analysand to improve her "persons" of others, to better accommodate to others, to do better reality testing in relating to others, and thereby to improve her relationships with others in general.

But how can the analyst help the analysand in this process? How can the analyst decide whether to attempt to change the analysand's 'person' of him, $W(pM)$, to fit more closely to his self-concept, $M(pM)$, or to change $M(pM)$ in the direction of $W(pM)$? The answer lies with the fact that, in order to have become a psychoanalyst, M must have undergone a much more extensive and intensive analysis than other people, in which he corrected his own transferences, that is, the distortions of his own "persons," including that of himself, $M(pM)$ (cf. 6.1.1). In spite of the precautions taken by their own analysis, psychoanalysts do not consider themselves immune to transferences. They refer to their own transferences upon their analysands as 'counter-transference.' This means that $M(pW)$ may be influenced by M's mother-"person." To check out this possibility, M continues his counter-transference analysis with a colleague or in small seminars. The counter-transference analysis is designed particularly to widen the framework in which the analyst is personicating his analysands.

Another safeguard designed to minimize M's influence upon $W(pM)$ consists in the relative 'anonymity' of M. Psychoanalysts make a conscious effort to reveal as little as possible about themselves, their likes and dislikes, values, and hypotheses and hunches about the analysand. They do so by remaining invisible behind the couch so that the analysand cannot get any cues from their facial expressions, and by keeping silent most of the time, even to the point of hardly ever answering any of the analysand's questions (cf. 5.1.1.1). Yet, psychoanalysts realize that their anonymity is never complete and that analysands personicate them on the basis of the location of the office, pictures on the walls,

FIGURE 5

Outline for a second-hand personicating model

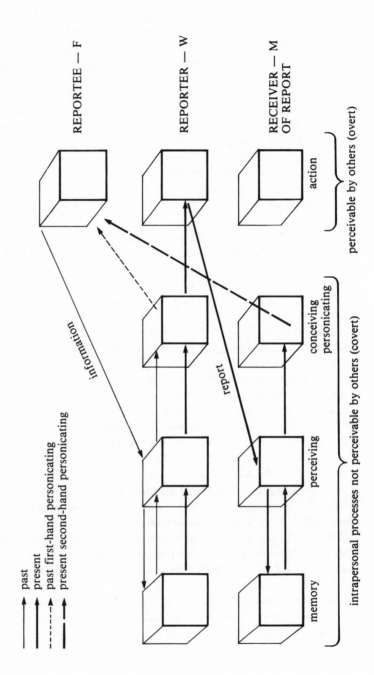

past
present
past first-hand personicating
present second-hand personicating

REPORTEE — F

REPORTER — W

RECEIVER — M
OF REPORT

action

perceivable by others (overt)

information

report

conceiving
personicating

perceiving

memory

intrapersonal processes not perceivable by others (covert)

publications by the analysts, and what the analysands have heard about them from common acquaintances.[11]

The arrangement of the analyst's office can provoke W(pM) and W's verbalization of her impression of the office may help shape M(pW). Two new analysands once came to my (L.W.B.) office one hour apart. They both came for their initial interviews. Nothing was changed in the room between the two appointments. One of them commented on entering the room how warm and friendly it looked. The other remarked that the office looked like a 'mausoleum.' Obviously, I personicated the two individuals differently.

8.2 PHENOMENAL ANALYSIS OF PSYCHOLOGISTS PERSONICATING SECOND-HAND ... In any form of counselling or psychotherapy which is not based on some kind of conditioning model, and particularly in psychoanalysis, the client, patient, or analysand (W) will sooner or later talk about people in her life – relatives, friends, acquaintances whom the psychologist has never met. The psychologist will then personicate, for example, W's father (F),[12] on the basis of W's description of her father, namely the *description* of W(pF). As long as M has not actually met F but merely heard about him from W, the psychologist's "person" of W's father is only second-hand. We write M's second-hand impression of W's father M[pW(pF)]. From M's perspective as second-hand personicator, W is a reporter and F a reportee. We have presented this situation in the form of a flow-chart in figure 5.

W collected information about F through interactions with F prior to telling M about F, that is, in the recent or more distant past. This information was stored in W's memory. Some of her total memories of F

---

11 L W B: I learnt in my own analysis with a woman analyst how far the anonymity of the analyst can nevertheless go. There was a *mazzuzah* (sacred Jewish word in a tiny metal container) at her entrance door, which made me wonder whether my analyst was Jewish or merely had left the mazzuzah which a former tenant had put there. Though I asked her about it in my analysis, I did not receive an answer. I criticized during that analysis a teacher I had at the training institute, but found out only much later that he was already then my analyst's husband.

12 F will always refer to the reportee, i.e., the second-hand personicatee. F may be W's father, mother, husband, daughter, boss, friend, enemy, cat, etc.

---

are actualized while talking (action) to M. These memories are of perceptions of what her father looked like, what he said and did. They probably include her pre-scientific theories about F's intentions, motivations, wishes, etc. In telling M about F, W reports some – never all – of her memories of F. M hears (perceives) what W says. W's report actualizes in M memories of other people, particularly fathers, M has known or heard about before. Out of this combination of memories of other people and of W's report about W(pF), M second-hand personicates F.[13]

Some highly important issues which seem to us not to have received the attention they deserve, are that (1) W has much tacit knowledge about F which is non-verbalizable (cf. 7.3.4 and 7.4), (2) W can verbalize at any given time (interview, session) only a small fraction of even the verbalizable part of her total W(pF), (3) M transforms that small fraction of W(pF) on the basis of many factors, some of which we shall discuss shortly.

8.2.1   *...in psychoanalysis* Psychoanalysis focuses on the analysand's (W) cognitions. The psychoanalyst (M) does not deal with the question of what W's father (F) is 'really' like (cf. footnotes 3 and 5 above). He is also not concerned with the question of how others personicate F, what F's self-concept, F(pF), is like, or how M would first-hand personicate F if M met F. F is of interest for W's analysis only in so far as the F in M[pW(pF)] can throw some light on M(pW) and on M[pW(pM)], that is, on W's transference of her father-imago on the psychoanalyst.

How little attention is usually paid to the distinction between W(pF), M(pF), and M[pW(pF)] can be illustrated by Sarbin, Taft, and Bailey's (1960) discussion of *identification*. They wrote: 'If Jones "identifies" with his father, he will be similar' (p. 233). However, they do not clarify what 'will be similar.' Is it (1) Jones's self-concept and Jones's father-"person": W(pW) = W(pF); (2) the psychologist's Jones-"person" and Jones's-father-"person": M(pW) = M(pF), which presupposes that M met the father; (3) M's first-hand M(pW) and his second-hand impression of Jones's father: M(pW) = M[pW(pF)]; (4) Jones's father's self-concept and impression of Jones: F(pF) = F(pW); or (5) Jones's and his father's self-concepts: W(pW) = F(pF)? From what we have written so far, it must be clear that M has no knowledge of (1), (4), and (5). The formulas

---

13 In order not to make the flow-chart too complex we omitted many aspects of personicating such as the transformations occurring in memory.

---

demonstrate the different meanings 'he will be similar [to his father]' can have. If M thinks that 'identification' means W = F, then he is a 'naïve' personicator and a 'naïve' psychologist, because he does not realize that he cannot 'know' either W or F but has only cognitions and cognitions of cognitions ("persons") which he can compare.

8.2.1.1 Psychoanalytic publications give the impression that psychoanalysts are no more aware of the difference between first- and second-hand personicating than other psychologists are. Yet, as we showed above, second-hand personicating takes place constantly in transference analysis.[14] All that is given to M in the analysis are M(pM), M(pW), M[pW(pM)], M[pW(pW)], and M[pW(pF)], plus M's memories from previous sessions with W (recent past), sessions with other analysands, his own analysis, his studies and readings, and his life experiences. We can now improve on our earlier phenomenal analysis of transference analysis (cf. 8.1.2) by adding the results of the analyst's second-hand personicating (1) himself through W telling him what she thinks of him, (2) the analysand through what she tells him about her self-concept, and (3) others in her life on the basis of what she tells him about them. We have tried to present in a very simplified flow-chart (figure 6) how the analyst arrives at an interpretation on the basis of his various cognitions.

In the distant past, W saw, heard, was touched by her father. She had many feelings about F. Over time, new experiences were added to her memories of F and transformed them to some extent. After having overcome some resistances, W had judged in her sessions in the recent past that she wanted to tell M about F. W did so. M both listened to what W said and her tone of voice and watched her gestures. Now, by piecing together what he remembers from past sessions with W and with other analysands, from his pre-scientific (everyday life) and his scientific 'knowledge,' and from his own analysis, by comparing those relevant cognitions which M is able to actualize at the present moment, he concludes that W relates to him as if he were her childhood-father. He then judges on the basis of his present M(pW) and his professional experience that this is a good time to communicate to W that he thinks

---

14 In the other part of psychoanalysis namely resistance analysis, M must compare merely M(pW) to M[pW(pW)] for determining whether he may be aware of something about W that W does not seem to be conscious of. There is no F involved.

FIGURE 6

Personicating between analysand and analyst leading to interpretation of father transference.

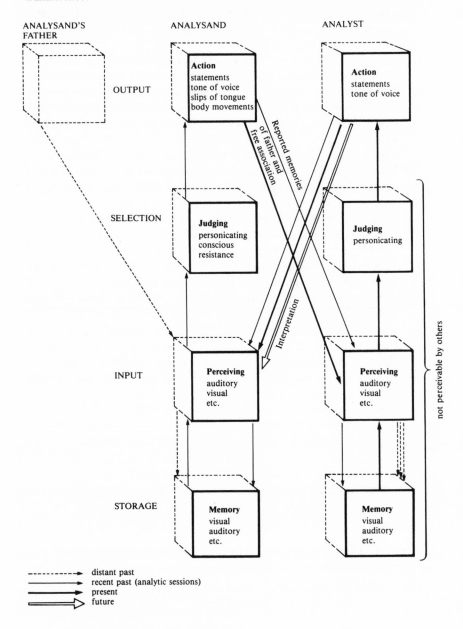

ANALYSAND'S FATHER   ANALYSAND   ANALYST

OUTPUT

Action
statements
tone of voice
slips of tongue
body movements

Action
statements
tone of voice

Reported memories
of father and
free association

SELECTION

Judging
personicating
conscious
resistance

Judging
personicating

Interpretation

INPUT

Perceiving
auditory
visual
etc.

Perceiving
auditory
visual
etc.

not perceivable by others

STORAGE

Memory
visual
auditory
etc.

Memory
visual
auditory
etc.

- - - - - - - - → distant past
—————→ recent past (analytic sessions)
══════► present
══════▷ future

PSYCHOLOGISTS CAUGHT 168

that the feelings W just expressed towards him correspond to feelings W once had towards her father (F) and that these feelings were not evoked by M. He then tells W his conclusion, that is, he gives her a transference-interpretation.[15] M's checking and re-checking of his various actualized past cognitions (memories) against one another is called the 'hermeneutic circle' (Radnitzky 1973).

Since psychoanalysis pursues a hermeneutic interest (cf. 3.3.1), psychoanalysts need not concern themselves with what F is 'really' like. M helps W only with respect to W(pF) and not with respect to F. In other words, psychoanalysts do not tell their analysands how to act towards others. This is one of the differences between psychoanalysis and counselling.

8.2.2   *... in counselling* Counselling is frequently pursued with a technical interest. W does not merely want to change her W(pW) and her W(pF) – as a matter of fact, she may not be interested in changing either – but she wants M to change either F or her or at least her relations with others. Most people coming for counselling – like most psychologists – are not aware of the difference between F and (pF) and between various (pF)s, though they have often been in situations where their own impression of someone conflicted with that of others.

Thus, many people go for counselling to receive advice as to how to deal with a son, a husband, a mother-in-law, a boss, a co-worker, etc. If M advises W how to act towards F without realizing that he, M, has no M(pF) but is giving advice on the basis of M[pW(pF)],[16] then M is a 'naïve' counsellor – and there may be more trouble ahead. In order to be useful to W, M must be aware of the limitations to the communication of W(pF) to him. As Ruesch and Bateson (1951) described it: 'Communication between [individuals] is of course pathetically impoverished compared with the richness of intrapersonal consciousness, which in its turn is but an impoverished and restricted version of the total psychic life of the [individual] ... The external communications are a codification of the

---

15 We can express the transference-interpretation by $M[pW(pM= pF)] \rightarrow$ $M(pM) \neq [pW(pF)]$.

16 The formula graphically shows the separation of M from (pF) by pW. M has no direct contact with (pF)!

---

internal psychic life and ... the recipient of such communication is receiving an already elaborated product from the psychic life of another individual' (p. 206).

Since many of the variables generally operating in both first- and second-hand personicating – for instance, purpose of personicating, expectations, interests, needs, attention, values, mood, stereotypes, beliefs, 'set,' perceived context – have been widely mentioned in the psychological literature (Kaminski 1959, 1963, 1970; Tagiuri 1969; Warr and Knapper 1968), we shall here do no more than refer the readers to these works. However, what has been overlooked in the past is that all of these variables are multiplied, that is, must each be entered more than once into any psycho-logical calculus of second-hand personicating. In order to clarify our last statement we must further extend and correct our formula of second-hand personicating.

When the counsellor or the psychoanalyst (M) personicates the client's (W) father (F) second-hand, M has already a client-"person," $M(pW)$. What W tells M now about F will be cognized by M under the influence of $M(pW)$. For example, in the extreme case where $M(pW)$ is a pathological liar, M may not believe what W tells him about F. Thus, $M(pW)$ and $M[pW(pF)]$ interact. On the basis of what M believes F to be like, M may change his $M(pW)$. The corrected formula for second-hand personicating is therefore $M\{(pW) \cdot [pW(pF)]\}$ where the dot is meant to indicate interaction between M's two impressions. In other words, M's impression of W's father is a combination and not the sum of $M(pW)$ and $M[pW(pF)]$.

It follows from $M\{(pW) \cdot [pW(pF)]\}$ that M must be aware not only of his purpose, expectations, interests, etc. in getting some impression of F and of his purpose, expectations, interests, etc. when he personicated W but also of the fact that W formed her impression of F on the basis of certain purposes, expectations, interests, etc. *and* that W tells (reports to) M – certain aspects of – $W(pF)$ with some purpose, expectations, interests, etc. in mind! The purposes, expectations, interests, etc. are certainly not identical in the four instances. To what extent W is aware of her purpose, interests, expectations, etc. is not relevant for this phenomenal analysis. To the extent to which M is not aware of the involvement of all of these issues – which we do not expect M to disentangle – M is a 'naïve' counsellor, psychotherapist, or psychoanalyst.

8.2.2.1 Let us put some flesh on M, W, and F. The client (W) asks the counsellor (M) what she should do when her husband (F) wants to have sexual intercourse with her several times a week and she does not want to. W's purpose in personicating F as oversexed may be to reassure herself unconsciously that she is an attractive woman, but her purpose in telling M about F may be to convince M that F exploits her. M's purpose in personicating F may then be to be in a position to advise W how to deal with F, while M's purpose in personicating W is to determine what kind of actions she is capable of towards F. The four purposes involved here are very different.

The difference in attention, in what M focuses on, can be illustrated by comparing the above counsellor to a psychoanalyst. The counsellor in the above situation must focus on the second factor of $M\{(pW) \cdot [pW(pF)]\}$, namely $[M(pW(pF)]$, if he wants to advise W how to change F's actions. The psychoanalyst, on the other hand, who wants to help W to gain insight about her relationship with F, must focus on the first factor, namely on (pW). The attention of the counsellor and of the psychoanalyst is thus directed to different aspects of W's communication.

The counsellor (M) may decide to do marriage counselling by seeing the husband (H) and the wife (W) together. By listening to both of them speaking about each other, M will form first- and second-hand impressions of both: $M\{(pW) \cdot [pH(pW)]\}$ and $M\{(pH) \cdot [pW(pH)]\}$, if M personicates the wife second-hand, disregarding his husband-"person," and the husband, disregarding his (M's) wife-"person." The counsellor can help the couple only to the extent to which he can keep $M(pW)$, $M[pH(pW)],)]$, $M(pH)$, and $M[pW(pH)]$ apart. Some interaction of these four "persons" seems to us inevitable however, since all four exist in one and the same mind.

The reader may try to figure out what a group psychoanalyst must do in order to be able to interpret the multiple transferences occurring among the usually eight members of a psychoanalytic group, as well as between each of them and the analyst – not to speak about the analyst's counter-transferences.

8.3   REQUESTS FOR ASSESSMENT Psychologists often receive requests to evaluate someone and then report to the individual who sent the one to be evaluated. For example, a teacher may want an evaluation of a pupil. The psychologist (M) evaluates the pupil (W) and sends an assessment to the teacher (T).

8.3.1   Whether or not M has met T personally or has even heard about T, the psychologist (M) will have some idea in mind as to what the teacher (T) wants to find out about the pupil (W). M will, therefore, personicate W with a specific purpose in mind, such as to personicate W in terms of 'intelligence' and not in terms of 'friendliness.' T's assessment request to

M must contain some information about W. For example, T may have written: 'Please let me know what the IQ of this 14-year-old girl is. I wonder whether it is advisable that she jump a grade.' On the basis of this request M will already ever so vaguely personicate W second-hand.

When the pupil (W) comes for the assessment, the psychologist has already a second-hand W-"person," M{(pT)•[pT(pW)]}, which will influence his actions towards W as well as his further personicating W. What M observes in W during the assessment, M(pW), will be coloured – among many other things – by the girl's (W) feelings and ideas about psychologists, W(pM), about her teacher, W(pT), and about the situation. M's final assessment, M[(pW)•(pT)] may be quite different from what he thought the girl would be like before meeting her (W). M(pT), the psychologist's impression of the teacher may also have changed in the process of his assessing W.

8.3.2   Many psychologists who have followed us up to this point may have thought that at least some of the problems we discussed could be solved by M using 'objective' tests to assess W. However, the solution is not that simple. 'Traits,' 'abilities,' and the resulting 'personality' are all hypothetical constructs, as evidenced by the fact that the concept of 'personality' does not exist for several hundred million Japanese. They conceptualize people merely in terms of roles. One man plays his role as father better than his role as a son. This absence of a personality concept is expressed even in the Japanese language. There exists no single Japanese word for self-reference, namely for 'I.' Depending on your and my respective status in society, I will refer to myself by a word indicating equal, lower, or higher status than yours (cf. 2.2.4 for the corresponding 'you').

8.3.3   Tests must consequently always be constructed on the basis of some concepts which psychologists use in personicating people, and of personicating some actual people in terms of one or more of such concepts. In order to construct a test intended to discriminate between 'normals' and 'neurotics,' a psychologist must first of all personicate some people as 'normal' and some other individuals as 'neurotic.' Only then can he invent test items and find out which ones are answered differently by those individuals whom he personicated as 'normal' and those human beings whom he personicated as 'neurotic.'

The test-constructor may personicate people who apply for admission at a mental health clinic as 'neurotic' and those who apply for admission to the armed forces as 'normal'. However, those individuals 'are' not necessarily 'normal' and 'neurotic' respectively, as evidenced by the episode reported below (cf. 8.5.1), and particularly by Rosenhan (1973) who, together with eight other people who had never sought help for any emotional problems, was diagnosed 'schizophrenic' and hospitalized – merely on the basis of telling a staff-member of a mental hospital of having once heard voices. It is also well known that a given individual often receives very different diagnoses (is personicated differently) from different psychologists and psychiatrists.

We expect a reminder from the reader that our last example did not refer to a personality assessment or an assessment of psychopathology but to an ability, namely a pupil's 'intelligence.' We reply that whereas we can *per*ceive someone's act *as* an intelligent act, no one can perceive 'intelligence.' Thus, even the construction of IQ tests rests in the final analysis on psychologists' *con*cepts of what 'intelligence' is, on psychologists personicating people as acting intelligently when given certain problems to solve. Which solutions to which problems are to be characterized as intelligent is an arbitrary decision by psychologists. All that can be determined empirically is that a certain age group or a certain percentage of a specified 'population' answered some test items and not others. As La Fave (1966) demonstrated, every answer to an analogies test is rationally justifiable; those answers which the test constructors consider to be 'right' require, however, less logical reasoning than the 'wrong' ones and may, therefore, be considered as less 'intelligent.'

8.3.3.1 Even assuming – as we do not after what we just wrote – that 'objective' tests did exist, many problems of personicating still remain when tests are used. The psychologist (M) personicates the girl (W) to whom he administers the IQ test as wanting to do as well as possible on the test. However, W may personicate her teacher (T) as wanting her to skip a grade, which W does not want because she would rather remain in the same class as her girl-friends. Under these circumstances, we personicate W as more 'intelligent,' if she obtains an average IQ on the test than if she obtains a high one. In other words, what Brandt and Maier (1976) demonstrated for the Eysenck Personality Inventory (cf. 7.1.5.4) applies equally to so-called ability tests: people answer test items in terms of the goal they pursue when taking the test. If the psychologist personicates the test-taker as having a different goal from the one the latter has in mind, if $M(pW) \neq W(pW)$, no 'objective' test 'measures' what M thinks it 'measures.'

FIGURE 7

Example of an experimental situation: s reports to e about direct observation of
"stimulus person" following earlier instructions from e; or graduate-student–e
reports to investigator about s following earlier instructions from investigator; etc.

REPORTEE	REPORTER	RECEIVER OF REPORT
"stimulus person"	subject	experimenter
OR	OR	OR
"stimulus person"	writer	subject
OR	OR	OR
subject	experimenter	investigator

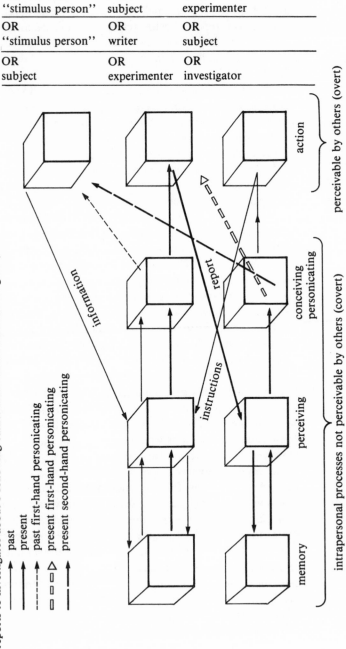

past

present

past first-hand personicating

present first-hand personicating

present second-hand personicating

information

report

instructions

action

conceiving personicating

perceiving

memory

perceivable by others (overt)

intrapersonal processes not perceivable by others (covert)

8.4 PSYCHOLOGISTS REPORT After the assessment M must write a report to the teacher (T). Teachers often complain that the reports they receive from psychologists are written in a psychological jargon which T does not understand and that the reports are, therefore, of no use to T. When this is the case, $M(pT) \neq T(pT)$ has led to communication problems. This leads us to the problems concerning the reporter and the report which are involved in all second-hand personicating and clearly distinguish it from first-hand personicating.

8.4.1 When the psychologist reports about the girl, M shifts from the position of second-hand personicator to the position of reporter.[17] We have indicated such shifts in figure 7. The pupil (W) is now the reportee and the teacher (T) the receiver of the report who second-hand personicates W on the basis of M's report.

M must present his report about W in such a way that T can get and make use of the information T wants – otherwise T will complain as we just indicated. In order to present his $M(pW)$ to T in a way which is useful to T, M must personicate T accordingly. The teacher's complaint is probably due to negligence by psychologists in personicating the individuals to whom their reports are addressed. If M does not realize the limitations of all verbal reports, namely that they can never communicate fully one's "person" of someone else, and if M does not at least verbalize his report in terms of his $M(pT)$, M is a 'naïve' reporter. The reporting problems can, however, be diminished through face-to-face contact between reporter (M) and receiver (T), where each can develop a more articulate "person" of the other, and where they can make their respective W-"persons" more congruent with each other through questions and answers. In the absence of such an interchange, the psychologist often remains 'naïve' to the fact that his $M(pW)$ critically differs from $T(pW)$. M misses the target, which is to enrich $T(pW)$.

The form and jargon of the report itself may draw the receiver's attention to it just as the tone of voice in which someone says something may detract a listener's attention from what is being said. In both

---

17 The shift is due to the fact that the three individuals do not actually stand in the linear relationship indicated by 'reportee → reporter → receiver of report,' but are personicating each other both first and second hand:
W M T

---

instances, the sender of the message is being personicated at the expense of the communication of the message.

8.4.2 In psychoanalysis, the analyst tries to listen to both what the analysand (W) says and how she says it. He also consciously chooses the tone of voice in which he asks a question or makes an interpretation. It is part of the contract between analyst and analysand that no reports will ever be issued to any third party. The issues of reports by M do not therefore arise in psychoanalysis, except when an analyst publishes his findings from a particular analysis in a professional journal. The identity of the analysand is always disguised in such publications, which are, therefore, not reports in the sense in which we discuss them here. Such case descriptions are not written for the purpose of conveying M(pW) to others but to illustrate a point in psychoanalytic theory.

8.4.3 Psychologists both write and read case reports. As readers (second-hand personicators) their attention may be drawn from the reportee to the reporter, if the report evokes strong feelings in them. They must be aware of this also when they are writers. The form itself in which W reports in speaking or in writing her W(pF) may lead M not so much to personicate F as to personicate W as hebephrenic, manic, depressed, paranoid, or as a pathological liar. The second-hand personicator must always at least minimally first-hand personicate the reporter when second-hand personicating the reportee. As our formula $M\{(pW) \cdot [pW(pF)]\}$ has shown, M gets at (pF) only via (pW), unless M has direct contact with F.[18]

8.5 EXPERIMENTERS AS PERSONICATORS When a line is drawn between experimental and applied psychology, between theory and practice, it is usually overlooked that *doing* research and *constructing* theories are also practice. It is unfortunate if psychologists do not also apply their psychological knowledge in their practice of research.

8.5.1 Experimenters too personicate those around them. They personicate some people as 'assistants,' some as 'confederates,' others as 'naïve,'

---

18 More examples and details of report and reporter problems appeared in our original publication on second-hand personication (Brandt and Brandt 1972).

'complaint,' or 'uncooperative subjects.' They usually arrive at their schizophrenic-subject-"persons" no more empirically than at their normal-subject-"persons." To the extent to which experimenters do not question their personicating of others in the experiment, they are again 'naïve' experimenters.[19] In the face of unexpected or undesirable results, experimenters may change their subject-"persons" from 'naïve' to 'defiant.' Sometimes the experimenter's subject-"persons" are called into question by colleagues, as in Orne and Holland's (1968) critique of Milgram's experiment: Orne and Holland second-hand personicated Milgram's subjects through Milgram's report as less deaf, dumb, and blind than Milgram seemed to have done.[20]

In many experiments, participants are personicated as 'normal' merely on the basis of being hospital staff members rather than inmates. No attempt whatsoever is made to obtain an 'empirical' foundation for that attribution. A colleague and one of us (L W B) once compared, after many years of experience as psychoanalysts, our "person" of a waitress in the coffee-shop of a mental hospital in whose out-patient clinic we were working. We both personicated the waitress as normal and then asked her whether any of the other waitresses there were inmates. She replied: 'We are all inmates. I am schizophrenic.'

A number of the personicating problems involved in psychological experiments have already been discussed within a different framework in chapter 7. In the meta-experiment (figure 3), the researcher personicates the 'experimenters' as personicating him as wanting to 'prove' his hypothesis in the pseudo-experiment at almost any price. This is partly the result of the fact that the researcher personicates the 'experimenters' as 'subjects' while the 'experimenters' personicate themselves as 'experimenters.' Similarly, Milgram assumed that the people whom he

---

19 In an excellent paper which is related to many issues in this book, Moore and Anderson (1962) tell of Yale freshmen interviewees for a psychological study who 'decided that each ... would manage *somehow*, in the course of the interview, to mention white horses,' which resulted in 'consternation of the interviewers when they compared notes' (p. 418).

20 If M stands for Orne and Holland, W for Milgram, and F for Milgram's subjects: $M[pW(pF)] \neq M\{pW[pW(pF)]\}$. If you find this difficult, be reassured that the '(fourth) level ("This is how I see you seeing me seeing you seeing me") is virtually beyond understanding' (Watzlawick, Beavin, and Jackson 1967, p. 266).

---

personicated as 'subjects' personicated themselves as 'teachers.' Whenever deception is used in this manner in a psychological experiment, the experimenter (M) attempts to make the subjects' (W) self-"persons" discrepant from his subject-"person." M attempts $M(pW) \neq W(pW)$,[21] while the goal of 'unobtrusive research' is $M(pM) \neq W(pM)$.

8.5.2   The various problems of second-hand personicating become even more entangled when we perform a phenomenal analysis of personicating experiments. Social psychologists (M) have typically tried to investigate how other people (W) personicate a third individual (F). M disregards the fact that M must personicate W in order to study $W(pF)$ and that $W(pM)$, the 'subject's' experimenter-"person," influences $W(pF)$. Furthermore, when using mere adjectives or descriptions of fictional characters as 'stimulus person' (F), the psychologist disregards the fact that W may personicate the author (T) of the 'stimulus material' and that, consequently, $W(pF)$ may be additionally influenced by $W(pT)$. The process which M studies exclusively on the basis of W's checkmarks on Semantic Differential scales (cf. Warr and Knapper 1968), and which M believes to be represented by those checkmarks as $W(pF)$, is thus in effect not $M[pW(pF)]$ but $M[pW(pF \bullet pM \bullet pT)]$. Most published research on personicating which we have seen gave us the impression that the author believed he was comparing F to $W(pF)$. For the reasons stated earlier (cf. footnote 5 and *passim*), we do not consider such a comparison possible. We believe that personicating research can compare qua data only $M(pF)$ to $M[pW(pF \bullet pM \bullet pT)]$, if mere descriptions of people are used as 'stimulus person,' and that the product in the round brackets cannot be taken apart into its individual 'factors.'

    Research on the process of personicating has been conducted within the experimental model discussed in the last chapter. That model excludes the experimenter, that is, the psychologist. It covers up the fact that the experimenter must form impressions; that his impressions are the only 'data' he has; and that the only data that are given to the readers of his journal articles are their impressions based on his words. The disregard for the part played by the psychologist may explain why the distinction between first-hand personicating and second-hand personicating has so far been overlooked.

---

21 This is the exact opposite of 'understanding,' which attempts $M(pW) = W(pW)$.

8.5.2.1 Warr and Knapper (1968) may have believed they made that distinction in what is probably the most meticulous collection of experiments on personicating to date. They distinguished between 'conception' and 'perception,' stating that: 'Judgments or impressions of a person when he is not serving as a stimulus will be referred to as conceptions and those judgments in his presence will be treated as perceptions' (p. 4). This distinction corresponds neither to ours between conceiving and perceiving, nor to that between first- and second-hand personicating. As the descriptions of Warr and Knapper's many experiments clearly indicate, their subjects perceived (in our sense of the word) nothing but pieces of paper with a text on it. The text consisted of various descriptions of people and events. The 'judgments in his presence' were made in the presence of only those descriptions. The only human beings present were the psychologists and other participants – who probably personicated one another but whose "persons" were not investigated by Warr and Knapper.

These authors also distinguished between 'direct person perception' and 'indirect person perception,' which they 'defined ... in terms of the presence or absence of an intervening communciation medium' (p. 28), and not of an intervening human being, a reporter. In Warr and Knapper's terms, my personicating someone on the basis of seeing and hearing her on my television screen is no different from my personicating someone I never heard about before on the basis of a news-report on television where I see and hear only the reporter. Both are instances of 'indirect person perception.' But the "person" resulting from a description on a piece of paper in front of me is considered 'direct person perception' by Warr and Knapper.

Obviously, Warr and Knapper did not personicate us when they wrote their book. Like every author, be s/he a psychologist or not, they must have personicated some general kind of reader. The problems we discussed earlier concerning the writing and reading of reports arise equally in relation to psychologists' professional books and journal articles. Reading and writing are aspects of many psychologists' practice.

8.6 DIFFERENCES BETWEEN FIRST-HAND PERSONICATING AND SECOND-HAND PERSONICATING It may be useful to summarize the main differences between first-hand and second-hand personicating:

1 In *first-hand personicating, a single process* of personicating takes place, whereas in *second-hand personicating, at least two* and usually

three or more such processes are involved: the reporter personicates at least the reportee, while the receiver of the report personicates the reportee and usually the reporter.

2 A *first-hand personicatee* is *perceived* (seen, heard, touched, etc.), whereas a *second-hand personicatee* is *reported* by a reporter and only the report may be perceived.

3 *Second-hand personicating* involves, in addition to perceiving and conceiving, also *communicating* from the reporter about the reportee to the receiver of the report, the second-hand personicator.

4 *Second-hand personicating* may involve an *interaction* between two *"persons,"* namely between the second-hand personicator's reporter-"person" and reportee-"person."

Thus: *second-hand personicating requires a minimum of three individuals, two of whom personicate the third, and one communciation.*

Our experimentally minded, logical empiricist, or positivist colleagues are not satisfied with a phenomenal analysis. They ask for experimental 'proof' that the differences between first- and second-hand personicating which we have pointed out show any effect in actual (preferably laboratory) situations. Amundson and Brandt (1972), therefore, investigated whether the above-discussed differences would show up in an 'experiment.'

8.6.1   Three social workers involved in parole granting were contacted, as well as three prison inmates who had very recently applied for parole but on whose fate no decision had been made yet. By rotation, the three inmates were paired with the three social workers (M) in such a way that each M had a face-to-face interview with one of the inmates, received only the file of a second inmate, and had a face-to-face interview with in addition to receiving the file of the third inmate. Thus, each inmate had one interview with two of the social workers while the third social worker received only his file. The rotation schedule is presented in table 1.

TABLE 1 Social workers personicating parole applicants

	Inmate 1	Inmate 2	Inmate 3
Social worker 1	1st hand*	2nd hand†	1st and 2nd hand
Social worker 2	2nd hand	1st and 2nd hand	1st hand
Social worker 3	1st and 2nd hand	1st hand	2nd hand

*1st hand = interview.   †2nd hand = file.

The entire 'experimental manipulation' consisted of the arrangement of the respective contacts and of obtaining the parole applicants' and social workers' permission to do a content analysis on the parole recommendations which the Ms made in writing, independently of the experiment, to the parole board. In his content analysis, Amundson used criteria set up by the parole service to decide on parole, namely (1) whether the applicant is likely to benefit from being paroled, and (2) whether granting him parole presents a likely danger to society.

The results clearly indicated differences between first-hand and second-hand personicating: (1) The files (second-hand personicating) did not change the first-hand personicating, that is, the results from combined first and second-hand personicating were the same as from first-hand personicating alone where M interviewed the inmate without seeing his file. (2) In the six interview situations in which the three Ms first-hand personicated the inmates, M found it more difficult to come to a clear-cut decision about recommending parole than when second-hand personicating an inmate solely on the basis of a report. This difficulty was independent of the direction of the recommendation (for or against granting parole). (3) When first-hand personicating an inmate, M tried to make a decision emphasizing the first criterion, namely whether the inmate might benefit from parole; when second-hand personicating the applicant, M tried to base his decision more heavily on the possible danger to society.

Our distinction between first-hand personicating and second-hand personicating is thus not merely a theoretical one but has been supported by an experiment in a real-life situation.

8.7   A GORDIAN KNOT: 'DOING' PSYCHOLOGY = PERSONICATING We have shown that psychologists personicate themselves, one another, and other people not only in everyday life, but also in their various activities as psychologists. Their tests, their theories of personality, their diagnostic categories are based, in the final analysis, on personicating other people. In their work as experimenters, as teachers who assign grades, hire colleagues, and research assistants, as counsellors, and as psychoanalysts, psychologists personicate others. In the course of their work, psychologists first-hand personicate the participants in their experiments and their colleagues; they second-hand personicate also many of their 'subjects,' who are 'run' for them by assistants, and students whom they admit for graduate work on the basis of grades and recommendations from reporters; and they are reporters when they give grades and when they write up their experiments for publication.

8.7.1   *Technical psychologists cut the knot* Technical psychologists have conducted an enormous amount of 'person perception' research. In it they did not separate perceiving from conceiving or first-hand from second-hand personicating. As in all of their work, they did not include themselves as either perceivers or conceivers, first-hand or second-hand personicators. Why not?

The models of technical psychology, whether of the S-R, S-O-R, S-C-R (Hein 1979) or R-R type, cannot include 'the "knower," without whom the knowledge is of no more significance than an undeciphered Etruscan inscription' (Bridgman 1959, p. 180). Even when technical psychologists call themselves 'cognitive behaviourists,' they study merely 'responses' and 'observable behaviour' and disregard cognitions, first of all their own. They do not reflect upon themselves and upon what they are doing. Technical psychology is geared towards changing others; not towards insights, not towards phenomenal analysis of the way in which oneself personicates, not towards psychoanalysis of oneself, but towards statistical analysis of one's 'findings.'

When psychoanalysts set as their goal to help the analysand adjust to society and its demands, they pursue a technical interest. Theirs too is a technical psychology. Only when they conduct an analysis for the purpose of better understanding, and the increased freedom such understanding may bring with it, is their work emancipatory.

8.7.2   *Psychoanalysts study the knot* In the course of truly trying to understand human minds better psychoanalysts like Ruesch and Bateson (1951), Watzlawick, Beavin, and Jackson (1967), and Menninger (1958) realized that personicating is not a linear process which can be broken down into its atomic components, but a highly complex process-structure with many feedback loops. They also realized that they themselves were involved in this Gordian knot.

8.7.3   *Kaminski and the Brandts map the knot* Kaminski (1970) laid a large number of the strands of that Gordian knot open and mapped them in his micropsychological phenomenal analysis. In this chapter, we mapped some additional strands. We tried neither to undo it nor to cut it. This Gordian knot of feedback loops may be studied and mapped. But alienation is the price for cutting it.

After tracing the roots of some psychologies in the next chapter, we shall return to the exclusion of technical psychologists from their own systems and discuss the resulting alienation.

9 Psychologists Caught in Different Historical Frameworks

Psychologists Caught in Different Historical Frameworks
The birth of psychology from the spirit of theology

9.0   'Can history be revised?' Boring began his 'Preface to the Second
Edition' of his *A History of Experimental Psychology* (1957), and replied
'Yes. As time goes on, there come to be second thoughts about the
interpretation of it.' Boring now 'wanted to get more into the dynamics
of history ... to speak of the rôle of the *Zeitgeist* and of the great
man ... two views ... [which] are not mutually exclusive but obverse and
reverse of every historical process' (p. xiii). Boring meant by *Zeitgeist* 'the
habits of thought that pertain to the culture of any region and period'
(p. 3). I would like to show in this chapter how different psychologies
can be understood to some extent as embedded in specific theologies,
which may also have influenced what Boring referred to as *Zeitgeist*.
Since the 'great man' aspect can be found in many histories of psychology, I shall largely disregard it here.

Psychologists are, like all other human beings, members of societies
in which they have been socialized (educated) and in which they communicate with colleagues and non-psychologists on many levels from
small talk to scientific arguments. Hence, any specific psychology can
be understood as 'a special configuration out of the context of life and
experiences of a historical-social group' (Mannheim 1964, p. 379).

I shall base this analysis to a large extent on my understanding of
Karl Mannheim's sociology of knowledge, which, in turn, is heavily
indebted to psychoanalysis and phenomenology and thus fits well into
my general approach in this book.

9.0.1   Mannheim's major work, *Ideology and Utopia*, appeared first in German in 1929 and in English in 1936. It contains brilliant analyses of
various psychologies but, though both editions have been republished
many times, it remains largely ignored by psychologists. Hence, some

preliminary discussion of Mannheim's approach appears necessary in a book for and about psychologists.[1]

Mannheim (1936) describes his sociology of knowledge as 'a method which will enable us, on the basis of increasingly precise criteria, to distinguish and isolate diverse styles of thinking and to relate them to the groups from which they spring' (p. 50). This relating is necessary because 'in every concept, in every concrete meaning, there is contained a crystallization of the experiences of a certain group' (p. 22) and because 'the derivation of our meanings ... plays an indispensable role, namely, it socializes events for a group' (p. 21). It is, therefore, not sufficient to trace certain ideas in psychology back to the individual history of the psychologist who first developed them, though such an investigation is useful too. But 'for a mode of behaviour of social significance, such as the transvaluation of values which transforms the whole system of life of a society in all its ramifications, preoccupation with the purely individual life-history and its analysis is not sufficient' (p. 27). 'It was the merit of the sociological point of view that it set alongside the individual genesis of meaning the genesis from the context of group life' (p. 28). Mannheim does not ask us to restrict our investigations to a single 'point of view' but fully recognizes the need for several independent approaches: 'The epistemological, the psychological, and the sociological ways of stating problems are the three most important forms of raising questions about and investigating the nature of the cognitive process' (p. 33).

9.0.2   Mannheim's sociology can be said to be psychoanalytic in the sense that it assumes that 'the examination of the object ... is coloured by values and collective-unconscious, volitional impulses' (p.5) and that it 'inevitably carries with it the gradual uncovering of the irrational foundation of rational knowledge' (p. 31). Whereas in psychoanalysis the modes of thought and feeling of an individual are understood in terms of the individual's personal origins, 'the principal thesis of the sociology of knowledge is that there are modes of thought which cannot be adequately understood as long as their social origins are

---

1   I recommend the reading of at least the first chapter of *Ideology and Utopia*, which Mannheim himself wrote in English and which, therefore, does not suffer from translation.

---

obscured' (p. 2). Hence, 'the sociology of knowledge seeks to comprehend thought in the concrete setting of an historical-social situation out of which individually differentiated thought only very gradually emerges' as 'every individual ... finds ... preformed patterns of thought and of conduct' (p. 3).

The role played by psychoanalytic concepts in Mannheim's thought becomes particularly evident in his 'illustration of how the extension of our knowledge of the world is closely related to increasing personal self-knowledge' and in his insistence that 'the stages of this understanding of the world are bound at every step to the process of individual self-clarification' (p. 48). Therefore, 'to live with the unconscious uncovered, is the historical prerequisite of scientific critical self-awareness' (p. 47).

9.0.3   This self-reflecting is a common denominator of psychoanalysis and phenomenology. Other characteristics of the phenomenological approach appear also in Mannheim's work. The sociology of knowledge is relational, studying knowledge always in relation to a specific group which developed and used it. It is, in other words, fully aware of the 'perspectivity of concepts which fixates certain sides of the same primary substance always differently ... The thought process which catches itself in this perspectivity of the concepts first closes for itself with all means the road toward a systematic total posing of questions' (1969, p. 90).

An outstanding characteristic of Mannheim's sociology of knowledge is that he applied this approach not only to other subject matters but also to the sociology of knowledge itself, as is required of a truly self-reflective and self-critical science which attempts to avoid false consciousness. Since his sociology of knowledge contains both psychoanalytic and phenomenological elements, the self-reflection of the sociology of knowledge can serve in part the understanding of both psychoanalysis and phenomenological psychology from the sociology of knowledge point of view.

9.0.4   'The sociology of knowledge actually emerged with Marx ... The other source ... is to be found in the flashes of insight of Nietzsche ... From Nietzsche the lines of development lead to the Freudian ... theories of original impulses and to the methods developed by them for viewing human thought as distortions and as products of instinctive mechanisms' (1936, p. 309f.). Thus, the precursors of Mannheim lived in the very recent past as 'the multiplicity of ways of thinking cannot become a problem in periods when social stability underlies and guarantees the internal unity of a world-view' (p. 6); but 'only when horizontal mobility is accompanied by intensive vertical mobility ... is the belief in the general and eternal validity of one's own thought-forms shaken' (p. 7).

Though Mannheim relates the development of the sociology of knowledge to 'a considerable social ascent ... a general democratization ... the rise of the lower strata' (p. 8) and 'the disruption of the intellectual monopoly of the church' (p. 12), he does not connect this analysis with those individuals whom he names as his precursors or with himself. Yet, it seems no coincidence that Marx, Nietzsche, Freud, and Mannheim had all rejected their respective religions and thus were not subject to any 'monopoly of the church.'

9.0.4.1 One of the sharpest attacks on the Christian churches was launched by Nietzsche, who wrote *Der Antichrist*. Of the four men he was the only one who was not a Jew, but he had the highest respect for the independent critical thinking of Jews: 'All Jewish scholars regard logic very highly, that is, the act of *forcing* agreement through reasons ... For nothing is more democratic than logic: it knows no social status of the individual and also accepts a crooked nose as straight. (As a side remark: Europe owes the Jews a great deal, especially with respect to becoming logical, to *cleaner* head-habits ... wherever Jews gained influence they taught to distinguish more finely, to deduce more sharply, to write more brightly and cleanly: their task was always to bring a nation to *"raison."*)' ('Die fröhliche Wissenschaft' No. 348)

Nietzsche's social mobility expressed itself in his separation from the Lutheran church in which his father and his two grandfathers had been ministers, by his becoming the most 'stringent critic of his countrymen [and] of the religion and morality of his fathers' (Kaufmann 1961), by dropping his middle name 'Wilhelm,' which was the name of the Prussian kings and later German emperors, by changing his citizenship from Prussian to Swiss, and by retiring after ten years as a professor at the University of Basle into utter solitude at the little mountain village of Sils-Maria. His writings were first ignored by the public until he was made world-famous through the Danish Jew Georg Brandes (Georg Morris Cohen), who lectured on Nietzsche at the Univeristy of Copenhagen. One psychologist upon whom Nietszche had a vastly greater influence than Mannheim's above quoted statement on 'the lines of development' indicates, and than has hitherto been examined, was Sigmund Freud (cf. Brandt 1961a, 1966a).

9.0.4.2 The social mobility of the Jews resulted from their emancipation after the French Revolution. But 'the multiplicity of ways of thinking' has had a tradition going back in history over millennia. I am referring to the hermeneutics of the Torah and the Prophets, and to the attitude that 'the ideal solution is ... an original synthesis that has never before been offered' and that 'this mental activity is a delight both to the performer and to his audience' (Zborowski and Herzog 1952, p. 98). This age-old Jewish attitude contrasts sharply with that of all Christian churches, where offering 'an original synthesis,' be it a new interpretation of the Bible by the Gnostics, the Albigenses, or Michael Servetus, or a new interpretation of aspects of the unvierse by Galilei or Giordano Bruno, was always considered heresy.

9.0.4.3 Now it seems to me that when Jews like Marx, Freud, and Mannheim – and Einstein, Husserl, Wertheimer, Popper, and innumerable others – were, partly as a result of the Age of Enlightenment and the subsequent emancipation of the Jews, partly as a result of the new social mobility, no longer concerned with finding new interpretations of the ancient Jewish texts, they sought instead 'an original synthesis that has never before been offered' in other fields: in economics and history, in psychology, in sociology – and in physics and philosophy. Thus, while renouncing the Jewish faith they still remained within the Jewish cultural tradition (cf. Bakan 1958).

The social mobility to which Mannheim ascribes the ascent of his own sociology of knowledge is concretely demonstrated in his own case though he makes no reference to it. He moved from Hungarian-speaking Budapest to the German-speaking Frankfurt, and later to English-speaking London. In Anglo-America neither his name nor 'sociology of knowledge' appeared in the 1961 edition of the *Encyclopaedia Britannica*. It required the new vertical social mobility brought about by the civil rights movement to give the necessary impetus 'toward a reflexive sociology' (Gouldner 1970) among Yankees.

9.0.5 Before proceeding to the sociological analysis of various psychologies, the Anglo-American reader who, in light of the above, cannot be expected to be familiar with Mannheim's approach must be introduced to two basic concepts of the sociology of knowledge which constitute the title of Mannheim's best known work: 'ideology' and 'utopia.' 'Ideology' implies 'that ruling groups can in their thinking become so intensively interest-bound to a situation that they are simply no longer able to see certain facts which would undermine their sense of domination

...[and] that in certain situations the collective unconscious of certain groups obscures the real condition of society both to itself and to others and thereby stabilizes it. The concept of *utopian* thinking reflects ...that certain oppressed groups are intellectually so strongly interested in the destruction and transformation of a given condition of society that they unwittingly see only those elements in the situation which tend to negate it' (1936, p. 40). With these concepts in mind a sociological analysis of some psychologies can now be undertaken.

9.1   THE BIRTH OF PSYCHOANALYSIS FROM THE SPIRIT OF MOSES The intellectual history of psychoanalysis, tracing many of Freud's ideas back to Darwin, Herbart, Fechner, Schopenhauer, Nietzsche, and others – including the French neurologists Bernheim and Charcot, whose works Freud translated into German – has been written and rewritten (e.g., Harms 1967; Jones 1957; Pongratz 1967; Wyss 1961). The social circumstances surrounding the development of psychoanalysis have also not been entirely ignored. The upper middle-class background of Freud's patients and Victorian morals have frequently been held responsible for the theory of infantile sexuality. It seems, however, problematic how 'Victorian' morality influenced Freud's ideas, which were derived from listening in Roman-Catholic-dominated Vienna to patients who came from Russian Orthodox nobility and from North America.

What has been said about the social origins of the sociology of knowledge applies largely also to psychoanalysis, which, as I showed, is closely entwined with the former and, like it, is predominantly a 'Jewish science.'[2]

9.1.1   Thinking and the use of language have been highly valued by Jews from time immemorial. The god of the Jews is a verbal god. Contrary to other gods he cannot be seen. He must not even be visualized in any shape or form. That he made man in his own image means that he gave man language so that man can understand him and communicate with him. Throughout the Jewish holy scriptures their god is reported to

---

2 Psychoanalysis has been jokingly called 'Jewish Science' in allusion to 'Christian Science.' The Swiss Jewish psychoanalyst Dr Raymond Battegay told me that he felt like being in a synagogue when he visited a psychoanalytic convention at New York.

---

have spoken and once even written to the Jews. To be fully initiated into the Jewish community a boy must demonstrate that he can read Hebrew. Eventually, he will be expected not merely to read the Torah but also to interpret it.

Since the end of the biblical kingdoms of Judah and Israel the boys also learned the language of the country in which they lived. In Eastern Europe they spoke Yiddish among themselves and Russian, Polish, Ukranian, or Rumanian with the gentiles. In the Balkan countries and Turkey they talked with one another in Ladino and spoke the national language with non-Jews. Jewish men thus had ample opportunities to become aware of different ways of thinking and of expressing one's ideas, of different shades of meanings, of various possibilities of interpreting what they heard or read. It seems only natural that those Jewish men who, like Mannheim, Marx, Einstein, Freud, and many others including myself, were no longer interested in re-interpreting biblical texts, applied their critical thinking, their analytically trained minds, to other fields.

In the psychology developed by the Jew Sigmund Freud interpretation plays a central part. His first book and by far his largest, if not most important work, is significantly entitled *The Interpretation of Dreams*. It was shortly followd by interpretations of everyday speech and actions. Interpretation – not manipulation, control, or 'behaviour modification' – became the tool of psychoanalysis.

Freud applied this tool in the first place to himself, to his own dreams, thought, feelings, speech, and actions. He helped his analysands interpret theirs. He interpreted myths, works of art, in short all products of the human mind.

But Jews do not value intellect at the expense of feelings. In contrast to the Puritans who will be discussed below, Jews freely accept and openly show their emotions (cf. Zborowski 1969). Emotions also play a central role in psychoanalytic theory and practice. They are considered to be the source of conflicts which create psychological symptoms. The psychoanalytic theory of development is a theory of emotional development. Fixations and regressions relate to early stages of emotional development. Resistance and transference, the two focal points of psychoanalytic work, concern emotions. All defences are defences against unacceptable anxiety-provoking emotions, and anxiety itself is an emotion. The superego is conceptualized as inducing the emotion of guilt. This concern with emotions contrasts strongly with other psychological theories in which emotions play a minor or no part.

What Jews all over the world have in common and what binds them together is no longer as much a common faith as a common history. Jews have a great sense of their history; they still celebrate their holidays by their own calendar, which counts the years from the mythological beginning of the world. Two of the main criticisms by others of psychoanalytic inquiry are that it delves into the analysand's earliest past history and that it takes such a long time. The investigation of the analysand's individual past can be well understood among people who spend a great deal of their lives studying the history of their forefathers. On the other hand, people with a long history – like the Chinese and the Indians – are not as much in a rush as newer nations. The sheer duration of an analysis is perhaps what distinguishes it most concretely from all other forms of psychotherapy.

This lengthy process, emotionally and usually financially costly, takes place in an atmosphere of great deprivation (cf. 5.1.1). One of its goals is to strengthen 'the reality principle,' the ability to postpone gratification. Psychoanalysis was developed before the foundation of the state of Israel, when large numbers of Eastern European Jews were still suffering under pogroms and living in poverty. Orthodox Jews were waiting for the Messiah to lead them back to their Holy Land, rather than seeking immediate gratification by moving there on their own.

The method developed to uncover unconscious motives, thoughts, and feelings consists of freely expressing what occurs to one ('free association'; cf. 2.5.2.1). It involves taking risks and reflects the struggle against 'censorship' and the 'resistance' against oppression and persecution in the political arena.

9.1.2   The psychoanalytic theory is a theory of internal mental conflict which reflects the conflict its founder was in for most of his life as a Jew in a very largely anti-Semitic environment. One of his earliest followers, and one of the tiny minority of non-Jews among them, the first president of the International Psychoanalytic Society, Carl Gustav Jung, later made common cause with the German National Socialists, though he was not even a German but a Swiss (Jung 1934).

Freud had already, before the First World War, emphasized the socio-economic influences on human functioning and had even mentioned them specifically as 'the sociological interest' in a paper on 'The Interest in Psychoanalysis' (1913). A direct socio-political influence on psychoanalytic theory is evident from the addition of the concept of a destructive drive, which resulted largely from observations Freud made during the First World War on shell-shocked patients who suffered from 'repetition compulsion,' the inability to stop reliving in fantasies and dreams some extremely painful experiences from the war. The further development of the theory of the destructive drive led Freud to his social critiques and critiques of religion, *The Future of an Illusion* and *Das Unbehagen in der Kultur* ('the discomfort in culture,' translated into English as *Civilisation and Its Discontents*). At the same time, several of his followers, such as Bernfeld, Fenichel, Fromm, and Reich, tried to combine psychoanalysis with Marxism and published the *Zeitschrift für Politische Psychologie und Sexualökonomie*, a line of thought carried much further by some contemporary West German psychoanalysts (cf. Brandt 1979b).

However, in a sociological discussion of psychoanalysis a strange paradox must not be overlooked: psychoanalysis has, on the one hand, widely influenced thinking in the social sciences and humanities, as reflected in novels, literary criticism, anthropology, and even to a certain extent academic psychology;[3] on the other hand, it is rejected as 'unscientific' by the vast majority of psychologists and psychiatrists. It is mainly relegated to a handful of private practitioners who have to do their research and teaching outside of universities. Psychoanalysis is psychology, as Freud again and again emphasized. The widely held idea that it is a medical discipline and that all or most psychiatrists are psychoanalysts does not correspond to any facts. Less than ten per cent of North American psychiatrists have any psychoanalytic training, as such training forms no more part of the training of psychiatrists than of that of psychologists.

According to one interpretation, the Jews chose to accept God's covenant and thereby became the chosen people. Similarly one can undergo psychoanalysis and become an analysand and perhaps a psychoanalyst only by one's own free choice. In both cases the choice involves responsibilities. Just as the Jews have always been a minority, only a small number of people can be analysed. According to Freud only few people are analysable and are willing to undergo analysis. Most people with problems in living seek other forms of help. The few who undergo psychoanalysis form a rather cohesive group whose members are in the majority of Jewish origin (Kadushin 1969). One cannot

---

3 Ironically, the public image of both psychologists and psychiatrists is of specialists in reading people's minds, i.e., 'vulgar psychoanalysis.'

---

expect a large following of a science which pursues an emancipatory interest within an increasingly other-directed society. A theory and practice which, in Riesman's (1950) terms, helps people to become more autonomous individuals can at best be vulgarized in a society flourishing from conspicuous consumption, but can never become the world-view or type of thinking of the ruling class.

While psychoanalysis has never dominated the thinking of those in power, its theoreticians and practitioners are neither socio-economically nor politically oppressed.[4] They cannot be said to 'unwittingly see only those elements in the situation which tend to negate it' (Mannheim 1936, p. 40). Hence, their thinking cannot be categorized as utopian in Mannheim's sense.

9.1.3   However, the thinking of North American psychoanalysts has to some extent become ideological. The bulk of Anglo-American psychoanalytic writings completely ignores not only the issue of personicating discussed in chapter 8 but most basic problems in general psychology. Most of these publications consist merely of exegeses of Freud's original works, resembling debates by medieval schoolmen. Psychoanalysis seems to have become an ideology, in Mannheim's sense, for the highly restricted group of members of the American Psychoanalytic Association. They give little evidence of self-reflection and self-criticism. They seem to strive for adjustment to the values and standards of the capitalist bourgeois society from which they profit, and to support the positivist domination of psychology. The members of the American Psychoanalytic Association form a small minority within psychiatry, which itself has little status within medicine. They are looked upon by other psychiatrists with much ambivalence and even hostility. In that situation they have tried to become some kind of an aristocracy 'monopolizing the right to preach, teach, and interpret' (Mannheim 1936, p. 10) and 'to cure ... patients [to achieve] an optimum of adaptation' (p. 20). They have done so by making most people in North

---

4   There are no more psychoanalysts in the Soviet Union since Stalin's consolidation of power and eradication of any critique. In the early 1920s the Russian translation of Freud's work was widely read in the U.S.S.R.

America believe that only physicians can be psychoanalysts and by suppressing all facts to the contrary.[5]

At the same time, more and more splinter groups formed among the remaining psychoanalysts which presents a picture very similar to that of the innumerable Christian churches. In both instances almost no dialogue takes place between the different sects, each of which claims to possess the only 'truth,' as revealed by Sigmund Freud and Jesus Christ respectively.

9.2 THE BIRTH OF GESTALT-PHENOMENOLOGY FROM THE SPIRIT OF LUTHER

9.2.1 Among the founders of gestalt-phenomenological psychology were also a considerable number of psychologists of Jewish origin: Rosa and David Katz, Koffka, Lewin, and Wertheimer. However, their group was not only less homogeneous in this respect than that of the early psychoanalysts, but it was also less isolated. Gestalt-phenomenology was developed within the university of predominantly Lutheran Berlin, from where it got its name 'the Berlin School' of psychology. Its roots lay in part in the 'Leipzig School' of Krueger, Sander, and Volkelt, located within another Lutheran university.

The basic characteristics of gestalt-phenomenology have been repeatedly stated in the pages of this book (cf. 0.3 and 5.1.2). The emphasis is on the organized, undivided, articulatedness of wholes as such, on the perspectivity of all knowledge, on the study of *Erlebnisse* (experiences) as part of behaviour, and of the consequent meanings attached to all phenomena. The origin of this kind of psychology in the Protestantism of Luther, and the Protestant Lutheran philosophies of Leibnitz and Kant, does not seem difficult to trace.

9.2.2 Luther's motto, 'everything believed or nothing believed,' represents the wholeness of faith. Salvation comes to the Lutheran through faith, whose wholeness must again and again be inspected by self-reflection. Faith is not intersubjectively observable. It is not based on consensus.

---

5 Sigmund Freud's daughter, Anna Freud, Ernst Kris, David Rapaport, Erik H. Erikson, Geza Roheim, and Theodor Reik are just some of the better known non-medical psychoanalysts.

Furthermore, since it is indivisible and must be undivided, it is not a composite of measurable charitable acts or of a number of good deeds. Correspondingly, gestalt-phenomenology conceptualizes human beings as wholes, and not as assemblages of traits, abilities, or factors which are randomly associated.

Lutherans can be in direct individual communion with their God. They need no priest as intermediary. As there exists no confessional in their church, they are directly responsible to themselves and their God. They must look into themselves to determine that they have undivided faith and to examine the meaning of their actions. Such self-examination leads to the recognition of problems. In contrast to logical positivism, for which no 'real' problems exist but only linguistic problems, real problems are what stand at the centre of the Lutheran philosophies of Leibnitz and particularly of Kant.

9.2.3   The Kantian tradition shows itself also in the importance given by gestalt-phenomenologists to *Grundlagenforschung*, the analysis of methodological and factual axioms by means of critical reasoning. This includes basic problems of definition of terms, of different meanings associated with the same word. As a consequence, a large number of psychological doctoral dissertations are theoretical, analysing problems – without necessarily leading to experiments.

The concern with problems pervades gestalt-phenomenology. Metzger's (1963) *Psychologie: Die Entwicklung ihrer Grundannahmen seit Einführung des Experiments* (psychology: the development of its basic assumptions since the introduction of experiments), a comprehensive presentation of psychology in its various aspects from a gestalt-phenomenological perspective, is entirely arranged by problems. This becomes immediately evident by looking at the chapter headings, each of which begins with *Das Problem*. They cover the problems of 'the psychically real' (*des seelisch Wirklichen*), 'characteristics' (*Eigenschaften*), 'connections' (*Zusammenhang*), 'frame of reference,' 'centring,' 'order,' 'effect,' and 'the body-mind problem.' Pongratz's (1967) history of psychology is entitled *Problemgeschichte der Psychologie*. It is not a linear history of psychology but traces the history of different problems in psychology such as 'soul and psychic life,' 'consciousness and the unconscious,' 'experience and behaviour.' Many of the chapters of the fifteen-volume *Handbuch der Psychologie* have titles like 'the problem of measurement,' 'abilities as a problem of personality research,' 'the problem of personality types.' Frequently, the chapters are further divided according to problems following an 'introduction to the problem.'

9.2.4   Luther's translation of the Bible from the original languages into German did not abolish the many German dialects. It made, however, one of them into the accepted written language. The dialect Luther selected was the one spoken at Prague, at the first German-language university. Thus, the German of the Luther Bible became the language of the German-speaking universities, in spite of the many political borders separating them and even despite the fact that many of them were in lands not converted to Lutheran Protestantism.

The language of Luther's translation of the Bible did not remain the only common ground of the German-speaking universities. Their entrance requirements became graduation from the *Gymnasium*, whose curriculum included ancient and modern languages and their literatures, in addition to German, history, geography, philosophy, chemistry, physics, biology, and mathematics, which together formed the subjects of the *philosophische Fakultät*. The latter consisted of two divisions, the *naturwissenschaftliche* and the *geisteswissenschaftliche*, each of which had a number of *Institute* corresponding roughly to Anglo-American departments. When Wundt founded the first *psychologische Institut* at Leipzig in 1875, it became part of the *geisteswissenschaftliche Abteilung* of the faculty of philosophy.

There was, however, one level on which room was left for great diversity. Each department had only one professor, who was its ruler – just like the hundreds of counts, dukes, princes, and kings who ruled their own lands within the loosely tied together Holy Roman Empire, and to some extent even after the foundation of the new German Empire in 1871. The professor hired his assistants, many of whom had already their PhD, and he decided on the teaching and research within his *Institut*. Thus developed the 'Leipzig School' (*Ganzheitspsychologie*), 'Würzburg School' (psychology of thinking), 'Berlin School' (Gestalt psychology), and even the French-speaking Swiss 'Geneva School' (genetic psychology). Only under the recent reorganization of many German-speaking universities, where more than one professor may be in the same department, have these 'schools' ceased to exist.

In spite of the development of the different schools, of the great diversity of the German-speaking countries,[6] and the fact that a

---

6 Austria was until 1918 a multilingual assemblage of nations kept together by a common emperor and with Roman Catholicism as the official state-religion. After the First World War Austria lost Hungary and

---

number of departments of psychology were in Roman Catholic lands, much common ground remained, laid by Luther and his translation of the Bible. In 1956, Hofstätter, a leading West German psychologist, admitted: 'I should get into serious embarrassment, if I had to name a typical representative of Roman Catholic thought among professional [as opposed to amateur] psychologists' (p. 367).

9.2.5

9.2.5.1 The common ground extended beyond the interest in problems and the analysis of basic assumptions. Allport (1957) pointed at the common philosophical assumptions going back to Leibnitz and Kant, the emphasis on the 'whole man' and generally on wholes rather than on elements, and the adaptation of methodology to the specific issue under investigation. With respect to the latter, W.A. Russell, who was guest professor at the psychological *Institut* of the *Universität Würzburg* during 1957–58, mentioned the 'interest in rational and intuitive methods' (Russell and Roth 1958). Metzger (1965) summarized the

---

the Slavic territories. German became the only official language, while the power of the Roman Catholic Church changed with the political parties in power. From 1938 to 1945 Austria was absorbed by Hitler Germany. Since 1945 Austria has been an independent, German-speaking republic. Switzerland is only regionally German-speaking, while parts have French, Italian, and Romansh respectively as their official language. It is one of the world's oldest democracies and consists of a federation of cantons (states), some of which are officially Roman Catholic while others are officially Zwinglian Protestant. From the time of Napoleon until 1871, there existed in Central Europe a large number of quite independent principalities and kingdoms which had previously been loosely united in the Roman Empire and formed the German Empire in 1871. In 1918 most of that general area became a German republic whose citizens were mostly Lutherans and Roman Catholics, neither of whom represented an official state-religion. After the Second World War that area was divided into two states along a north-south line. East Germany became officially part of the 'socialist' countries, while West Germany became affiliated with the U.S. The western and southern parts of West Germany are predominantly Roman Catholic, while the rest of that country is predominantly Lutheran.

---

characteristics of German-language psychology as the emphasis on the study of personality carried out generally with 'an inclination to phenomenology,' 'a deep rooted distrust in purely empiristic views,' 'a certain reserve against elementarist assumptions,' and 'a considerable reserve against an excessive and, as we believe, in its extreme forms suicidal objectivism' (p. 110). I would like to add to these shared aspects of German-language psychology the absence of *Rattus norvegicus*, which must have swum against the Gulf Stream from its end to its origin without ever getting on land in between.

9.2.5.2 An additional joint aspect of German-language psychologists is that they are psychologists *tout court* rather than 'social psychologists,' 'learning psychologists,' 'developmental psychologists,' etc. The 'whole man' aspect, to which Allport pointed in terms of their object of study, and which I traced to Lutheran Protestantism, extends also to the psychologists themselves as subjects. Thomae, the editor-in-chief of the fifteen-volume *Handbuch der Psychologie*, for example, worked and published in the areas of motivation, personality, development including aging, conflict resolution, and decision-making. Metzger published in such different areas as visual perception and education for creativity. Graumann worked in social psychology, perception, consciousness, motivation, and personality.

9.2.5.3 Two important roots of gestalt-phenomenology in particular have not yet been mentioned: Goethe and Romanticism. Goethe, who is mainly known as a poet and the author of 'Faust' outside German-speaking countries, considered himself primarily a scientist. In his work on comparative anatomy (1795) he wrote about *Gestalt*, demonstrating that the *os intermaxillare* which he discovered in the human skull could not be understood by disregarding the whole of which it formed a part both phylogenetically and ontogenetically. His four-volume *Zur Farbenlehre*[7] begins with systematic phenomenological experiments on colour vision, during which Goethe (1810) discovered the colours of shadows and the law of the size of after-images, which was later mistakenly attributed to Emmert.

---

7 '*Lehre*' has no English equivalent in this combination. It corresponds to the suffix 'ology' in psychology. It is derived from the German word for 'teaching.' The 'teachings on colour' include research and theory construction, as well as a critique of Newton's theory of colours.

9.2.6 Though Romanticism looked back at medieval chivalry, its 'values of emotion, instinct, intuition, fantasy, becoming (*Werden*)' and its 'pitting in almost all areas of the mind and of life the lasting against progress, the organic against the mechanic, what is original and primitive against what is artificial' (Schmidt 1934) do not conflict with Lutheran Protestantism. Mannheim (1969) stated more specifically: 'It is no coincidence that exactly that trend of thought was first taken hold of by Romanticism which stressed again the specific value of insight [*Erkenntnis*] which lies in the qualitative and holistic aspects of understanding, i.e., by that modern counter-current which signified in Germany also politically the counter-attack against the bourgeois-rationalizing world goal. Furthermore it is also no coincidence that today gestalt-perception, morphology, personality theory [*Charakterologie*], etc. launch their scientific-methodological counter-attack against the positivist methodology in an atmosphere which receives its world view and its political stamp from neo-Romanticism' (p. 145).

9.2.6.1 The Lutheran emphasis on wholeness and the Romantic values mentioned by Schmidt are also reflected in an area whose research and theories fill an entire volume of almost 600 pages of the *Handbuch der Psychologie*, namely *Ausdruckspsychologie*. In English-speaking countries there is no sub-area corresponding to *Ausdruckspsychologie* (concerning which Allport [1957] wrote 'So far as we handle problems of expressive behavior ... our concepts are importations' [p. 19]) which covers the study of facial expresions, tone of voice, body posture, gestures, and handwriting, the last of which used to be a required course for all psychology majors.

9.2.7 To the extent to which 'the inclination to formulate general theories without wanting to collect empirical data degenerates in its worst form to nothing but romantic personal fantasy' (Russell and Roth 1958, p. 228), gestalt-phenomenology can be categorized as both ideology and utopia. Russell was, however, aware that such degeneration was rather the exception. In general, the self-reflective and truly critical (cf. chapter 2, footnote 4) attitude of gestalt-phenomenological psychologists protects them from ideology and utopia to the extent to which any scientist can escape this Scylla and Charybdis.

9.3 INTERLUDE: OTHER PERSPECTIVES 'The mere defining of a concept and the shading of its meaning which one uses contain already to some extent a prejudgment of the results of the reasoning built upon that concept' (Mannheim 1969, p. 173). The general idea of perspectivity thus applies also to my analysis of the various psychologies discussed in this chapter.

9.3.1   For instance, Zellinger (1972) thematizes the similarities rather than the differences between psychoanalytic, gestalt, genetic, and behaviourist psychology. He considers as a common basis for these four psychologies that they conceptualize human beings as motivated to adapt in order to re-establish a disturbed equilibrium. Zellinger traces these psychologies back to Darwin and refers to the training in biology received by both Freud and Piaget. He contrasts these psychologies with those of Gordon Allport, George A. Kelly, and particularly contemporary Soviet psychologists. The latter have severely criticized the four psychologies which Zellinger lumps together, but particularly behavourism and psychoanalysis. Soviet psychology considers the four psychologies 'bourgeois ideologies.' If one agrees with Zellinger that all four of these psychologies rest on an equilibrium-adaptation model, it then follows that they are all conservative, since adaptation for the achievement of equilibrium cannot bring about anything but the status quo again.

9.3.2   Zellinger's perspective thus differs from that of Mannheim, Habermas, the Marxist psychoanalysts, and myself. Zellinger does not seem to differentiate between Cannon's static concept of homeostasis and von Bertalanffy's (1956, 1962) concept of *Fliessgleichgewicht* (steady state), which refers to a dynamic equilibrium. I understand the latter to be the concept underlying psychoanalytic, gestalt, and genetic psychology. In particular, Freud's and Piaget's respective ideas about developmental stages which are not merely maturational, but result from new structures of inter*action* with the environment, and which cannot be explained by a merely *re*active model of human beings, contradict Zellinger's analysis.

That psychoanalytic, gestalt, and genetic psychologies postulate a human being who is both active and *re*active is also the understanding of Overton and Reese (1970, 1973). With respect to Freud, Mischel (1974) points out that psychoanalytic theory underwent changes in line with the observations of its practitioners, and that defence mechanisms 'are to be understood by analogy, not to physiological processes, but to normal purposive and intentional behavior' (p. 255). Moreover, the concepts of 'alloplasticity' and 'autoplasticity' imply, especially in the work of Hartmann (1939), an active alteration of both self and environment by the individual.

9.3.3   If, then, diamat psychology agrees with psychoanalysis that human beings are active, 'why does Soviet psychology reject Freud's teachings? Above all, we have the incompatibility of the entire methodology of Freudianism with generally accepted methods for the establishment of scientific data ... the demoralizing influences spread by psychoanalysis, especially in the younger generation, which give eroticism the place of a leading social principle and encourage the very worst forms of decadent literature and art ... the reactionary role which this point of view plays by masking the true causes of social disasters ... instead of concentrating on the tasks related to the struggle against class exploitation and other negative aspects of the capitalistic system' (Bassin 1969, p. 402). What strikes me in this 'Critique of Freudian Theory' by a Russian psychologist who works at the Institute of Philosophy in Moscow is that it attacks psychoanalysis exactly from that standpoint which Zellinger criticizes as the method fetishism of behaviourism, from a Victorian-bourgeois anti-sexuality view, and from a pragmatic, 'doing'-oriented perspective. What this Russian critique, like Zellinger, disregards are the basic dialectic-materialist similarities between psychoanalysis and Marxism.

9.3.3.1 These similarities are equally ignored by Soviet psychologists and by bourgeois-capitalist psychoanalysts. Yet, once one is aware of them they are quite striking, though there seems to be no indication that either theory has borrowed from the other.

According to Bekker (1940), Marx's basic philosophical concepts are 'dialectic forms of movement,' as expressed in the dialectical relationships between 'theory and practice,' 'quantity and quality,' 'measurements and measuring instruments,' 'possibility, reality, and necessity,' 'the singular, the particular, and the general,' 'contradiction and conflict,' and 'differentiation and integration.' Other central concepts of Marx's philosophy are 'false consciousness,' 'the negation of the negation,' 'the identity of opposites,' and 'the role of history.' The central role of all these concepts, though by different names, in psychoanalysis can easily be shown. The 'dynamic view' (Rapaport 1960) deals specifically with the 'dialectic forms of movement.' Psychoanalytic 'theory and practice' (technique) are completely interdependent, each deriving from and in turn advancing the other. From the 'economic view,' the 'quantity' of drive energy cathected in any particular manner determines the 'quality' of affect or of a symptom. Since all 'measurements,' that is, diagnoses, are made by human beings qua 'measuring instruments,' the counter-transferences of those human beings (the analyst) must be analysed to disentangle as far as possible the dialectics between the instruments and what they measure. By making what was unconscious conscious, 'possibility' (potentials) becomes 'reality' and 'necessity' becomes distinguishable from mere wishes. Both theory and practice of psychoanalysis are advanced on the basis of observations made on 'the singular' (the individual), who is considered to be a 'particular' instance of 'the general.' 'Conflict' is recognized through 'contradiction' in the free-associations of analysands. Becoming aware of contradictions may lead to new conflicts. These express themselves particularly in resistances, which contradict the avowed desire for greater self-understanding. Analytic work (working through), which recapitulates and continues arrested emotional growth, progresses through 'differentiation and integraton' of previously unconscious content. The purpose of this work is to become aware of 'false consciousness' and thereby correct it. 'The negation of the negation' consists of making repressed (negated) thoughts and feelings conscious. The 'identity of opposites,' which Freud discussed specifically in his paper on the contradictory meaning of the primal words (1910), is affirmed in what psychoanalysis calls the 'primary process.' As to 'the role of history' in psychoanalysis, the 'genetic point of view' (Rapaport 1960) deals specifically with ontogenesis, while poligenesis, the history of the society in which the individual is socialized, is frequently neglected by non-Marxist psychoanalysts.

On the basis of the foregoing comparison between Marx's fundamental concepts and basic characteristics of psychoanalytic theory and practice, I consider dialectical materialism similar to psychoanalysis in important respects. This view is not in agreement with that of Zellinger or with that of most psychologists in the 'socialist' countries, or with that of most psychoanalysts in the capitalist countries. Nor have I found the parallel I have drawn in Mannheim's work. Our differences are easily explained on the basis of the concept of perspectivity. As Popper (1959) stated, 'things may be similar in *different respects*, and ... any two things which are from one point of view similar may be dissimilar from another point of view. Generally, similarity ... always presuppose[s] the adoption of *a point of view*: some similarities ... will strike us if we are interested in one problem, and others if we are interested in another problem' (Appendix *x, p. 421f.).

9.3.3.2 As I have attempted to show, the rejection of psychoanalysis by Soviet psychology is based in part on the same positivist arguments with which behaviourists reject the former. It can further be understood in terms of the ideologies of both Soviet psychology and behaviourism, neither of which is interested in self-reflection and in questioning its basic assumptions, as both represent respective groups in power in their countries. *Mutatis mutandis* the opposition of psychoanalysts in the capitalist countries to diamat is understandable as the utopian thought of a group which – though not socially, economically, and political-ly – is academically oppressed by its very limited access in capitalist countries to teaching in university departments of psychology as well as of psychiatry. Thus Mitscherlich (1970) wrote: 'In our opinion one weakness of the Yankee group of psychoanalysts proved to lie exactly in the fact that their naïve identification with the bourgeois role of the physician lasted ... relatively long beyond the end of World War II and with it the idea that it is also the task of the physician to reconcile the suffering human being with her or his society as it just happens to be' (p. 45). Yankee psychoanalysts attempted to strengthen their position 'scientifically' by emphasizing in their publications the similarities rather than the differences between psychoanalysis and behaviourism, and they tried to fortify their position politically by pressuring the training institutes affiliated with the International Psychoanalytic Association not to accept trainees without a medical degree, despite what Freud had written in 'The Problems of Lay-Analysis.'*

9.3.4   Using a different frame of reference from Zellinger, Bassin, or North American psychoanalysts, I come to see an important similarity between diamat and behaviourist psychology: Each is the dominant psychology in a certain socio-economic system and in a country functioning under that system. The difference between the two psychologies lies in the fact that diamat psychology is officially imposed and supported by the political party in power, whereas behaviourism is unofficially supported by and in turn supports the capitalist system.

9.4   THE BIRTH OF DIALECTIC-MATERIALIST PSYCHOLOGY FROM THE SPIRIT OF MARX

9.4.1   Contrary to psychology west of the Iron Curtain, psychology in the self-styled 'socialist countries' does not claim to be independent of an under-

---

* P.S. (1980): In the fall of 1979 an international group of psychoanalysts met in the U.S.S.R. at Tbilisi (Tiflis) for a conference on 'the Unconscious.' I have not yet seen a report from that meeting.

---

lying *Weltanschauung*. Thus, the introduction to the East German *Wörterbuch der Psychologie* (dictionary of psychology) (Clauss 1976) explicitly states: 'The dictionary is intended to be a representative reflection of dialectic-materialist psychology.' Correspondingly, the articles in the dictionary, like the publications of psychologists from 'socialist countries,' reflect in both form and content the dialectic between theory and practice, quantity and quality, measurements and measuring instruments; possibility, reality, and necessity; the singular, the special instance, and the general; and differentiation and integration. Books and journal articles from those countries not only state openly their philosophical and methodological underpinnings, but exemplify them also through the application of such concepts as the negation of the negation, the identity of opposites, contradiction and conflict, and the role of history, of the relations of production, and of false consciousness.

9.4.2   As these concepts indicate, diamat psychology is predominantly cognitive. It has been so since Pavlov introduced the concept of the 'second signal system,' through which he categorically distinguished human from animal psychological functioning. Consciousness plays a central role in diamat psychology, as shown by the entries in the East German dictionary of psychology. This role is also demonstrated by the fact that the articles on 'aphasia,' 'cybernetics,' 'educational guidance,' 'inner speech,' and 'thinking,' in addition to those on the 'frontal lobe,' 'localization of psychological functions,' the 'orienting reflex,' and the 'restitution of psychological processes,' were entrusted to psychologists from the 'socialist' countries by the editors of the West German *Lexikon der Psychologie*, which appeared in English translation as *Encyclopedia of Psychology* (Arnold et al. 1972).

Another aspect of Marxism reflected in diamat psychology is the emphasis on work, activity, and action, which are central to diamat theory and research on thinking, being, and consciousness (cf. Rubinstein 1958).

9.4.3   In so far as diamat is openly acknowledged as the basis for all of psychology in the 'socialist countries,' one cannot speak of false consciousness. However, diamat psychology becomes an ideology when its concepts are not applied to itself, when it does not reflect upon itself, when its critique is directed '*only at the opponent*... because one was probably subconsciously afraid... to get to the point of posing the question *in principle* and thereby think those problems through which would unsettle one's own position' (Mannheim 1969, p. 238). In order to stop being an ideology, diamat psychology would have to acknowledge 'the basic insight of the sociology of knowledge that all human thought *in general* is bound to [the conditions of] existence' (ibid.). It would have to recognize its own historical position and development, and particularly its own negation. But already half a century ago Mannheim found that 'as soon as Marxist-proletarian strata rise to the top they shake off the dialectic element in the theory ... and think in line with the generalizing, nomothetic method of liberalism and democracy' (p. 116). One may wonder to what extent the bureaucratization of the 'socialist countries' has led to a 'bureaucractic-conservative mentality' (p. 102f.). I found some indication of such a mentality in the frequent references to Pavlov and to diamat which seem merely to give lip service to an ideology without contributing to the issue. Particularly in both empirical and theoretical articles in cognitive psychology, for instance, analyses of thought processes, 'the dialectical materialism is only called materialism' – to paraphrase Mannheim (p. 219). What effect the recent more open-minded discussion in East Germany of psychoanalysis will have on the self-reflection of diamat psychology cannot yet be predicted.

I am also not in a position to place diamat psychology into its proper historical perspective. To do this seems to present a special difficulty in view of the fact that, contrary to Marx's prediction, the proletarian revolution did not take place in the highly industrialized countries in which its philosophy had been developed, but in countries to which that philosophy was not indigenous and from which it was then exported as a consequence of the Second World War. The sociology of diamat psychology is thus enmeshed with the history of Eastern Europe, a discussion of which would go beyond the scope of this book.

9.5   THE BIRTH OF BEHAVIOURISM FROM THE SPIRIT OF CALVIN Behaviourism originated in the U.S. in 1913. Today, almost seventy years later, it not only dominates in one form or another Anglo-American psychology, but has spread to many countries outside North America. Boring (1957) informed us that 'Watson founded behaviorism because everything was all ready for the founding' (p. 506). 'Watson was a functionalist (with a small *f*)' (p. 641), which means one who wants to predict the future and change it, if it does not look promising (p. 551). To the 'question why American psychology went functional in this broad sense,' while Germany and England did not, Boring replied: 'American psychology went functional because functionalism ... [was] natural to the temper of America' (pp. 506ff.).

In this section I shall attempt to show that that 'temper' resulted from four roots of the Yankee way of life: puritanism, the pioneer mentality, industrialization, and the melting-pot ideal.[8] Of these, puritanism was the first, from which the other three branched off. Yet, Boring did not mention it.

9.5.1   As the sociology of knowledge implies perspectivity and perspectives always require some distance, it is not astounding that the sources for such an analysis of behaviourism are to be found largely in works of authors like Erikson (1963), Ruesch (and Bateson 1951), and Hofstätter (1956), who were not raised and educated in the U.S. though they spent some time in that country. Thus, Erikson pointed to 'puritanism as a decisive force in the creation of American motherhood' (p. 292) and claimed that 'the American ... lives with two sets of "truths"': a set of religious principles or religiously pronounced political principles of highly puritan quality, and a set of shifting slogans, which indicate what ... one may get away with ... Without any pretense of logic or principle, slogans are convincing enough to those involved to justify action' (p. 286). After discussing in some detail the influence of the frontier upon 'the American Identity,' Erikson points at 'industrialization [which] brought with it mechanical child training' and 'clocklike punctuality in order to make [the human organism] a standardized appendix of the industrial world ... creating ... a mass-produced mask of individuality' (p. 294f.). According to Ruesch 'pioneer and puritan morality is the core of the American value system ... Today, there exists a pride in this core of the culture' (p. 97).

What are the characteristics of puritanism which have pervaded the lives of Yankees, both in the narrower (New England) and wider sense of this word? Puritanism is an offshoot of Calvanism. At the centre of Calvinist dogma lies

the doctrine of ... unconditional election – God determines that certain persons (the elect) shall be saved despite their inability to save themselves

---

8   I disregard the Deists because they had no deep influence on the Yankee way of life. Their main force, Freemasonry, deteriorated in the U.S. from its philosophical, anticlerical origins into social and charitable organizations which discriminate against atheists and blacks. The metric system, a tangible sign of the Age of Enlightenment, was not introduced in the U.S. by either Franklin or Jefferson.

---

through performance of good works; others shall be condemned to damnation ... These elect alone are ... granted power to attempt to follow godly ways ...

These abstractions, which the New Englanders modified somewhat, were given vitality through the actions and the writings of the Calvinists – Pilgrims and Puritans alike. Their lives were devoted to searching out clues to the divine will ... revealed in the daily affairs of mankind ... Finally, each one of them searched his own behavior to test its significance [as an indication of either salvation or damnation] and, for the same reason, scrutinized that of his friends and compatriots ... The Puritans ... necessarily became more worldly. They still clung fundamentally to their Calvinistic creeds. (Hart and Gohdes 1955, pp. 6ff.)

As expressed in the term 'Protestant work ethic,' 'work was one of the cardinal Puritan virtues, and ... very often made a man and his many sons comparatively well off in a surprisingly short time' (Horton and Edwards 1967, p. 41). At the same time, 'the Puritans strove for simplicity and coherence [and] originated rigidities of behavior in order to obtain a long-lost security.' Under the 'hardship [of] hostile Indians and ... a rigorous climate ... the Puritans developed ... the pioneer morality' (Ruesch and Bateson 1951, p. 96f.).

As proverbial as the puritan attitude towards work is that towards sex. Here, too, puritan and pioneer values supported each other. 'The initial shortage of women, especially in frontier outposts, reinforced the rigid rules regarding behavior toward the opposite sex, which the Puritans brought with them' (ibid.). Eventually, 'the combination of puritan with pioneer psychology seems to have created human beings who are less sensitive to sensory and aesthetic pleasures and who prefer work and action to meditation' (p. 131f.).

With industrialization, which resulted largely from the puritan work ethic, the pioneer mentality which produced 'personalities fascinated with action' (Ruesch and Bateson 1951, p. 131), and with the melting-pot ideal to absorb new immigrants, the Yankee value system has changed but little over the centuries. For the Yankee 'melting pot' does not produce an alloy, a mixture or compromise, but melts all newcomers down, 'adjusts' them to fit the existing society. As the U.S. congressional system, which was designed to make coalition governments impossible, shows and as U.S. foreign policy demonstrates, Yankees compete and do not compromise. The loser must smile and adjust to the rules of the winner.

The continued influence of puritanism upon Yankee life can still be seen in many of the campaign slogans of the 1980 U.S. presidential candidates, in the drawers of every hotel and motel room of the U.S., and in dividing mankind into the 'free world' which may have received grace and the 'communists' who are damned, or into whites and blacks (without mulattoes) or friends and enemies (without acquaintances in between, since puritans know no purgatory). The free expression of feelings which was condemned by puritans and pioneers alike is still inhibited, as shown in the studies by Zborowski (1969) and Argyris (1969) and by the popularity of encounter-groups, T-groups, etc., where the emphasis is on adjustment and acting. The strong puritan taboo on enjoying sex as an expression of deep feelings of involvement, concern, affection, and love continues to pervade life in the U.S. despite the large sales of sex magazines and books teaching the readers 'how to do' it and thereby perpetuating 'mechanical' and 'clocklike' performances. In line with the strongest verbal Yankee expression of anger, new 'do it yourself' manuals appear constantly. Social psychologist William McGuire admonishes students and colleagues: 'In case of doubt, do anything, but do something' (1967).

9.5.2   Because, as English and English (1958) have pointed out, 'the term has lost most of its distinctive reference,' I shall briefly remind the reader what I mean by 'behaviourism.' I refer to a psychology which is considered to be an 'objective' science reducible to and using methods derived from physics, such as 'measurements,' and based on 'operational definitions,' 'controlled, repeatable experiments' with 'naïve subjects' or with animals selected on purely practical and not on ethological grounds, and 'inter-subjective verification.' 'Parsimony' and 'logical consistency' are its guides. Its aims are 'prediction' and 'control.' To achieve these the 'associations' between 'stimuli' and 'responses' must be studied. Past 'associations' represent the only history of concern. The establishment of such 'associations' or 'bonds' between 'stimuli' and 'responses' is called 'learning.' 'Reinforcements,' sometimes called 'rewards' and 'punishments,' strengthen those 'bonds.'

In this sense, 'cognitive' and 'subjective' behaviourism are behaviourism more than in name, as demonstrated by Hein (1979). Similarly 'social learning theory' contains the essential ingredients of behaviourism. Even the research done concerning Rogerian, Maslowian, Kellyian, and other concepts from 'humanistic' psychologies is behaviourist because it is carried out with behaviourist tools. Such tools can provide only behavourist data – just as a thermometer can only provide one with temperature data and not with lengths, weights, or experiences.

All of these concepts, principles, and methods are taken for granted by behaviourists, most of whom cannot even imagine any other form of a 'science of psychology.' They either are not even aware of the existence of such methods as ethological observation, content analysis, the hermenuetic circle, and phenomenal analysis, or consider them 'unscientific.' They ignore equally psychoanalytic, gestalt, genetic, and diamat learning theories by referring to 'learning theory' in the singular as if theirs were the only one.

It is now possible to relate behaviourism to Yankee values and to answer such questions as: 'The Americans travelled to Leipzig to learn about the new psychology from Wundt; they came back fired with enthusiasm ... and then, with surprisingly little comment on what they were doing and probably but little awareness of it, they changed the pattern of psychological activity from the description of the generalized mind to the assessment of personal capacities in the successful adjustment of the individual to his environment ... Why?' (Boring 1957, p. 507). And why had the phenomenological-gestalt psychologists and the psychoanalysts who emigrated to the U.S. as a result of Nazi persecution hardly any lasting impact upon Yankee psychology, while the ideas of the *Wiener Kreis* were gobbled up?

9.5.3   A psychology made 'objective' through the introduction of the crucial experiment from the natural sciences cannot be traced to Wundt, for whom 'the experimental technique used ... to analyse mental processes is a profoundly different technique, both in principle and in concrete practice, from the experimental technique used by a behaviourist to predict and control behaviour' (Danziger 1979, p. 38). 'Objective' experimental psychology originated in the U.S. and can be understood in terms of the puritan mentality.

9.5.3.1   Contrary to Lutherans who can obtain salvation and escape damnation by having true faith, and to Roman Catholics who can obtain salvation through faith and good deeds in this life, Calvinist puritans have no means of influencing their fate after death. Whether or not they receive divine grace is predetermined and depends on neither faith nor good deeds. All that Puritans can do in this life is to 'test' by 'experiment' whether or not they are damned for eternity. That means to predict.

The test must be 'objective.' Introspection does not suffice for determining whether one has the right faith. Hence the test consists of doing work. If the puritan's work leads to success, this is an indication that he has been elected. If in spite of working hard he fails, he probably has been damned. Thus, for the puritan there exists no freedom. God's will becomes law, natural law, in physics, chemistry, astronomy, biology, and in psychology. In the puritan experiment, behaviour is the independent variable, success or failure the dependent variable which must be measured 'to test its significance' of rejecting the null hypothesis that equal numbers of puritans and non-believers will go to hell.

That behaviourists consider the results of their experiments as 'crucial' as the puritans considered theirs is shown by the statement of the well-known social psychologist Robert Rosenthal that 'no scientist would select intentionally a procedure likely to show his hypothesis in error' (1969, p. 195). In other words, as scientists psychologists are likely to produce self-fulfilling prophecies (cf. 7.1.6.1).

In order to test a hypothesis one must control the conditions surrounding the experiment as strictly and as rigorously as possible. Control of the environment and of oneself is a primary feature of puritan life and of behaviourist experimental psychology. Only such rigorous controls permit reliable measurements. Control and measurement are the criteria for 'scientific' psychology among behaviourists. This relationship between the puritan mentality and behaviourism becomes clearer when one contrasts it with the Lutheran mentality and *geisteswissenschaftliche Psychologie*. Since faith, upon which salvation depends for the Lutheran, cannot be measured but only qualitatively evaluated, precise definitions based on phenomenal analysis became the criterion for 'scientific' psychology among getalt-phenomenological psychologists.

9.5.3.2 The puritan and pioneer emphasis on doing and the corresponding disregard for feelings are reflected in the Yankee distrust of intuition. This distrust led behaviourists to the invention of a myriad of 'objective' tests. That these tests must necessarily be subjective (cf. chapter 8) is simply overlooked. The mistrust of intuition, in one's own thoughts and feelings, strengthens the use of measuring instruments. Such behaviourist 'tools' have typically no place for the expression of doubt, ambiguity, ambivalence, or indifference (cf. the Semantic Differential). Most frequently, they have only two categories: 'true' and 'false.' If they have a third one like the MMPI has, it represents ignorance but none of the above feelings. Nor is there a place for doubt, ambigiuity, or ambivalence in such Yankee psychologies as Rokeach's (1960, 1968) belief systems.

For behaviourists and puritans there exists only one 'truth.' It is revealed to them in the 'Acts,'[9] by what has been done and what worked. What works is the result of good works. When 'it works' the behaviourist has found the truth and publishes it (cf. 3.2.1). When it does not work (negative results) there is nothing to publish. Success is, thus, the proof of the truth for puritans, pragmatists, functionalists, and behaviourists alike. 'The proof of the pudding lies in the eating' means that when the rat eats the food which the behaviourist experimenter had prepared for it and placed at the goal of the maze, the behaviourist theory has been proved to be true. Now the behaviourist's work is finished successfully.[10]

9.5.3.3   'In America success is a yardstick with which the value of an individual is measured ... Objective and quantifiable terms had to be used, and thus a man's position was determined by his measurable success rather than by convention and tradition. The tendency toward quantification was further promoted by the whole economic trend ... Once the

---

9 'The Acts of the Apostles' are called *Apostelgeschichte*, i.e. 'Apostle story,' in Luther's translation.

10 These criteria for 'truth' and 'work' stand in flagrant contrast to some Jewish ones. With respect to 'truth,' one can compare the behaviourist view to that of Popper (1934/1959), according to whom scientists must attempt to falsify their theories and not to verify them. As long as a theory can not be falsified it may be kept while further falsifications are attempted. 'In the logic of science here outlined it is possible to avoid using the concepts "true" and "false"... The old scientific ideal of *epistēmē*–of absolutely certain, demonstrable knowledge–has proved to be an idol. The demand for scientific objectivity makes it inevitable that every scientific statement must remain *tentative for ever*' (1959, pp. 273ff.; emphasis in original). Concerning 'work' Bakan wrote: 'The main work of the scientist is thinking and making discoveries of what was not thought of beforehand. Psychologists often attempt to "play scientist" by avoiding the main work' (1967, p. 44f.). Behaviourists disparagingly call such work 'armchair-psychology.'

---

tendency toward quantification was established, this tendency became self-promoting' (Ruesch and Bateson 1951, p. 114f.).

Such 'objective' quantification is concrete and independent of ideas. It eliminates differences in values and points of view. By counting hands one determines intersubjective 'objective' 'truth' (cf. Brandt 1968). Looking at a problem from different perspectives may create discord and confusion. It is also uneconomical. Consistency and parsimony make life simple instead of complex, as demonstrated by the puritans who 'followed a strict and closely regulated habit of life' (*Encyclopaedia Britannica* 1961).

The role of measurement in behaviourism is emphasized in every Yankee textbook in psychology. The emphasis on measurement has led to ever new statistical methods. 'All that can be said here is that this reduction of everything to a measurable or inventory-like describability is significant as a serious attempt to determine what is unambiguously ascertainable and, further, to think through what becomes of our psychic and social world when it is restricted to purely externally measurable relationships ... What is left of [a 'situation'], or is it even at all intelligible when it is reduced to an external constellation of various reciprocally related but only externally visible patterns of behaviour? It is clear ... that a human situation is characterizable only when one has also taken into account those conceptions which the participants have of it, how they experience their tensions in this situation, and how they react to the tensions so conceived' (Mannheim 1936, p. 43f.). As Mannheim and others have recognized, this obsession with measuring, or 'metromania' as I call it, requires the neglect of qualitative differences. One can count only on the basis of common characteristics and must disregard all qualitative differences in order to assign numbers – which by themselves have no qualities. But measurement is by no means an absolute requirement of science. There are purely qualitative analyses made in chemistry as well as in biology. That Yankee psychology did not follow the example of these branches of science can be understood in terms of the puritan desire to measure the results of work in order to ascertain unambiguously God's will. In the industrialized society which resulted from the puritan's work, measurement could also be used to measure the amount of work done and to assign status by measuring the amount of money earned and saved. That measures have a strong irrational and mystical aspect for Yankees is demonstrated by their resistance to abandoning an irrational, impractical, and complicated conglomeration of measures for the highly rational, practical, and simple metric system which was introduced in Europe 200 years ago by the French Revolution. The inconsistency which lies in that resistance compared to the very values of puritan and pioneer morality is merely one of the indicators of false consciousness. (See also 4.3.4 and 4.3.5.)

9.5.3.4 When the puritan 'searched his own behavior to test its significance and, for the same reason, scrutinized that of his friends and compatriots' (Hart and Gohdes 1955, p. 6f.), that 'behaviour' had to be 'intersubjectively verifiable through observation.' The same holds true, though for different reasons, for the present-day other-directed melting-pot society. Here 'behaviour' must be 'intersubjectively observable' to find out how to 'behave' and to obtain approval from others for one's 'behaviour.' 'Intersubjectively observable and verifiable behaviour' is all behaviourists are interested in. Faith, thoughts, and feelings are 'private events.' They are of concern neither to puritans nor to behaviourists. Since private events can, by definition, not be intersubjectively observed, they may at best be inferred as 'intervening variables.' If they were obtained by introspection, psychology could not be reduced to physics, since physical objects cannot introspect. The behaviourist unified-science ideal could never be reached. Thus, behaviourists study only what people and rats do, how they 'respond' to 'stimuli.'

This concern with doing shows up not only in strict behaviourism but even in various psychotherapies in which the clients are required to do something, to role play, to touch one another, etc. This contrasts clearly with both individual and group psychoanalysis, where the analysands are strictly forbidden to act out and are allowed only to verbalize their thoughts and feelings. Analysands are even requested not to change any of their usual modes of action, because once these modes have changed there is no longer any motivation for the analysand to investigate and try to understand them.

Lack of interest in thinking and feeling is evidenced by the almost complete absence of Yankee research into these human functions. When research was undertaken it consisted of the measurement of supposed physiological correlates. Since, however, such correlates have not yet been found for emotions like guilt, joy, boredom, awe, relief, surprise, disappointment, they have simply been ignored by behaviourists.

In line with the puritan attitude, sex was also not studied by behaviourists in its relation to feelings and thoughts. Such a study would have emphasized one of the basic differences between humans and animals, namely that the latter perform sexual acts only when the female of the species is in heat, while humans perform sex for pure pleasure, which had no place in puritan morality. In addition, a close look at human sexual functioning would have revealed the fact that thoughts and fantasies can, without external 'stimulus,' bring about physiological changes like an erection and vaginal secretions. This evidence of 'mind over matter' would have destroyed some basic behavourist assumptions.

It may be objected that in behaviourist deconditioning therapy the client is asked to think of, to fantasize anxiety-provoking situations. This is merely one of the many contradictions of behaviourism which cannot justify this method within its own theoretical framework, since the behaviour therapist has no means of observing what the client thinks of. The behaviourist's answer to this argument is 'But it works.' However, the observation of the results does not indicate what brought the results about (cf. Klein et al. 1969).

9.5.3.5   The neglect of feelings in behaviourism is particularly evident in the role 'reward' and 'punishment' play in it. These two concepts, without which behaviourism and its 'learning theory' cannot be imagined, were also at issue in puritanism. Calvin's God does not reward or punish on the basis of the deeds of his flock. He decides beforehand whom he will reward with grace and whom he will punish by eternal damnation. In just the same way, the behaviourist experimenter decides when the rat will receive a shock and under what conditions the autistic child will be given a piece of candy. The rat and the child must try to figure out what the experimenter has in mind, as the puritan tries to find out God's inscrutable ways.

It is inconceivable for the puritan that some souls might get bored in heaven and might find hell exciting. Correspondingly, behaviourists do not question whether what they set up as punishment is experienced as such by their 'subjects' and whether the latter feel rewarded by whatever the experimenter decided to be a reward for them. They do not consider that someone who feels guilty may experience a gift as punishment because it increases the guilt feelings, and may feel rewarded by an electric shock because such 'punishment' relieves some guilt. Behaviourists ignore that a gift may be insulting and therefore experienced as a punishment.[11]

---

11 For a detailed analysis of this issue, see my 'Reward and Punishment or Bribe and Extortion?' (Brandt 1977).

The renaming of reward and punishment as positive and negative reinforcement merely masks the theological origin of the concepts. It also brings to the fore the disregard for feelings. One rewards others because one enjoys what they did. One punishes others because one feels angry. One *feels* rewarded or punished. 'Reinforcement' is a technological term, as in 'reinforced concrete' or 'troop reinforcement.' Just as the puritan God does not punish out of anger but on the basis of his plan for the world, the technical psychologist reinforces according to 'schedules' which the experimenter predetermines. Reinforcement functions mechanically, for instance, in the Skinner box, just like predestination. Both function according to design.

9.5.3.6 Consistency and parsimony (Occam's razor) are the basic criteria which behaviourists took over from the pre-quantum, outdated natural science paradigm. Neither of these values is ever questioned in Yankee psychology. They are taken for granted – as they must be or else be abandoned because they have no empirical base. Nature is prodigal, wasteful, producing millions of sperms only one of which fertilizes an ovum, drones which never reproduce, different kinds of eyes for vertebrates and insects, and so on. Consistency and parsimony are religious and aesthetic (cf. chapter 11), and not scientifically based values when examined more closely. They are not necessary requirements for science, as evidenced by the theory pluralism of modern physics (cf. 4.3.3), by the five different viewpoints of psychoanalysis (Rapaport 1959), and by phenomenology with its infinite number of possible perspectives. Nor is life consistent even in the U.S. with its patent contradictions between avowed individualism and practised conformity, efficiency and laisser-faire, equality and oppression, 'cleanliness is next to godliness' and water, soil, and air pollution.

But consistency and parsimony fitted well into the puritan mentality. The puritans believed 'that theirs was exclusively the right faith and that all who held other tenets – Quakers, Baptists, and the like – should be severely punished' (Hart and Gohdes 1955, p. 11). This intolerance was continued by the pioneers when dissent and resulting conflict could not be tolerated at the frontier. It became today's melting-pot ideal, which shows up in many guises. One of these is the intolerance towards other languages. Bilingual children are considered 'handicapped' by educators in the public school system of the U.S. Earlier school regulations prohibited children from speaking their mother tongue (Spanish, American Indian languages) in school even during recess. This intolerance resulted in the abolition of foreign language requirements by behaviourists in their departments in the U.S. universities, the oldest of which, Harvard and Yale, were founded by puritan ministers. At the same time, most non-English psychologial publications are not translated into English unless they promote behaviourism. Other developments in psychology are being ignored, as is the critique of behaviourism even by Yankee psychologists like Koch, MacLeod, Bakan, Silverman, Rychlak, and Carlson, and that by others who publish in English like Bannister, Harré, and myself.

Consistency and parsimony explain why textbooks like the first edition of the one by Krech and Crutchfield (1960), which was representative of gestalt psychology, were later revised to fit behaviourism. The same principles led to the behaviourization of psychoanalysis and Piagetian psychology (cf. 2.5.2). They help one understand why Bridgman's suggestion in 1927 to define concepts through physical operations, that is, through a description of what one does, fitted well into the behaviourist mentality and was promptly accepted by behaviourists, whereas his own rejection of operationalizing concepts less than twenty years later (Bridgman 1945, 1959) not only has been entirely disregarded, but is not even mentioned in Boring's 1957 revision of his widely quoted book, although Boring (1945) chaired the 'Symposium on Operationism' at which Bridgman denounced his earlier ideas.

Similarly, the dogma of consistency and parsimony explains the marriage between the *Wiener Kreis* and behaviourism. The behaviourists used logical positivism wherever possible to support their methodologies and their cosmology rather than change these as a result of that philosophy. 'Here LE [logical empiricism] has been influenced by pragmatism and by behaviourism as a school of psychology. The idea is that only behavioral psychologists talk about "mind" (!) in a "scientific" way, i.e. in a way which is empirically "verifiable"; that talking about mind in a scientific (scientistic) fashion is equal to talking about things which are intersubjectively "observable" – about *perceptual* (or physical) entities. Thus the Principle of "Verification" leads to a behaviouristic philosophy of mind (the early positivists, Feigl, Quine, etc.),' (Radnitzky 1973, p. 28). Radnitzky sees a 'complex interaction' between behaviourism and logical empiricism and by no means a simple linear relationship. As a result of that interaction '*philosophical* behaviorists (materialists) hope that eventually behavioral science will confirm that man is but a cross-breed of computor and rat' (p. 259f.; emphasis in original).

Parsimony and consistency led to using Darwinism to eliminate distinctions between human and animal psychology and to use the rat as the naïve subject par excellence for psychological research. That rats were in this process anthropomorphized and humans myomorphized has been ignored. As Hofstätter (1956) discussed, the fate of the rat is as predetermined by the experimenter as the Calvinist's fate by God. Hence 'rat: psychologist = human: God' (p. 363). Hofstätter points out the slang meaning of 'rat' when applied to someone, and the parallel with the puritan who only in rare instances has been destined to receive divine grace. 'Calvin's God does not ask man questions and also does not answer any of man's questions – for him the case of the individual is already closed before the life of the latter even begins. He has placed the individual into an apparatus and decided beforehand whether it will starve there or not ... Within this apparatus exists, however, the possibility to learn; this is the grace God has given to the selected.' Hofstätter quotes the seventeenth-century puritan minister R. Baxter as having said: 'When God shows you a way through which you can rightfully achieve more than through another way and when you refuse to go that way then you sin with respect to your calling; you refuse to serve the will of God' (p. 364). Hofstätter adds that 'Baxter's statement is not quite correct: Calvin's God does not show the individual any way, he merely equips it with the possibility of finding such a way.'

Parsimony further led behaviourists to espouse the simplest possible explanation for all 'behaviour,' the S–R formula, which continues to underlie all their research, while Thurstone's 1923 critique of 'the stimulus-response fallacy in psychology' is never mentioned by behaviourists and came to my attention only through an Austrian psychologist. That the terms 'stimulus' and 'response' are so ambiguous that they can serve for neither the description nor the explanation of *any* human or animal function is merely another one of the contradictions of behaviourism which my students realize when I tell them to look these terms up in English and English (1958).

The desire for consistency has also led to such Yankee psychological theories as those by Festinger and Rokeach whose relationship to a particular kind of society Argyris (1969) pointed out.

9.5.4
9.5.4.1 The emphasis on parsimony and consistency contributed as well to making the U.S. into a melting-pot, while Canada strove to remain a multicultural mosaic with a multiparty parliamentary rather than a two-party presidential system, and with bilingual psychological journals. To achieve and maintain the melting-pot in the face of constant immigration people had to be adjusted to become 'average Americans.' Behaviourism tried to contribute to such adjustment by conditioning

through reinforcement. Adjustment was also required by ever increasing industrialization which was largely the result of puritan work. Industry needed naïve subjects who learned simple tasks and could be controlled by rewards and punishments or by bribes and extortions. First the pioneers and then industry changed the environment and eventually brought about tremendous technological changes. In that atmosphere people had to be made to adjust to those changes. Learning through insight for a mere increase in knowledge, as investigated in gestalt-phenomenological, genetic (Piagetian), and psychoanalytic psychology, has no value in either a pioneer or an industrial society.

9.5.4.2 In a society of immigrants who ran away from an unpleasant past and who want their children to have a better life and to become part of a melting-pot, in a fast-changing, upward mobile, progress-oriented society with a short history compared to Asia and Europe, people cannot be proud of their past. In a melting-pot history must be forgotten, otherwise the country becomes a mosaic like Canada where each ethnic group is proud of its history. The U.S. contrasts in this respect also with Mexico, which is proud of its long pre-Columbian history, its ancient, truly American cultures.

The lack of a sense of history is also reflected in behaviourism, which is an ahistorical psychology. It reproaches psychoanalysis for the latter's emphasis on the individual's history and it misunderstands genetic psychology, in which behaviourists are interested merely to speed up learning and thus adjustment to the melting-pot. Merely to understand the past as Piaget has tried to do during most of his life is not 'doing something.' History has no intrinsic value for Yankees. Thus all Yankee psychotherapies reject the psychoanalytic interest in the individual's past and the individual's unique development. This rejection of the past was emphasized even by Gordon W. Allport despite his profound understanding of European psychology.

History – whether phylogenetic, poligenetic, or ontogenetic – is an organic development. 'History of reinforcements,' which by definition are random associations, is no true history. It is a mere conglomerate of events. It has nothing in common with the process of growth and maturing. Thus behaviourism remains ahistorical. It must remain so as long as it uses the experimental method and group data. One cannot experiment with growth but must wait for it to happen, and one cannot average the histories of a group. One can merely disregard them, as both the industrialized melting-pot society and experimental behaviourists do in order to go on 'doing something.'

As quoted above, Erikson mentioned 'the industrial world' and Ruesch 'modern technical civilization' in connection with the characteristics of present-day Yankee values. Industrialization and technology form the material ground, the existence (*Sein*) in Mannheim's terms, on which the predominant ideas rest. Bakan (1966) discussed in detail the relation between behaviourism and industrialization from the point of view of the movement from a rural to an urban society. I do not want to repeat his excellent analysis. I rather want to add some further aspects of that relationship.

9.5.4.3   As is well known, the capitalist system is built on consumerism. The products of industry have become more and more intricate gadgets, from automobiles, washing machines, and television sets to ever larger computers. In order to consume these gadgets one need not know what is inside the 'black box.' One need know only how to 'stimulate' them, that is, turn them on, and to watch the 'response,' namely, whether they 'work.' It is not in the interest of the manufacturer that the buyer know what is inside the machine. Its structure is irrelevant for the buyer as long as 'it works.' When it no longer works the consumer will buy another gadget.

Until workers can be replaced in any given industry by automation they are objects for the entrepreneur, like the machines which will eventually replace them. The workers can, therefore, also be treated like black boxes about whom one need only know how to 'turn them on' in order to obtain the desired 'output' or 'response.' All that is of interest to the entrepreneur and the psychologist working for him is how people 'function,' and not what their 'structures' are. What the entrepreneur wants to know from the psychologist is how to 'control' the workers and how to 'predict' their 'behaviour.' What the workers think and feel is of no interest to the entrepreneur, who does not hire psychologists to do research on thinking and feeling.

9.5.5   Behaviourism has made considerable inroads into West German psychology during the last three decades. It has, however, not achieved the hegemony it has had in the U.S. for three quarters of century. An explanation for its success in the land of the *Dichter und Denker* (poets and thinkers) seems nevertheless required in this chapter on the sociology of psychological knowledge.

Like most developments, the relative success of behaviourism among West German psychologists is overdetermined. Germany was defeated in 1945 through the use of arms 'made in U.S.A.' and largely occupied by Yankees. Yankee success proved that pragmatism and behaviourism 'worked.' With the Yankee occupation of Western Europe came what the British called the 'cocacolonization,' the flooding of the rest of the world with U.S. soft drinks, hot dogs, gadgets, and *Readers' Digest* propaganda.

The rebuilding of the destroyed cities and rearmament led to a large-scale re-industrialization with the help of U.S. capital and vast numbers of immigrant workers from other cultures who had to adjust to the new industrial society. The situation became similar to that in which behaviourism flourished in the U.S..

Moreover, German psychology was in some disarray. Psychoanalysis had been banned by the Nazis despite Jung's collaboration with them. Many other German psychologists had emigrated. Those who had remained in German universities had either taught 'master-race' theories or were at least suspect because of their silent support of the Nazi regime. There existed then some kind of a vacuum in psychology in post-war West Germany.

Many of the characteristics of behaviourism favoured its entrance into that vacuum. Its ahistorical aspect was particularly propitious for its acceptance in a society which wished to forget important periods of its past. The simplicity of the S–R model was just right for the new kinds of students from the new mass society, who attended new universities with administrative and architectural structures which have entirely broken with the historical past.

Many of these psychology students go with Yankee scholarships for a few semesters to U.S. universities or study under West German professors who spent some time in the U.S. after the Second World War. When they attend international psychological congresses they must be able to understand English because of the mass of Yankee symposia and presentations of papers. Contrary to their older professors, who learned French as a first foreign language, their first and often only foreign language is English. Even their West German psychological journals contain many articles in English. Under this combination of circumstances it is easy to understand that behaviourism has made a considerable inroad into psychology in West Germany.

9.5.6   By Mannheim's (1936) definition, behaviourism is clearly an ideology. It has 'become so intensively interest-bound to a situation that [behaviourists] are simply no longer able to see certain facts which would undermine their sense of domination ... The collective unconscious ... obscures the real condition of society both to itself and to others and thereby stabilizes it' (p. 40). The facts which behaviourists are no longer able to see have been discussed in various places in this and other chapters. This view of behaviourism as an ideology seems to be shared by Hilgard (1972), who stated that 'the major contribution of behaviourism may have been to give confidence to students of human and animal nature that they were dealing with a subject-matter sufficiently like that of other sciences to place them in the tradition of Darwin, Mendel, Newton, and Einstein.'

The utopian thinking of behaviourists is shown both in their experiments on learning and particularly in the therapies derived therefrom. 'They are not at all concerned with what really exists; rather in their thinking they already seek to change the situation that exists. Their thought is never a diagnosis of the situation; it can be used only as a direction for action.' (Contrary to the ethologists, behaviourists do not study what animals *do* but what they *can* do under the controlled experimental conditions.) 'In the utopian mentality, the collective unconscious, guided by ... the will to action, hides certain aspects of reality' – for instance, the qualitative differences between humans and rats, between beings which learn mainly through language and can pass on to the next generation what they individually have acquired, and beings who are incapable thereof. 'It turns its back on everything which would shake its belief or paralyse its desire to change things' (Mannheim 1936, p. 40).

Finally, behaviourists have a false consciousness when they consider themselves to be representatives of a value-free natural science which is independent of the society in which it developed and which through 'empirical proof' establishes 'truth' about 'behaviour,' while 'instead of attempting to discover what is most significant with the highest degree of precision possible under the existing circumstances, [they] tend to be content to attribute importance to what is measurable merely because it happens to be measurable' (p. 51f.).

9.6   RELATIONISM VS. RELATIVISM In this chapter I have tried to show that any psychology, like any other science, develops within a specific society, namely, in a given historical epoch and within certain geographical confines, and therefore reflects a specific perspective. As a result of that perspective it focuses on particular aspects of psychological functioning in general. I have tried to show this by highlighting a few psychologies. By selecting certain psychologies and disregarding others (for instance, existential, individual [Adlerian], analytic [Jungian], or genetic [Piagetian] psychology) I too have taken only a limited number of perspectives. Furthermore, I have discussed these psychologies in the framework of Mannheim's sociology of knowledge as I understand it. One could have taken other perspectives like that of Marxism and discussed these psychologies in terms of means and relations of production.

Whatever framework one uses, one must eventually arrive at the conclusion that a perspective-free, absolute psychology is not achievable. 'In this context one ought to ask again and again whether the concept of knowledge [*Erkennen*] is even concretely conceivable without the premise of the total constitution of the human being and whether it can be even thought of, not to speak of carrying it through, in any manner which is for us meaningful' (Mannheim 1969, p. 255). This does not mean 'a relativism implying the randomness of any claim; the relationism in our sense says rather that any statement can essentially be formulated only relationally. Relationism turns into relativism only when one combines it with the older static ideal of eternal, desubjectivized unperspectivist truths and measures it against this disparate ideal (of absolute truth)' (p. 258).

The question may be raised whether my analysis of the relationships between certain psychological systems and certain cultures means that 'Calvinist psychology [is] only valid for Calvinists? Is there some absolute sense in which any of these psychologies is more true than another? Does Jewish psychology have anything relevant to say to non-Jews?' as Kurt Danziger asked me in a letter after reading the first draft of this chapter.

From my perspective, the answer to these questions must also be relational, namely in relation to the interpretation of the questions. If 'valid for Calvinists' means that Calvinists can be understood only in terms of a Calvinist psychology, the answer is 'no!' If one interprets 'valid for Calvinists' as meaning that the explanation of human functioning in general given by Calvinist psychology is meaningful only to Calvinists, the answer is 'yes!' This does not mean that a Calvinist cannot like anyone else step into another framework and understand, for example, Jewish psychology as many non-Jews have done. *Mutatis mutandis*, a Jew may step into the Calvinist framework to understand Calvinist psychology as I have attempted throughout this book. Whether someone finds a psychology from a different culture relevant for understanding human functioning raises the issue of relevance which I have touched upon in chapter 3. I shall return to the question of 'truth' in chapter 11.

10 Psychologists Caught in Different Autistic Frameworks

Psychologists Caught in Different Autistic Frameworks
L'aliéniste aliéné

10.0 FROM ALIENATION TO IDENTITY In the first chapter of this book I showed how I had been alienated from my Jewish roots, cut off from my German *Heimat*, lost most of my family, and how, in search for authenticity and identity, I recaptured my Jewish heritage through assimilation of and accommodation to the ideas of many Jewish thinkers, how I renewed my ties with German culture through its psychology while finding a new *Heimat* in Canada, and how I founded my own home by marrying Elisabeth Pasztor, a rediscovered friend from the most unsettled period of my life. The present chapter was written with her (cf. chapter 8, footnote 1). In it we shall explore the different aspects of alienation we see in many colleagues.

10.1 THE EVIDENCE Without using the word 'alienation' Mannheim (1936) described the kind of psychologist we are referring to. According to him, these psychologists make

the attempt to construct a sort of mechanical science of elements of psychic experience which have been formalized and emptied of meaning (psychic mechanics) [The attempt has as its] aim ... not the exact comprehension of qualitative peculiarities and unique constellations, but rather the determination of the most obvious regularities and principles of order obtaining between formalized simplified elements ... The mechanistic method, in spite of the concrete achievements for which we are indebted to it, has, from the point of view of life-orientation and conduct, contributed very much to the general insecurity of modern man. The acting man must know who he is, and the ontology of psychic life fulfils a certain function in action. To the extent that mechanistic psychology and its parallel in actual life, the social impulsion towards all-embracing mechanization, negated these ontological values, they destroyed an important element in the self-orientation of human beings in their everyday life. (p. 24)

10.1.1 *The meaning of 'alienation'* The quote from Mannheim illustrates mainly one aspect of alienation. However, the word 'alienation,' like its counter part 'identity,' has a number of distinguishable though related meanings. As far as possible and useful, we shall differentiate between these various meanings – using different subscripts to refer to them – and present for each examples of psychologists' alienation.

10.1.1.1 What Mannheim described was the lack of wholeness which, in our culture, is usually associated with the concepts of self and identity in one sense. Such identity$_1$ means that different, even conflicting and contradictory facets of one individual like the Jew, the German, the Canadian, the artists' son, the linguist, the psychoanalyst, the phenomenologist, the dialectical materialist, as well as one's espoused theories and one's theories-in-use, all belong together in a common I, a unified whole of which they are merely subsystems. The corresponding alienation$_1$ is expressed by Faust's famous words *'Zwei Seelen wohnen, ach! in meiner Brust, die eine will sich von der andern trennen.'* (Two souls live, alas! in my breast, one wants to separate from the other.) It may be expressed by denial of some of the facets of oneself. Alienation$_1$ was typical of the assimilated German Jews who did not consider themselves as Jews, who thought that the Nazis would not persecute them, and who were murdered in gas chambers. As this example shows, one need not be aware of one's alienation in order to suffer from its consequences. In its extreme form, alienation$_1$ means depersonalization and leads to multiple personalities. It always includes some form of false consciousness.

We consider human beings who rely on introspection to determine how they feel, what they think, what they want, whether they are truthful or lie, etc., and who declare introspection to be an invalid method for gaining information, to be alienated$_1$. The same applies when these psychologists communicate their thoughts, feelings, sensations, observations, etc. to others including other psychologists, and when they accept what others tell them as reports about facts but reject such 'free descriptions' as useful data in their work. We consider them alienated$_1$ when they personicate relatives, friends, acquaintances, and strangers in everyday life without any of the questionnaires, tests, and other devices they use in their work for forming impressions of others, and when they continue such unaided personicating even after they have found out that they grossly misjudged others. These examples point to a split between a psychologist who is a human being like other human beings ($E \equiv S$) and one who is fundamentally different from people ($E \not\equiv S$). Further examples of this split were already discussed in the context of research frameworks (cf. 6.2.2 and 6.2.3).

This alienation$_1$ of the psychologist from him/herself as a human being is promoted by the predominant school of Yankee academic psychology and by the mandarins of the American Psychological Association. They also contribute to the alienation of psychologists in a second sense through rejection of methodological and theory pluralism.

10.1.1.2 Alienation$_2$ and identity$_2$ refer to an individual's sense of being unique. Someone who knows and accepts that s/he differs in some or in many aspects from all others can be said to have an identity$_2$. Alienation$_2$ is the result of an other-directed culture, of a melting-pot society, of an effort to produce identical, interchangeable workers for the assembly line and co-workers who 'won't rock the boat.'

The professors of psychology who are alienated$_2$ do not emphasize the unique aspects of their respective approaches with pride. Rather they contribute to the mass production of future alienated$_2$ psychologists by rejecting critical theoretical dissertations and other novel perspectives in the study of psychological issues.

We consider it also a sign of alienation$_2$ when psychologists assume that $E_1 = E_2 = E_3$, namely, that the personal charcteristics of each psychologist are irrelevant to the results. This applies equally to results of experiments, of diagnoses, and of any form of treatment. When psychologists disregard their mannerisms, attire (cf. 7.2.1), etc. as extraneous to the situation and as not impinging upon the experiences of the 'subjects,' 'clients,' 'patients,' etc., the psychologists are alienated$_2$ in our terms.

10.1.1.3 Yet another concept of identity – and its converse, alienation$_3$ – is implied in the feeling that, despite many changes, one remains the same individual over a lifetime and that memories of one's childhood are, indeed, memories and not fantasies. We refer to the lack of this sense of continuity as alienation$_3$.

Consequently, psychologists seem to us alienated$_3$ whenever they commit adultomorphisms, be it in explanations of children's 'behaviour' or in designing programs for children and disregarding their own childhood joys, hates, and fears. Alienated$_3$ psychologists consider only children's actions and whether or not these are desirable from an adult perspective.

Alienation$_3$ refers not only to being emotionally cut off from one's childhood, but to a break with any period in one's ontogenesis. Thus, psychologists are alienated$_3$ whenever they disregard any of their own life experiences in their work. This seems to have happened, for example, in the designing of the experiments on hurting others in the name of some higher aim (cf. 6.3.1) and in the development of the 'lost-letter technique' (Milgram 1969).[1] Both what we call alienation$_3$ and identity$_3$ appear to play a part in either placing too high or too low demands on one's students, particularly one's doctoral candidates.

10.1.1.4 The professor who has forgotten his own experiences as a doctoral candidate and places unreasonable demands on his supervisees may over-identify with his/her new role as psychology professor. We label such role identification identity$_4$ and the absence of a clear role identification alienation$_4$. In the framework of this book, we are concerned with alienation$_4$ only in so far as it refers to the role of psychologist.

The problem with psychologists' identity and alienation with respect to their role is that there seems to be no uniform role definition for psychologists. To be sure, technical and hermeneutic psychologists conceptualize their roles differently. Technical psychologists see as an important aspect of their role 'to obtain a control over human conduct corresponding to that of physical science over the material world' (Cattell 1917, quoted by Danziger 1977, p. 8) 'for the sake of ultimate human betterment' (APA 1973, p. 7). Hermeneutic psychologists consider their role largely to consist of promoting the understanding of the human mind. Furthermore, among technical psychologists different role concepts exist depending on whether they consider themselves to be 'scientists' or 'practitioners.' The role concept of the 'scientists' conflicts, in addition, with the popular view of psychologists as people who help others solve their personal problems.

This situation, combined with the low status of the 'scientists'

---

1 During a conversation at the 1975 Alpbach Symposium (cf. Koestler 1973) Professor Graumann drew my attention to the absurdity of the lost-letter technique by asking me how often in my past I had found a stamped, addressed envelop in the street. He told me he never had and he had never met anyone else who had.

---

compared to natural scientists and of the 'practitioners' compared to physicians and particularly psychiatrists, leads to a number of contradictions and corresponding conflicts. On the other hand, it seems illogical to speak even of identity and alienation in relation to a role which is not clearly defined. On the other hand, it seems psycho-logical to assume that some role-alienation may result exactly from the absence of a clearly defined role. At the same time, some psychologists seem to over-identify with their poorly defined role, as we shall attempt to show when we discuss the interrelationship between the various identities and forms of alienation (cf. Lumpkin 1970).

One indication of alienation$_4$ and its relation to the vagueness of role definition is the general lack of interest by psychologists in the history of psychology and the onesidedness of their corresponding knowledge (cf. Danziger 1979).

10.1.1.5 So far, we could relate various forms of alienation to different meanings of 'identity' which particularly Erikson (1959) discussed without, however, clearly separating them in the way we do. All of the above four aspects of alienation are estrangements from different features of the self: alienation$_1$ from its wholeness, alienation$_2$ from its uniqueness, alienation$_3$ from its continuity, and alienation$_4$ from roles which are parts of it. We shall now discuss three further meanings of alienation which, rather than standing in opposition to aspects of identity, are different kinds of lack of involvement and are related to Marx's concept of alienation.[2]

Work can be fun. One can be absorbed by it and enjoy it. This capacity of being involved in one's work was probably what Freud referred to when he said that the three signs of normality are to be able to enjoy work, leisure, and intimacy. By alienation$_5$ we then mean estrangement from one's work. We realize that a society such as ours with a strong division of labour develops many kinds of work which cannot serve as sources of intrinsic gratification and pride to the

---

2 Many readers may find this phenomenal analysis of alienation something new. It is, however, quite common in German-language psychology. Metzger (1963) distinguished five meanings of reality (Brandt and Metzger 1969), Bischof (1966) six meanings of inside and outside, Graumann (1966) eight different meanings of conscious and unconscious, and Brandt (1977b) six meanings of reward and punishment.

---

workers. However, psychologists need not be alienated$_5$ from their work: the study of human beings raises an infinity of fascinating questions and can be highly gratifying.

We consider psychologists alienated$_5$ when they discuss their salaries and grant moneys rather than 'talk shop' at coffee-breaks, social gatherings, or even their professional conventions, and when they do not attend or even set up colloquia for the purpose of exchanging experiences and ideas.

As on the assembly line, this alienation of human beings from their work seems related to the division of labour in many areas of psychology. It occurs when experiments are merely designed by psychologists but carried out by graduate students whose actual interactions with the 'subjects' escape the investigator's observation; when 'objective' tests are used which the investigator not only did not himself design but frequently understands only poorly in terms of their underlying assumptions (cf. Brandt 1972a) and their validation; when others perform blind diagnoses on the basis of test data obtained by one psychologist; and when the results are analysed by computer according to a programme someone else designed using statistics which the researcher does not fully comprehend. Under such circumstances alienation$_5$ can hardly be avoided.

10.1.1.6 Alienation$_5$ from one's work is closely related to but not psychologically identical with alienation$_6$ from the products of one's labour. Whenever psychologists make findings which, as has been shown in previous chapters, cannot be applied to them as human beings, they are alienated$_6$. This is particularly striking in all aspects of both classical and operant conditioning which 'eliminate[s] ... the concretely appraising and volitional human being in us' (Mannheim 1969, p. 147).[3] The 'mechanistic psychology' Mannheim wrote about largely conflicts with the experiences and feelings of the psychologists who pursue it. Its findings can, therefore, not be made use of by psychologists in their daily lives or even in their actual work situations, because the findings

---

3 Some German-speaking psychologists refer to conditioning and particularly to 'behaviour modification' as *Verhaltenszirkus* = 'behaviour circus.' As in English, the German word has the slang meaning of circus: 'Any large, colorful spectacle' (Wentworth and Flexner 1960).

---

are based on assumptions which do not fit the psychologists' experiences.

When psychologists rely on statistics as the exclusive criterion for accepting or rejecting hypotheses, we consider them alienated$_6$ because, paraphrasing Agnew (1977), a statistic is 'not really empirical, it's an artificial corset for data' (p. 40) into which one cannot squeeze one's real life. These psychologists are caught on the horns of a dilemma: they can either make use of the products of their labour for themselves and thus 'contribute very much to the general insecurity of modern man' including their own, or remain alienated from the results of their efforts.

10.1.1.7 Half a century has elapsed since Mannheim argued that mechanistic psychologists exerted a destructive influence upon society. Yet, these psychologists seem to be as alienated as ever from the prospective consumers of their 'scientific' (scientistic?) endeavours which aim at 'ultimate human betterment.' This is alienation in a seventh sense of the word: a rift separating an individual from others. Psychologists label an individual 'autistic' who is alienated$_7$ in the extreme.

Alienation$_7$ of mechanistic psychologists begins with their definition of psychology as 'the science of behaviour.' This definition implies a denial of any concern for human beings as experiencing, intentional actors. In line with this definition, flatworms, rats, and pigeons are studied – but without the ethologist's interest in the psychology of animals. They are studied merely after having been anthropomorphized and for the purpose of making ill-founded analogies with humans. Alienation$_7$ is clearly expressed by Skinner's (1959) warning against 'the flight to real people' (p. 249).

When alienation$_7$ does not take the form of animal experiments it frequently consists of investigations of a grin without a cat:[4] of isolated physiological functions, incoherent acts and experiences like single emotions, independent motives, and unrelated memories – as if emotions,

---

4 Martin Gardner comments in *The Annotated Alice* (Carroll 1960): 'The phrase "grin without a cat" is not a bad description of pure mathematics ... Mathematical theorems ... are abstractions that belong in another realm "remote from human passion," as Bertrand Russell once put it ... "remote even from the pitiful facts of Nature..."' (p. 91).

---

motives, and memories did not always occur in systems and were always *someone's* emotions, motives, and memories. In addition, what kind of common human experience is the learning of nonsense syllables, the autokinetic effect, or even the finding of a lost letter in the street?

Whenever psychologists investigate merely the 'behaviour' and 'responses' of groups of people and disregard their individual 'life space,' such research exemplifies alienation$_7$ because the psychologists do not enter into a dialogue with the research participants qua individuals in order to obtain information from them about 'their worlds' and their relations to those worlds.

Psychologists' alienation$_7$ is particularly striking in personicating-research (cf. chapter 8), where the psychologists' impressions of others and the impressions these people form of the psychologists and of one another do not form part of the investigation, which usually centres on the participants' impressions of non-existing, imaginary people. In the vast majority of such research (Warr and Knapper 1968; Tagiuri 1969), the individuals who are asked to report their impressions of others never see or hear those others even if the latter exist. Frequently personicating is investigated merely on the basis of words, usually adjectives (Asch 1946), while the psychologist claims to be interested in the personicating, that is, in how real human beings form impressions of other real human beings in everyday life.

Psychologists are also alienated$_7$ when they treat phobias, learning disabilities, depressions, homosexuality, impotence, etc. instead of total human beings who happen to have some 'problems in living' (Szasz 1961) like most people do. In these instances, psychologists disregard the identity$_1$ of other people. Alienation$_7$ is also expressed through psychologists' unconcern for the uniqueness, identity$_2$, of people whom they treat on the basis of 'reinforcement schedules' derived from animal experiments. The identity$_3$ of 'clients' or 'patients'[5] is not respected when a psychologist does not take their personal histories and their ethnic, social, and educational backgrounds into account in making a diagnosis or counselling them. The alienated$_7$ psychologist disregards

---

5 Psychologists' identity$_4$ (with their role) is not strengthened by using terms from lawyers' ('client') or physicians' ('patient') relationships and having no corresponding term of their own.

---

differences among clients or 'subjects' as well as the differences between her/himself and them. Any disrespect for any aspect of the identity of others represents some alienation$_7$ of the psychologist, namely, alienation from other human beings.

10.1.2 *The dialectics of alienation* We discussed four different meanings of the word 'identity' and seven meanings of 'alienation' – without claiming that we have exhausted the ways in which these words can be used. As the last examples indicate, one's alienation from others is related to one's respect for other people's identity. But one's own 'identities' and one's own 'alienations' are also dialectically interrelated. They are different aspects of experience. The conscious acceptance of one's identity in its four aspects is what Sartre (1946) called 'authenticity.'

We shall now illustrate the dialectics of alienation by discussing the typical publications of alienated psychologists. Psychologists' publications form the common basis for all psychologists. In the course of becoming a psychologist, one must read publications by other psychologists and contribute to them at least through a thesis. Published and unpublished reports – research, test, case reports – are the most ubiquitous products of psychologists. They seem to us, therefore, a concrete[6] basis for a discussion of the interrelationship between the different aspects of alienation outlined so far.

The more psychologists protect their identity$_4$, their identification with the predominant image of the role of psychologist, by writing their reports according to prescribed rules, the more they are alienated from themselves, their work, and from non-psychologists. We find the most striking sign of this role over-identification to be the use of 'the author' for 'I' and the omission of what we consider pertinent information about the researcher.

---

6 I (LWB) consider their publications as the only widely available, intersubjectively observable 'hard,' 'empirical' givens ('data') psychologists have. I see it as one of the paradoxes of positivist empirical science that published reports, like all other data, must be subjectively interpreted by every reader. This applies to test and case reports as much as to the numbers contained in figures and tables, whether these represent 'raw data' or 'grouped data.' The numbers themselves *are* the data the reader receives and *represent* the data the writer wants to report about. Thus, hermeneutics enter into all technical science.

The only information psychologists commonly reveal about themselves in their reports is their name and place of work. By omitting all other aspects of themselves, of their identity, they appear alienated$_1$, $_2$, and $_3$, because they are actually whole human beings with unique combinations of interests, values, knowledge, etc., and with unique histories, even as far as their psychological education and training are concerned. At the same time, they are alienated$_6$ because the product of their labour becomes something impersonal, and alienated$_7$ because they are unrecognizable to others. This is particularly obvious when publications are judged by others after the author's name has been removed from the work. The taboo against the *ad hominem argument* (Brandt 1970b) isolates the worker from the product of his/her work. Alienation$_5$ (from work) is indicated by the presentation of scientific research as a business enterprise: the name of the financial sponsor usually appears in a footnote but not the names of the 'subjects,' the participants who were used as 'the things' (cf. 6.2.1), as the material on which the psychologist worked. Here, we see, at the same time another indication of alienation$_7$.

Whereas the use of the third person ('the author') makes a 'thing' of the psychologist also, the use of 'we' by a single author, who refers to the participants as 'the subjects,' reads like a *pluralis majestatis*. Perhaps this interpretation of the 'we' does not seem as far-fetched if one realizes that experimenters give orders to their 'subjects' without discussing with them the rationale of what 'we' tell them to do. Majesty does not interact with subjects, but is alienated from them through identification with a role. Correspondingly, any human interaction which took place in the actual experiment is eliminated from the published report by means of such phrases as 'the subjects were run' and 'the experimenter presented the stimulus' without ever clearly indicating who did what to whom. Such combination of alienation$_2$ (from one's uniqueness), alienation$_3$ (from one's individual history), alienation$_6$ (from the product of one's labour), and alienation$_7$ (from others) is exemplified by Michael Wertheimer's 'Relativity and Gestalt: A Note on Albert Einstein and Max Wertheimer' (1965), which contains no indication that the author wrote about his own father!

The interrelationship of various aspects of alienation appears also in such phrases as 'the findings make it clear that' and 'the results revealed.' Since only human beings can 'make clear that' and draw conclusions from results, psychologists who use such expressions are alienated in the different meanings of that word.

Usually a 'paper'[7] about an experiment contains very little information about the various inevitable communications between 'E' and 'S.' Pictures, words, or syllables used as 'stimulus material' are rarely reproduced in full in journal articles. (The exact amount of money, but not the exact wording of messages, exchanged between employer-psychologist and employee-subject may be reported.) However, the physical paraphernalia are described in great detail: recording devices and projectors with manufacturer's name and serial number, room and paper size, thickness and weight of cards on which something is printed, exposure time, etc. The writers thereby provide support for our contention that they are mainly involved in the mechanistic, technical aspects of their work and are alienated$_5$ and $_7$ from its genuinely psychological features.

Alienation$_7$ seems to us most evident in the use of statistics by psychologists. When groups of data are compared, no people are left behind those figures. An 'average neurotic,' an 'average eight-year-old,' an 'average male,' an 'average schizophrenic' exist no more than an 'average psychologist.' The 'average human being' has 0.873 breasts, 0.946 testicles, and 9.899 fingers. Poor 'thing'! The chasm between the psychologist and real human beings – as opposed to the caricatures psychologists create through quantification and 'measurement' – widens even further when quantified and grouped observations are analysed by computer and turned into orthogonally rotated factors.

Psychologists' alienation$_4$ from their reference group expresses itself by the narrowness of their interest areas and the consequent inability to understand and communicate with colleagues specializing in another sub-area. This lack of communication between psychologists can be seen from the lists of references in journals containing almost exclusively articles published in the same journal. The same applies to Anglo-American psychology as a whole with its complete alienation$_4$ from the world-wide community of psychologists, which includes many who publish in languages other than English.

10.2   SCIENCE = OBJECTIVITY = ALIENATION? The psychologists whom we described as alienated may argue that what we call alienation is

---

7 The word 'paper' stands for a material, for pure form, and not for content. The term used by French psychologists and other scientists for their research reports is *communication*.

---

merely a result of the requirements of science; that they apply 'the scientific method'; that science requires objectivity, and that objectivity means to stand at a distance, to be aloof from what one investigates, not to be involved with the objects of one's research. We shall counter such an argument point for point and try to show that it is fallacious, both in general and with particular respect to the forms of alienation we discussed above.

10.2.1   We hope that every reader will agree that science is not something given to us by the world, something people discoverd, but that it is a human activity. It is furthermore an activity pursued by people in co-operation with other people and therefore according to certain rules. These rules, the rules according to which the game of science is to be played, are made by people. Once one has outgrown Piaget's second stage of moral development, one realizes that rules can be changed as long as all players agree to the new rules. In other words, one realizes that rules are neither sacred nor inviolable. If one knows the history of science, one also knows that the rules of science have been changed in the past. Lewin (1935) discussed this issue with respect to the Aristotelian and the Galilean rules of science. Certainly Titchener and Skinner did not play by the same rules and both are considered scientists, at least by some people.

Hence, there exists no *one* 'method of science,' but there are *many* method*s* of science. What behaviourists mean when they speak of 'the method of science' is not the method Darwin or Linnaeus used. Whoever insists on 'the method of science' merely ignores 'that our concept of science is much narrower than the scope of the actually existing kinds of knowledge and that possible and communicable knowledge ends by no means where the area of our present sciences ends' (Mannheim 1969, p. 144). As Jaspers (1963) pointed out, a combination of different methods increases rather than diminishes 'the understanding and explanation of human behavior' which, according to Fincher (1972), is 'the ultimate objective – implicit or otherwise – [of] all schools or systems of psychology.'

10.2.1.1 Nor do we accept the argument that alienation is a necessary corollary of objectivity. According to both Bridgman and Piaget, objectivity does not mean to stand at *a* distance but to stand at *various* distance*s*, that is, to consider an object from different perspectives. Such an understanding of objectivity implies nothing about scientists' involvement or non-involvement with their research. As was argued in chapter 3, we cannot imagine human beings doing anything without motivations and emotions – not even scientific work. Scientists who are not alienated from their work to the extent of being interested merely in financial profit derived from it *feel* curious. It is precisely their involvement in obtaining more 'objective' knowledge in the sense of Bridgman, Piaget, and Popper that can lead psychologists to reflect upon their involvement and take it into account instead of denying it. Such self-reflection upon and accounting for one's involvement can further enhance the objectivity of one's research and thus make it more scientific.

10.2.2 Definitions of psychology like Fraisse's (1963) as 'the science of human personality in all its aspects' show that the alienation resulting from its definition as 'the science of behaviour' can be avoided. Fraisse's definition clearly establishes psychology as a human science and thereby as one which includes the scientist. It also establishes the uniqueness of psychology, as the definitions by Metzger and Bischof (cf. 3.3) do even more explicitly.

Thomae (1968) demonstrated how psychologists can do research on total individuals and their subjective worlds. He and his co-workers conducted a longitudinal study involving full-day interviews with about 3000 West Germans repeated during eight- to twelve-year periods. From the taped interviews, of which long excerpts appear in his book, Thomae developed a new personality theory (cf. Brandt 1976a).

10.2.2.1 From Fraisse's, Metzger's, and Bischof's definition of psychology, as from that of many other psychologists, it follows that experiments with animals do not make psychology any more scientific. When inferences are drawn from animals to human beings such inferences must rely on inductive reasoning. However, Hume already acknowledged that induction is not logically justifiable. More recently such philosophers of science as Kuhn (1970b) and Popper (1959) therefore rejected induction as a form of scientific reasoning.

That 'the flight to real people' against which Skinner warned can increase psychological knowledge in ways in which Skinner's alienation could not must be evident from the work of Piaget and that of many psychoanalysts. The avoidance of 'real people' through the investigation of their physiological processes is also not prescribed by any dictates of 'science.' As Holzkamp (1964) and Bannister (1968) demonstrated, physiology represents a different dimension and a different universe of discourse from psychology. The two fields have separate subject matters, as acknowledged by such eminent neurosurgeons as

Penfield (4.3.3) and Pribram who are 'ready (and capable) to defend spirit as data' (Pribram 1976, p. 312).

10.2.2.2 Nor is it necessary, in order to be scientific, to study a grin without a cat or the learning of and short-term memory for nonsense syllables. Much of such experimentation about unrelated titbits of psychological functions is based on a poorly defined concept of 'learning' rather than on a clear concept of science. Much more psychological knowledge than that gained from 'learning' experiments has been derived from research on action (Langenheder 1975; Kaiser and Werbik 1977), on thinking (Piaget, Vygotsky), on problem-solving (Rubinstein, Wertheimer), on decision-making (Thomae 1974), and on personality (Thomae 1968), where total human beings were studied in real-life situations and not as unrelated 'abilities' of conceptually dismembered 'organisms.'

We have empirically demonstrated that Rokeach's, Eysenck's, and Osgood's 'scales' are invalid (Brandt 1978; Brandt and Maier 1976). Holzkamp (1964), Thomae (1968), and others demonstrated on epistemological grounds that the use of such 'instruments' as questionnaires and inventories cannot be justified. Without *Eichung* (standardization of measuring instruments – for which English has no special word) there exists nothing to measure – unless one is satisfied with 'measuring' length with tape-measures made of rubber.

10.2.2.3 There are other reasons why the grouping of data, quantification, and the use of statistics are not indicated in psychology, and why alienation resulting from these procedures is unnecessary. Every event is unique. Any event occurs and can be observed only once. Since induction is not justifiable by the logic of science, one can no more generalize scientifically from umpteen events than from a single one. As Holzkamp (1964) argued convincingly, if one studies a single case which typifies certain characteristics, one can say something at least about those characteristics.

The quantification of human experiences for the purpose of analysing psychological data conflicts,moreover, almost always with the basic rules of mathematics. The mathematical requirements for the application of parametric statistics can almost never be met by psychological givens (cf. Siegel 1956). Actions and experiences do not consist of equal units. The assumption of a normal curve on which actions and experiences are distributed cannot be supported empirically. Consequently psychological data also do not meet the requirements for factor analysis as Kempf (1972) and others have shown. Nor is the rejection of the null hypothesis any indicator of 'truth' (Bakan 1967; Clauss 1976). Quantification and statistics serve psychologists mainly for the preservation of a myth. They protect scientism against science. The hermeneutic psychologies discussed in earlier chapters have, however, contributed to psychological knowledge in various ways without quantification. For example, Ivo Kohler's subjective study of his hallucinations while he was treated with a new drug in a hospital may shed some entirely new light on the voluntary control of perception, though Kohler kept records merely of the qualities and characteristics of his experiences and did not 'measure' anything.[8]

Whether one considers the research made by Kohler on and by himself more or less scientific than experiments in which the psychologist is separated from the experiences s/he studies by graduate students serving as assistants is a metaphysical issue. That such alienating separation does not make psychological research automatically more scientific was shown in the chapter on research (7.1.5.2 and 7.1.5.3). The same applies to diagnoses made by independent testers and to blind test evaluations. These are not necessarily more valid than diagnoses and prognoses at which a psychologist arrives during an interview.[9] One can try to understand a total individual and need not treat separate symptoms.

10.2.2.4 As far as psychologists' reports about their research are concerned, we find it equally difficult to discover any scientific justification for the alienation described earlier. Even the American Psychological Association discovered eventually in 1974 that 'I' is more appropriate for reporting what *one* did and observed in an experiment than 'we' or some passive construction. Other scientists like Bridgman (1959) have,

---

8 Professor Kohler told me about this research when I visited him in the hospital at Innsbruck, Austria. (LWB)

9 Only twice during my years of work as a psychoanalyst did I send analysands for testing because I did not feel sure enough about my diagnoses. In both instances, the testers were very experienced psychologists whose test diagnoses disagreed with mine. Unfortunately, my diagnoses solely on the basis of analytic sessions proved correct. One analysand quit the analysis and committed suicide two weeks later; the other proved to be a psychopath as I had suspected. (LWB)

---

for years, considered 'I' the scientifically correct form for reporting, as evidenced by the prescriptions for authors of *Science*, the official organ of the American Association for the Advancement of Science. Yet, a search through a number of 1977 issues of different APA journals did not turn up a single 'I.'

The omission from scientific reports of details about the communications and other transactions which took place between the psychologist and others cannot be justified on scientific grounds either. Whether the purpose of publishing research reports is to inform other scientists or to enable them to replicate the research, in either case the omission of psychological events from the reports is indefensible. In view of the kind of detailed information which psychological research reports usually contain, it seems difficult to attribute the omissions to such non-scientific practical considerations as space-shortage. In order to save space one would rather omit the name of the university at which the research was carried out, since that information is useless for replication of the experiment: insiders know where the work was done and outsiders cannot replicate it at the same place nor would they want to repeat the experiment with the same students. From a scientific point of view, the exact wording of the instructions is at least as important for a replication of the research as the make and serial number of the instruments, and the word or design presented to the participants at least as important as the size and whiteness of the paper on which it appeared.

The omission of detailed indications about the psychological investigator is not only scientifically unjustifiable but contradicts all dictates of the logic of science. The investigator's sex, age, size, etc., as well as his/her momentary state of health, mood, fatigue, etc., may have an effect on both the other participants in the experiment and the observations made of them. In addition, the training and experience and certainly the expectations of the psychologist enter into the analysis, interpretation, and discussion of his/her observations and the conclusions drawn from them. The role of the scientific observer has been discussed in detail by Ruesch (Grinker 1967). It has also been recognized by such psychological publications as the *Journal of Phenomenological Psychology, the Psychoanalytic Review, Psychological Issues*, and *Psyche* which, contrary to most 'scientific' psychological journals, provide some personal information about their authors.

Knowledge about the psychologist is particularly important in personication research, where 'traits' and 'personality' attributed to someone depend not only on the one who is said to 'have' the 'traits' and 'personality' but also on the attributor (Kaminski 1959, 1970; Ruesch and Bateson 1951; Sullivan 1953). It therefore seems to us that, in line with the generally accepted logic of science today, psychologists ought to provide as detailed descriptions as possible of themselves as 'the ultimate instruments' (Bridgman 1959).

When 'the ultimate instrument' performs a 'crucial experiment' on itself, testing thereby one of its theories – when a physician cures himself, when a dentist successfully treats his own teeth or pulls them, when a psychoanalyst solves some of his problems in living through analysis of his dreams and his *Fehlleistungen* (parapraxes; literally, erroneous achievements or actions), when Wolfgang Metzger (1966b) after having lost one eye discovered the cues for monocular depth perception – the scientist-practitioner becomes a 'whole' human being, integrating the professional role identity$_4$ into his/her identity$_{1, 2}$, and $_3$, and identifying with his/her work and its products without losing contact with the rest of mankind.

In summary, psychologists' alienation from themselves, their work, and from other people is not a necessary concomitant of the pursuit of scientific psychology but leads to

10.2.2.5 *The alienation paradox*: People who enter a field of study in order to understand themselves and other human beings better become, through their studies and their work in this field, more alienated from themselves, their work, and other human beings.

10.3   SOME SPECULATIONS FOR PSYCHOLOGISTS' ALIENATION We can explain the alienation of certain psychologists in a number of ways. Referring back to the sociology of knowledge (cf. 9.5.3.6), we can point at the stimulus-response dogma and show that it entails a concept of human beings as incapable of determining their own destiny, which, in the capitalist, free-market economy, depends on the 'demands' of the market, of industry, of technology, etc. The corresponding self-concept of the members of such a society excludes exactly that kind of freedom and responsibility which could make them feel uniquely human, that is, give them identity$_2$. The high competitiveness among the members of a society from which only few are chosen by their God, and whose hierarchical structure contains only few places at the top of the pyramid, can explain alienation$_4$. Other people are used for gaining approval and acceptance but not for emotional involvement in such an other-directed society. Even for approval and 'unconditional acceptance' one looks only to one's own subgroup, and, if one does not get it there, one buys it from a psychologist. It is not economical, psychically or otherwise, to invest emotionally in human relationships in a geographically highly mobile society spread over a vast country. In a society where fund-raisers and advertisers address completely anonymous strangers by 'dear friend,' and where integrity and dignity are no primary values, alienation must be quite general.

The understanding and explanation of human 'behaviour' is, in such a society, based on answers to such questions as: 'How can human beings be more efficiently and effectively manipulated?' and 'How can people be better adjusted to the existing norms?' In order to manipulate people – including oneself, for instance, by biofeedback or yoga exercises, without deeper understanding of either – one must keep at a certain distance from people and remain 'objective' in the sense of not becoming emotionally involved (not in the sense of assuming different perspectives to gain deeper insights). Thus, the technical psychologists' alienation does not present a paradox, if their aim is merely better manipulation.

If, however, psychologists want to learn more about how human beings experience life and act in it, and not only about what people can be made to do, then the alienation of psychologists represents a paradox. This paradox can be explained not only from a sociological but also from various psychological perspectives.

The choice of a profession whose avowed goal is the understanding of human beings, and the simultaneous avoidance of intimate contact with human beings in the pursuit of that profession, can be conceptualized as presenting an 'approach-avoidance conflict' in Lewinian terms. However, for us, such labelling does not yet constitute an explanation. It is merely a description on a more abstract level. It throws no light on what may create the conflict.

Those psychologists who, in their work, keep at a distance from others and from themselves as human beings are usually not aware of the fact that their scientific methods represent an alienation. Thus, they have no conscious conflicts. For an explanation of those conflicts we shall therefore resort to theories which include concepts about unconscious psychological dynamics.

10.3.1 Sullivan (1953) dealt with what he termed 'social isolation' and contended that the avoidance of close contact with others helps people with low self-esteem to reduce their anxiety. In line with Sullivan's theory, the question then arises whether it is reasonable to assume that the psychologists whom we describe as alienated have a low self-esteem. We have a number of reasons for this assumption. The general public knows almost nothing about experimental psychology, as many of its representatives have experienced. When these are introduced to strangers as psychologists, the strangers say to them: 'Can you read my mind?' or 'I have a neighbour who needs your help' or 'I have to tell you that dream.' In other words, psychology is commonly equated with psychoanalysis, that is, with that approach to psychology which is most strongly rejected as unscientific and most widely ignored by most psychologists. In addition, many laymen believe that they know enough to discuss psychological issues as experts, whereas they have no such pretensions with respect to other sciences which they have not studied.

Among scientists the psychologist has a very low status. Since psychology is, in Kuhn's (1970a) terms, still in the 'pre-paradigm' stage, it cannot measure up to other sciences. Among professionals the psychologist has lower status than the psychiatrist, who himself sits at the bottom of the totem-pole among medical specialists.

It also does not increase the self-esteem of the psychologist that his scientific knowledge and training does not distinguish him from others in daily life by better insights into himself and others and by better relationships with people (Zellinger 1970).

The attempt to apply their scientific theories to themselves can only further lower the self-esteem of most psychologists, as those theories declare people to be mere mechanisms which react automatically to their environments and whose achievements are merely the results of 'reinforcements.' A further decrease in self-esteem can thus be avoided by these psychologists only by not applying their theories to themselves (cf. 5.1), that is, by avoiding a reflexive psychology (Bannister 1970). The pursuit of a science of human beings which psychologists cannot apply to themselves qua human beings cannot raise their self-esteem qua psychologists. Thus, Sullivan's theory explains to some extent the above described alienation of certain psychologists from other people. Sullivan did not, however, indicate where the specific anxiety originates which social isolation is intended to decrease, nor does his theory account for alienation from oneself.

10.3.2   We therefore turn to psychoanalytic theory to attempt to throw some further light on the issue of the psychologist's alienation. 'What follows is speculation, often far-fetched speculation, which the reader will consider or dismiss according to his individual predilection. It is further an attempt to follow out an idea consistently, out of curiosity to see where it will lead' (Freud 1920, p. 23). Freud considered anxiety as a signal of the impending danger of being overwhelmed by aggressive and/or sexual drives. These drives may appear in consciousness in the form of fantasies and wishes. They can, however, also be excluded from consciousness by means of defence mechanisms. Similarly the anxiety which results from the above mentioned danger can be kept from reaching conscious awareness, as can perceptions in instances of hysterical blindness or deafness. In such cases the unconscious processes can only be inferred from the logical contradictions between an individual's actions and the explanations s/he gives for her/his actions. Whether or not someone considers those inferences to be satisfactory explanations for the logical contradictions depends on what that individual accepts as a scientific explanation. As the conservative philosopher Braithwaite (cf. Taylor 1970) stated in his corresponding article in the *Encyclopaedia Britannica* (1961) an 'explanation' is what 'provides any sort of intellectual satisfaction.'

According to psychoanalytic theory, the most widely used defence mechanisms in highly technological societies are reaction formation, rationalization, isolation, and denial. Reaction formation consists in acting contrary to one's underlying drives. By concentrating on an approved course of action, one shuts conflicting fantasies and wishes out of one's consciousness. Applying this hypothetical construct to the alienated psychologists, we conclude that they chose a field which in name deals with the 'psychic' so that they would not become aware of the anxiety which contact with other people and with the human psyche arouses in them, a field which keeps them from actually entering into such contacts. If they had been aware of their fears of close human contact, many psychologists might have chosen different careers.

Rationalization seems involved in psychologists' justification of methods which entail alienation both from oneself and from others without being appropriate methods for the study of human beings qua human beings and without being scientifically sound.

Isolation consists in the separation of thoughts from other, usually related, thoughts and from feelings. As we pointed out, one of the reasons for alienation in various forms is the implicit, namely, unconscious, assumption $E \neq S$, which consists in separating the thought that one is a human being from the thought that the people who volunteer to work with a psychologist, be it as participants in an experiment or as clients in a counselling situation, are similar human beings who have thoughts, feelings, intentions, curiosity, motivations, etc., like oneself, and who no more merely respond to stimuli than oneself. Such isolation, which also expresses itself in unawareness of the feelings one has in performing one's work as a psychologist, protects one's unconscious wish for omniscience and omnipotence as a scientific psychologist.

$E \neq S$ can also be explained in terms of the denial of one's common humanness, and again as a defence against the loss of feelings of omnipotence, that is, against feeling helpless. Such denial of being human leads to alienation$_1$ by not integrating one's humanness into one's self-concept, to alienation$_2$ when one pretends not to differ from rats, to alienation$_3$ by rejecting one's human development, and to alienation$_4$ by separating one from the rest of mankind.

In order to be more specific in our psychoanalytic explanation of the alienation of certain psychologists we would have to investigate the life histories of individual psychologists as well as their human relationships in general. One would have to determine whether alienated psychologists went through particularly fierce power struggles in their childhood and developed obsessive-compulsive personalities. However, such childhoods seem very likely for people brought up in a society dominated by a combination of puritan, pioneer, and capitalist morality as discussed in the preceding chapter.[10]

---

10 After completion of this book we noticed James A. Schellenberg's *Masters of Social Psychology: Freud, Mead, Lewin,* and *Skinner* ((New York: Oxford University Press 1978), which relates some biographical material to the respective theories. It lacks, however, the kind of detailed and objective childhood and background material required for an in-depth study of the genesis of those approaches to social psychology.

---

11 Psychologists Caught in Different Aesthetic Frameworks

Psychologists Caught in Different Aesthetic Frameworks

Science for art's sake

Verweile doch, du bist so schön! (Goethe, *Faust*)

11.0 All science begins and ends with events which can be investigated only by empirical phenomenological idiographic psychology. It begins with 'a free creative choice that is different from the artist's only in the kinds of evidence upon which it focuses and the grounds upon which its fruitfulness will be judged' (Hall and Lindzey 1957, p. 11). It ends with the entirely private experience of 'proof' (Bridgman 1959). The logic of science provides no answers concerning the creation of theories or the establishment of 'proof.' Popper (1959) made perfectly clear that even the logic of science itself consists of 'proposals ... guided, in the last analysis, by value judgments and predilections' (p. 38). The uniquely human activity called 'science' can, therefore, be understood, if at all, only in terms of some psychology which does not attempt to reduce itself to some other science like physics, chemistry, or physiology. While other sciences can escape to psychology, there is no escape for psychology beyond itself.

11.1 As long as psychologists continue trying to ascertain 'the truth,' they are attempting to pull themselves up by their own bootstraps and will always end up in the liar paradox. Even Hall and Lindzey (1957) agreed that 'theories are never true or false' (p. 10). Furthermore, any theory concerning the creation of theories becomes problematic when applied to its own creation. The problem, as I conceptualize it, is not so different from that with which Roman Catholics must struggle when they attempt to deal with both the omniscience and the omnipotence of God. If God is truly omniscient, he must also know the entire future. Consequently, God has no free choice. Hence, God is not omnipotent. If God is truly omnipotent, God can act in the future in any possible way – and is not omniscient because he does not know now how he will act later. The belief in both God's omniscience and omnipotence must thus lead to *credo quia absurdum*, to the belief that God is beyond human comprehension.

11.1.1   Even Hall and Lindzey (1957), whose 'point of view ... is ... admittedly colored heavily by the teachings of logical positivism' (p. 10), concede that 'there is no formula for fruitful theory construction any more than there is a formula for making enduring literary contributions' (p. 11). They do not, however, point out that, if the creation of new theories followed some psychological law, that is, if there were a 'formula,' the creation of a new theory would be predictable. If the creation of a new theory were predictable, the new theory itself might also be predictable. More concretely, assuming that I knew enough about my colleague X to be able to predict that Professor X will invent a new theory, I might also be able to collect sufficient 'data' about psychologist X to predict the content of the forthcoming Xian theory. In that case, I already know the Xian theory before X invents it – which means that by the time X creates the theory, it is no longer a new theory – except if X meanwhile collected the necessary and sufficient 'data' about me to be able to predict that I would predict the Xian theory.

I believe, as Hall and Lindzey do, that 'theories are not "given" or predetermined by nature, the data, or any other determinant process. Just as the same experiences or observations may lead a poet or novelist to create any one of a multitude of different art forms, so the data of investigation may be incorporated in any of countless different theoretical schemes' (pp. 10-11). However, contrary to Hall, Lindzey, and other logical positivists, I am willing to draw both the logical and psycho-logical conclusions from this belief.

11.1.2   It follows from their statement that one can at best reconstruct *ex post facto* how our colleague X went about creating a new theory. Such reconstructing in psychology can, like reconstructions in archaeology, history, and literature, take only the form of a hermeneutic circle. My reconstructions can never be experimentally tested because in an experiment one must predict the outcome, which is, in this case, the new theory to be created by someone else in the experiment. 'The fact that a theory is a conventional choice, rather than something that is inevitable or prescribed by known empirical relations, emphasizes the lack of appropriateness of truth or falsity as attributes to be ascribed to a theory' (ibid.).

11.2   The problem of the creation of theories itself thus points to the problem of proof. (How can X 'prove' that X created some new theory in the way X claims X created it?) Psychologically the question is now no longer 'How can one prove that p is true?' but 'How does X become convinced that p is true?' or 'How does p make sense to X?' While there can also be no definitive answer to this question, I shall attempt to throw some light on it. If I am even to the least extent successful in this attempt, it will also make sense to the reader that there is as much disagreement among psychologists as I have shown in the preceding chapters. If the reader has disagreed with many of my earlier interpretations and if my explanation for such disagreements makes sense to him, I am highly successful in my attempt without even removing or nullifying such earlier disagreements.

11.2.1   It seems to me that 'proof' in the sense of 'these observations prove the theory T' or 'these arguments prove that p is true' is a very complex feeling – just as complex as the feeling of doubt and the feeling of ambivalence. The feeling of proof seems to be what the gestaltists call an aha-experience or an experience of closure. Something falls into place. Kuhn (1970a) has described science as 'puzzle solving.' Consequently one may say that 'proof' is putting that part into a puzzle which gives one a picture of the whole.

Two kinds of words are used for making sense out of some events. One kind of word refers to physical actions: I *grasp* the meaning of something. The other kind refers to some passive perception: I *see* (cf. Hanson 1969); I have some in*sight*. The equation of seeing and knowing is reflected in the frequent use of 'perceiving' for 'conceiving' or 'conceptualizing,' even in scientific psychological writings, and by the Sanskrit word *veda* which means 'knowledge' and whose Latin cognate is *videre* = 'to see,' with the English cognates 'wit' and 'wise.' There is further the saying 'seeing is believing.' Yet, not all seeing is believing.

11.2.2   After having measured the two horizontal lines in the Müller-Lyer 'illusion,' one still sees them as of different length but no longer believes that they are of different length. Most psychologists, believing that the two lines 'are' of identical length, also believe that the only possible problem is why they see the two lines as diferent. However, one can also ask the question why they do not believe what they see, namely that the one line is longer than the other. Why do they not consider the equal measurements with a yardstick an 'illusion'? And why do they not consider the possibility that the two lines 'are' of different length when compared to each other directly, and 'measure' the same when each is compared to a yardstick separately? – an idea which I owe to Professor Otto Heller of the University of Würzburg, who was a professional magician before becoming a psychologist. I can rephrase my question by asking why most psychologists take it for granted that measuring the two lines of the Müller-Lyer 'illusion' 'proves' that the two lines are of equal length. If intersubjectivity is considered as the criterion of objectivity, the two lines are 'objectively' of unequal length, since most observers report seeing them as of unequal length.

The pat (and pet) answer to my question is that to explain the difference between the seen and the measured lengths of the two lines by assuming the measurements to be 'true' and the perceptions without yardstick to be an 'illusion' is more 'consistent' with other observations and more 'parsimonious' than any of the alternative explanations I have offered. This answer begs the question as to why one accepts the most consistent and most parsimonious explanation as the 'true' one. If the reply to this question is that consistency and parsimony are two basic rules or principles of 'science,' the psychological question still remains as to why scientists set up and adhere to those rules.[1]

11.2.3   As ought to be evident from preceding chapters, I believe that more than one explanation can be given for any human action. Consistency and parsimony, as well as the explanations based on them, can be understood on the basis of the history and sociology of psychology, of drives and defence mechanisms, of the means and relations of production, and in a number of other ways. At this point, I want to propose that what makes sense to someone, what someone experiences as proof, what someone considers to be true, can also be conceptualized in terms of aesthetics: *An individual accepts that explanation of events which most closely fits his/her sense of beauty.* This formulation will be less objectionable to many psychologists if I restate it by writing that 'the most elegant explanation is the most acceptable.' One reason why this formulation is more acceptable to some psychologists is that it eliminates the subjective factor. It implies that some explanations 'are' more elegant

---

1   The most parsimonious and consistent explanation is always God. The difference between theology and science lies merely in the absence of critique in the former.

---

than others. Since I consider elegance, like relevance (cf. chapter 3), not to be inherent in an explanation but as resulting from an interaction, I do not wish to reformulate my statement in terms of elegance. Moreover, the statement in terms of 'elegance' may give the impression of being synonymous with 'consistency and parsimony.'

11.3 Like most ideas, the idea of relating science to aesthetics is not Brandt-new. In a lecture entitled 'Die Bedeutung des Schönen in der exakten Naturwissenschaft' (the relevance[2] of beauty in the exact sciences) given at the Bavarian academy of fine arts in 1970, the physicist Werner Heisenberg, whose 'uncertainty principle' I have mentioned repeatedly in these pages, traced the relationship between science and beauty back to the ancient Greeks. According to them beauty is the proper conformity of the parts to one another, and to the whole; knowledge (*Erkenntnis, Verstehen*) can mean only 'to recognize connections, that is, coherent features, characteristics of relationship within variety [*Vielfalt*]' (1971c, p. 98). Heisenberg stated that 'mathematical pictures ... prove to be the true ideas underlying nature not only through their correct representation of experience but above all through their simplicity and beauty' (p. 100f.) and that 'the relevance of the beautiful for the discovery of the true has at all times been recognized and emphasized' (p. 102), as expressed in the Latin maxim *pulchritudo splendor veritatis* (beauty is the splendour of truth). He quotes Kepler's statement *'geometria est archetypus pulchritudinis mundi'* and warns against 'the misunderstanding that natural science and technology deal solely with exact observation and rational, discursive thought' (p. 107) – a myth James D. Watson's (1968) *The Double Helix* tried to evaporate.

The relation between science and art can be conceptualized as a dialectic one. Pythagoras conceptualized such an interaction between mathematics and beauty. Greek sculptures were based on geometrical principles such as the 'golden section' governing the proportion between the parts and the whole. In the late nineteenth century, the French Impressionist painters aimed at painting *la vérité vraie* (the true truth) by attempting to represent the diffraction of light by the air. In

---

2 *Bedeutung* can mean 'relevance,' 'meaning,' 'significance.' Heisenberg's (1974) translator, Peter Heath, alternates between 'meaning' and 'significance.'

---

the early twentieth century, the German expressionist painters tried to picture an internal truth. The cubists sought to represent the true picture of aspects of the world by combining several perspectives. Thus, even the least realistic painting can give the viewer the feeling that it is a true representation of some part of the world. If science is a search for truth, a truth which can never be fully attained but can, perhaps, be more and more closely approximated, so is art. Just as science is by no means entirely rational, art is not entirely irrational.

11.3.1   When it became evident that the rational strain of neither the impressionists nor the expressionists could attain an ultimate truth, the attempt to strengthen the irrational aspects of art led to Dadaism. When it dawned on scientists and philosophers of science that science too cannot reach any ultimate truth, that rationality and ever more rigorous Dataism (Bunge 1967) do not bring about that truth, the most revolutionary philosopher of science, Paul Feyerabend, turned 'Against Method' (1970, 1975) and proposed a 'Dadaist' and 'an anarchistic theory of knowledge.' Feyerabend came to the conclusion that, in scientific research, 'what remains are aesthetic judgements, judgements of taste, and our own subjective wishes.' He continued:

It seems to me that an enterprise whose human character can be seen by all is preferable to one that looks 'objective,' and impervious to human actions and wishes. The sciences, after all, are our own creation, including all the severe standards they seem to impose upon us ... It is good to be constantly reminded of the fact that science as we know it today is not inescapable and that we may construct a world in which it plays no role whatever (such a world, I venture to suggest, would be more pleasant than the world we live in today) ... The choice between theories which are sufficiently general to provide us with a comprehensive world view and which are empirically disconnected may become a matter of taste ... Matters of taste are not completely beyond the reach of argument. Poems, for example, can be compared in grammar, sound structure, imagery, rhythm, and can be evaluated on such a basis. (1970, p. 228)

Hall and Lindzey (1957) wrote: 'The theorist in choosing one particular option to represent the events in which he is interested is exercising a free creative choice that is different from the artist's only in the kinds of evidence upon which it focuses and the grounds upon which its fruitfulness will be judged' (p. 11). The logical and psycho-logical conclusion from this statement is that there is no difference between the scientific and the artistic process. The difference lies merely in the material which is processed and in the evaluation of the results, just as the difference between eating meat and eating vegetarian food lies not in the digestive process, but in the material and the evaluation of the consequences of the process, the digestive activity.

It follows, therefore, not only from the ideas of such revolutionary scientists and philosophers as Pythagoras, Heisenberg, and Feyerabend, but also from the pronouncements of such conservative psychologists as Hall and Lindzey, that science and art are not miles apart.

11.3.2   Popper's description of 'science [as] essentially critical; ... it consists of bold conjectures, controlled by criticism, and ... it may, therefore, be described as revolutionary' (1970, p. 55) also does not stand in flat contradiction to considering science an art. Art has frequently been critical and revolutionary. I am reminded here of the frescos by Orozco in the New School for Social Research which had to be covered by drapes during the communist-hunts of the 1950s. Much of the literature of all ages has been critical. And the line between science and art is not easy to draw in such books as Lucretius' *De rerum natura* (of the things of nature), Goethe's *Die Wahlverwandtschaften* (selective affinities) and *Die Metamorphose der Pflanzen*, Galilei's dialogues, Alfred Renyi's *Dialogues about Mathematics*, and Sigmund Freud's works for which he was honoured by the Goethe Prize, the highest German literary award. I have gained at least as much psychological knowledge from novels and plays as from textbooks. The 'truth' of that knowledge is conveyed to the reader by the same private feeling as 'scientific proof,' a feeling of which William James (1890) probably presented the most detailed and clear phenomenal analysis.

11.4   To some readers the view of science as an art may seem outrageous. It may no longer seem so when science is considered as a game played according to agreed-upon rules. In his *Logik der Forschung* (logic of research, translated under the title *The Logic of Scientific Discovery* [1959]) Popper (1935) set up the rules according to which he was willing to play the game. What are usually considered to be various research methodologies are rules for the science game. Now, the distance between games and art is not always that great. In the rowing contests between Oxford and Cambridge the winning crew was not necessarily the fastest one. The teams were also scored for style, that is, on aesthetic criteria. In chess too, one player may play more elegantly than the other. Similarly, in scientific research the 'design' and its execution can be evaluated as more or less beautiful. Certainly, theories can be more or less appealing.

11.4.1 To accept 'truth' as a complex feeling comprising personal taste does not solve the problem of self-reference but raises further questions for psychology. These questions are, like those with which I started this chapter, questions for individual psychology. What in the individual history of one psychologist induces her or him to accept the most consistent and parsimonious explanation of events as the 'true' one and what in the make-up of another psychologist leads him or her to consider a more complex explanation of the same events more beautiful 'because reality is not always as simple as we should like it to be and because unfortunately one cannot represent it correctly more parsimoniously than it happens to be' (Metzger 1962, p. 107)? Thus, we get right back into the vicious circle of personicating and the concomitant paradoxes.

Some of the paradoxes of self-reference can be easily solved by introducing the fourth dimension. The Cretan who said 'All Cretans are liars' does not necessarily mean that all Cretans lie at all times. When I say 'I am taking myself too seriously' I take myself seriously in making that statement. When recognizing myself to be a fool I feel insightful and not foolish in relation to that recognition.

11.4.2 Psycho-logic frequently does not correspond to classical logic. An individual and his/her self are not sets in the sense of classical logic. The boundaries fluctuate almost constantly. Something is, in one sense, part of me and, in another sense, not (James 1890; Brandt 1967a).[3]

Many paradoxes result from our frameworks of logic. In recent years, an attempt has been made to construct a new logic called 'fuzzy logic' which may lead us out of the dilemma because it is closer to 'psycho-logic' (cf. Gaines 1976). I can do no more here than indicate that 'fuzzy reasoning' is not based on the old either/or dichotomy but on a more-or-less continuum. Judgments of 'truth' made on the basis of 'fuzzy set theory' seem to me not too different from aesthetic

---

3 Many writers have rejected the idea of a unified personality, e.g., Goethe in *Faust* and Hesse in *Steppenwolf* and other works of his based on Jungian psychology.

---

judgments. In fuzzy logic, a statement may be more or less true just as something may taste more or less good or be more or less beautiful.

11.4.2.1 The difference between classical logic and psycho-logic can, perhaps, be best elucidated through the problem of the importance of being earnest. According to the Aristotelian law of contradiction, nothing can be A and non-A; in other words, nothing can be earnest and in jest at the same time. However, play is characterized exactly by being both serious and playful. If someone takes a game too seriously, it is no longer fun. In the extreme, it becomes an issue of life and death – as it almost does when hockey players beat each other up on the ice. On the other hand, the players must take the game seriously enough to follow the rules. Otherwise it becomes clowning and the game cannot continue. The game is most aesthetically appealing when all players are both serious and not serious.[4]

11.4.2.2 In 1974 a group of leading German-language psychologists and philosophers published, under the editorship of the past president of the West German psychological association, a very scholarly book entitled *Dichotomie und Duplizität: Grundfragen psychologischer Erkenntnis – Ernst August Dölle zum Gedächtnis* (Dichotomy and duplicity: basic questions of psychological knowledge – in memory of Ernst August Dölle). The more than a dozen scholars presented Dölle's life and work, argued whether he was a phenomenologist or an experimental psychologist, discussed his contributions to 'binaural rivalry,' to learning theory, to educational psychology, to psycholinguistics, and to a number of other areas, and speculated on his relation to women, to psychoanalysis, and to positivism. The number of cross-references between the various chapters indicate close collaboration between the authors, who also set up the Dölle-Archives and founded the Dölle-Society. Finally, the scholarly work contains a complete bibliography of Dölle's publications and all his unpublished manuscripts to which the contributors to the book frequently refer.

The book was immediately reviewed in all German-language psychological journals. When I visited the four German-speaking coun-

---

4 The game character of psychology is implicitly acknowledged by the use of judges (cf. Brandt 1968).

---

tries in 1974, it was the most discussed work among psychologists. Many respectable books and articles published since then refer to Dölle's contributions to our science.

Though nothing in the book or in any of the scholarly reviews states so, none of us believes that Ernst August Dölle, the typical German psychology professor, who even received a posthumous honorary doctoral degree from the University of Karlsruhe, ever lived.

Are the authors of the book, including the philosopher Hans Albert who confessed to me that he wrote not only a chapter under his real name but three additional chapters under three fictitious names, liars? Is the book a scholarly work? a work of art? a game? a joke? none of these? all of these? The last answer is the correct one.

11.5   Some psychologists are *Fachidioten*: they are so preoccupied by their field to the exclusion of everything else that they have become ἰδιώτης, withdrawn in their private worlds. Others have become σχιστός, split into a psychologist and a completely unrelated citizen interested in anything except psychology. One need be neither.

Accepting judgments about 'truth' as aesthetic judgments leads me to include my own subjectivity in my science. I have done so in the chapters of this book from the perspectives of (1) my unique history, (2) the languages I am familiar with and think in, (3) my values and interests, (4) my picture of the physical world, (5) the theories which appeal to me, (6) my interpersonal relations, (7) my ways of conducting research, (8) my personicating myself and others, (9) the period of history I have been living in, and (10) my search for my own identity. I have thus tried to integrate various aspects of my life.

I have tried to avoid the 'pretence of knowledge ... the scientistic prejudice and ... specious claims of what science can achieve' and tried instead to 'debunk such arrogations, some of which have by now become vested interests of established university departments' (Hayek 1975, p. 440). I have attempted not to imitate those who 'please their lower instincts, their craving for intellectual security in the form of clarity, precision, "objectivity," "truth"' (Feyerabend 1975, p. 27), because I have come to the conclusion that security and freedom are rarely reconcilable in this world. I have tried to heed the 'principle of *anything goes*' (ibid.).

In the course of writing this book I found that *psychology can be a beautiful game.*

12 Conclusion: Psychologists Released from Different Ethical Frameworks

Conclusion: Psychologists Released from Different Ethical Frameworks

All art is quite useless. (Oscar Wilde, *The Picture of Dorian Gray*)

12.1   The psychologists who formulated the *Ethical Principles in the Conduct of Research with Human Participants* (APA 1973) for psychologists stated that 'it is one of their obligations to use their research skills to extend knowledge for the sake of ultimate human betterment' (p. 7).

Hindus, Buddhists, Taoists, and Jews do not feel such an 'obligation.' Their respective philosophies contain the 'ethical principle' to work on their own individual 'betterment.' Their ethics do not include any obligation to control others in order to better them. 'Ultimate human betterment' is an obligation of Christian ethics. In the name of this lofty end heretics were burnt at the stake and pagans were massacred in order to save their ψυχή. Christians have received the Word which Hindus, Buddhists, Taoists, and Jews ignore, namely what 'ultimate human betterment' consists of. The illustrious anonymous members of the Ad Hoc Committee of the American Psychological Association who wrote the *Ethical Principles* therefore needed not define – operationally or otherwise – what they meant by 'ultimate human betterment.'

The *Ethical Principles* represent an attempt to keep psychology from being 'the science of MIS-behaviour.' Such an attempt must be condemned to failure because the 'obligation to use' one's skills 'for the sake of ultimate human betterment' sanctifies, in the last analysis, all means. For such a laudable end any lie becomes a 'white lie,' cheating becomes 'withholding of information,' hurting others becomes an 'unfortunate necessity.' For, what does 'ultimate human betterment' mean, if not PROGRESS?

12.2   The ethical principle which follows from considering scientific psychology an *autotelic* activity, that is, an activity undertaken solely because it is enjoyable (Moore and Anderson 1962), is rather mundane and pre-scientific. That principle requires that *all* participants understand and agree to the rules and are free to stop playing when they no longer enjoy the game. Such an ethical principle of 'fair play' can make the science of psychology into a *fröhliche Wissenschaft, la gaya scienza.*

Epilogue

Over two years have passed since I considered this book ready for publication – well aware that it would always remain improvable. In the meantime, of those mentioned in this book my uncle Hans Jacoby, my only close relative, Wolfgang Metzger, with whom I exchanged many ideas, and Jean Piaget, whom I regret never to have met, are dead. Piaget was still alive when I had the pleasure of meeting his former student and interpreter Rémy Droz in May 1980. The latter encouraged me not to change my chapter on 'truth' (chapter 11).

As a consequence of comments by readers of the manuscript, particularly by one anonymous reviewer for the Social Science Federation of Canada, I made a number of changes buttressing my arguments rather than recanting. The doctoral dissertation which Ted Hein wrote in the meantime under my supervision strengthened my view that recent developments in Yankee psychology, particularly the new fad of so-called cognitive psychology, represent no actual break with behaviourism, whatever the members of the Society for the Prevention of Cruelty to Dead Horses (Koestler 1967) may say.

Those who think that my considering psychology as a beautiful game destroys all arguments in my book are reminded that paradoxes are meaningless or problematic only within classical logic but not within psycho-logic; that a game must be taken seriously while being only a mere game; and that the rules of the game of science as I play it require constant critique and self-analysis. In the final analysis, the 'truth' of my arguments stands in relation to my own development which I described at the beginning.

Bibliography

Works marked * contain information about recent German-language psychology.

Agnew, N. McK. 1977. 'On Data: Does Science Have Holes in Her Pockets?' *Ontario Psychologist* 9 (2): 33-51

Allport, G.W. 1957. 'European and American Theories of Personality,' in H.R. David and H. von Bracken, eds, *Perspectives in Personality Theory.* New York: Basic Books

American Psychological Association. 1963. *Ethical Standards of Psychologists.* Washington, DC: APA

- 1973. *Ethical Principles in the Conduct of Research with Human Participants.* Washington, DC: APA

Amundson, N.E., and Brandt, L.W. 1972. 'Methods of Personication in the Parole Process,' *Canadian Journal of Criminology and Corrections* 14: 109-19

Anastasi, A. 1970. 'On the Formation of Psychological Traits,' *American Psychologist* 25: 899-910

Anderson, R. 1971. 'Attribution of Quotations from Wundt,' *American Psychologist* 26: 590-3

Argyris, C. 1968. 'Some Unintended Consequences of Rigorous Research,' *Psychological Bulletin* 70: 185-97

- 1969. 'The Incompleteness of Social-Psychological Theory,' *American Psychologist* 24: 893-908

- 1975. 'Dangers of Applying Results from Experimental Social Psychology,' *American Psychologist* 30: 469-85

- 1976. 'Theories of Action That Inhibit Individual Learning,' *American Psychologist* 31: 638-54

Arnold, W., Eysenck, H.J., and Meili, R. eds. 1972. *Lexikon der Psychologie*. Freiburg: Herder

Asch, S.E. 1946. 'Forming Impressions of Personality,' *Journal of Abnormal and Social Psychology* 41: 258-90

Bakan, D. 1958. *Sigmund Freud and the Jewish Mystical Tradition*. Princeton, NJ: Van Nostrand

– 1966. 'Behaviorism and American Urbanization,' *Journal of the History of the Behavioral Sciences* 2 (1): 5-28

– 1967. *On Method*. San Francisco: Jossey-Bass

– 1971. 'The Social Context of American Psychology,' Presidential address, Division of the History of Psychology, September 7, 1971, American Psychological Association Annual Convention, Washington, DC (mimeo)

Bandura, A. 1969. 'Social-Learning Theory of Identificatory Processes,' in D.A. Goslin ed, *Handbook of Socialization Theory & Research*. Chicago: Rand, McNally

Bannister, D. 1968. 'The Myth of Physiological Psychology,' *Bulletin of the British Psychological Society* 21: 229-31

– 1970. 'Science through the Looking Glass,' in D. Bannister ed, *Perspectives in Personal Construct Theory*. London: Academic Press

Barber, T.X., and Silver, M.J. 1968. 'Fact, Fiction, and the Experimenter Bias Effect,' *Psychological Bulletin* 70: 1-29

Bassin, F.V. 1969. 'Consciousness and the Unconscious,' in M. Cole and I. Maltzman eds

Bateson, G. 1951. 'Conventions of Communication: Where Validity Depends upon Belief,' in J. Ruesch and G. Bateson

Bateson, G., Jackson, D.D., Haley, J., and Weakland, J. 1956. 'Toward a Theory of Schizophrenia,' *Behavioral Science* 1: 251-64

Bekker, K. 1940. *Marx' Philosophische Entwicklung, sein Verhältnis zu Hegel*. Zürich: Oprecht

Bertalanffy, L. von. 1956. 'General Systems Theory,' *General Systems Yearbook* 1: 1-10

– 1962. 'General Systems – A Critical Review,' *General Systems* 7: 1-19

Bieri, J., Alkins, A.L., Briar, S., Leaman, R.L., Miller, H., and Tripodi, T. 1966. *Clinical and Social Judgment*. New York: Wiley

Bischof, N. 1966. 'Erkenntnistheoretische Grundlagenprobleme der Wahrnehmungstheorie,' in W. Metzger ed

Böll, H. 1971. *Gruppenbild mit Dame*. Köln: Kiepenheuer & Witsch

Born, M. 1969, *Albert Einstein – Hedwig und Max Born – Briefwechsel 1916-1955*. Munich: Nymphenburger Verlagshandlung

Boring, E.G. 1957. *A History of Experimental Psychology*, 2d ed. New York: Appleton-Century-Crofts

Brandt, L.W. 1960, 'Freud and Schiller,' *Psychoanalysis & Psychoanalytic Review* 46 (4): 97-101

- 1961a. *'Some Notes on English Freudian Terminology,' *Journal of the American Psychoanalytic Association* 9: 331-9
- 1961b. 'Some Notes on Penis Loss Anxiety,' *American Journal of Psychotherapy* 15: 246-50
- 1963. 'Psycholinguistic Analysis of Statements of Problems from Applicants for Psychotherapy: A Comparison of a Group Who Rejected and a Group Who Accepted Treatment at Three Outpatient Mental Health Clinics.' PHD dissertation. New York University (University Microfilms No. 64-6548)
- 1966a. *'Process or Structure?' *Psychoanalytic Review* 53: 374-8
- 1966b. *'Life in a German Clinic. Review of *Die psychosomatische Klinik und ihre Patienten* by C. de Boor & E. Künzler,' *Contemporary Psychology* 11: 108-10
- 1967a. 'The Phenomenology of the Self-Concept,' *Existential Psychiatry*, 6 (24): 422-32
- 1967b. *'Wanted: A Representative Experiment. Review of *Theorie und Experiment in der Psychologie* by K. Holzkamp,' *Contemporary Psychology* 12: 192-3
- 1968. 'A Note on the Use of Judges,' *Journal of Psychology* 68: 261-6
- 1970a. 'The Behaviorist's Leap: An Inquiry into What Attitude Researchers Measure,' *Journal of Social Issues* 26 (4): 163-6
- 1970b. 'The argumentum ad hominem Taboo,' *Contemporary Psychology* 15: 589-90
- 1971a. 'Science, Fallacies, and Ethics,' *Canadian Psychologist* 12: 231-42
- 1971b. 'Subjective Time and Decision Making,' *Psychological Review* 78: 81-2
- 1972a. 'Questions Concerning Some Assumptions Underlying the Semantic Differential,' *Psychologische Beiträge* 14: 61-7
- 1972b. *'The Will to Be Human. Review of *Wollen und Wert* by Peter Keiler,' *Contemporary Psychology* 17: 351-2
- 1974. 'Experiments in Psychoanalysis,' *Psychoanalytic Review* 61: 95-8
- 1975. 'Experimenter-Effect Research,' *Psychologische Beiträge* 17: 133-40
- 1976a. *'Contemporary German-Language Personology,' in D. Schultz, *Personality Theories*. Marterey, Calif.: Brooks/Cole
- 1976b. *'Socialization for Emancipation. Review of *Sozialisationsforschung* edited by H. Walter,' *Contemporary Psychology* 21: 701-2
- 1977a. 'Psychoanalyse *versus* Psychoanalysis: traduttore, traditore,' *Psyche* 11: 1045-51

- 1977b. 'Reward and Punishment or Bribe and Extortion?' *Journal of Phenomenological Psychology* 7: 195-208
- 1977c. *'Marxist-Leninist Psychology – What Is It? Review of *Lexikon der Psychologie* by W. Arnold, H.J. Eysenck & R. Meili – *Psychologisches Wörterbuch* by F. Dorsch – *Wörterbuch der Psychologie* by G. Clauss,' *Contemporary Psychology* 22: 660-1
- 1977d. *'Gesetze des Sehens* by W. Metzger,' *Journal of Phenomenological Psychology* 8: 115-19
- 1978. 'Messung eines Masstabs: Empirische Untersuchung des Semantischen Differentials (SD),' *Probleme und Ergebnisse der Psychologie* 66: 71-4
- 1979a. *'Behaviorism – The Psychological Buttress of Late Capitalism,' in A.R. Buss ed, *Psychology in Social Context*. New York: Irvington
- 1979b. *'German Language Psychoanalysis Today,' *Psychoanalytic Review* 66: 591-616
Brandt, L.W., and Brandt, E.P. 1972. 'Second-Hand Personication: A New Model for "Person Perception" Research,' *Canadian Psychologist* 13: 217-38
Brandt, L.W., and Maier, G.R. 1976. 'Was misst Eysencks Persönlichkeitsinventar (EPI)?' *Archiv für Psychologie* 128: 112-18
Brandt, L.W., and Metzger, W. 1969. *' "Reality", What Does It Mean?' *Psychological Reports* 25: 127-35
Bridgman, P.W. 1927. *The Logic of Modern Physics*. New York: Macmillan
- 1959. *The Way Things Are*. New York: Viking
Broglie, L. de. 1937. *Matière et lumière*. Paris: Albin Michel
Bronfenbrenner, U. 1977. 'Toward an Experimental Ecology of Human Development,' *American Psychologist* 32: 513-31
Budilowa, E.A. 1974. 'Über die Wechselbeziehung von Theorie und Geschichte der Psychologie,' in E.W. Schorochowa ed
Bunge, M. 1967. *Scientific Research*. Berlin: Springer
Carroll, L. 1960. *The Annotated Alice*. Edited by M. Gardner. Harmondsworth, Middlesex: Penguin Books
Clauss, G. ed. 1976. *Wörterbuch der Psychologie*. Leipzig: VEB Bibliographisches Institut
Cole, M., and Maltzman, I. eds. 1969. *A Handbook of Contemporary Soviet Psychology*. London: Basic Books
Criswell, J. 1958. 'The Psychologist as Perceiver,' in R. Tagiuri and L. Petrullo eds, *Person Perception and Interpersonal Behavior*. Stanford, Calif.: Stanford University Press

Danziger, K. 1977. 'Images from the Past: The Dialectics of Control,'
Ontario Psychologist 9 (2), 6-15

- 1979. 'The Social Origins of Modern Psychology,' in A.R. Buss ed,
Psychology in Social Context. New York: Irvington

Deese, J. 1969. 'Behavior and Facts,' *American Psychologist* 24: 515-22

Dorsch, F. ed. 1976. *Psychologisches Wörterbuch*. Bern: Huber

Dschuang Dsi. 1951. *Das wahre Buch vom südlichen Blütenland*. Translated
by R. Wilhelm. Düsseldorf: Eugen Diederichs

Duncker, K. 1945. *On Problem-Solving*. Translated by L.S. Lees.
Psychological Monographs 58 (5), 1-114

Einstein, A. 1923. *The Meaning of Relativity*. Princeton, NJ: Princeton
University Press

English, H.B., and English, A.C. 1958. *A Comprehensive Dictionary of
Psychological and Psychoanalytic Terms*. London: Longmans

English, O.S., Hampe, W.W. jr, Bacon, C.L., and Settlage, C.F. 1961.
Direct Analysis and Schizophrenia. New York: Grune & Stratton

Erikson, E.H. 1959. *Identity and the Life Cycle*. Psychological Issues,
monograph 1. New York: International Universities Press

- 1963. *Childhood and Society*. 2d rev. and enl. ed. New York: Norton

Eysenck, H.J., Arnold, W., and Meili, R. 1972. *Encyclopedia of Psychology*.
New York: Herder & Herder

Eysenck, H.J., and Eysenck, S.B.G. 1963. *Eysenck Personality Inventory*.
San Diego, Calif.: Educational & Industrial Testing Service

Farthing, G.R. 1971. 'Sex Differences in Personication.' MA thesis,
University of Saskatchewan, Regina Campus

Feyerabend, P.K. 1970. 'Consolations for the Specialist,' in Lakatos and
Musgrave

- 1975. *Against Method*. London: NLB

Fincher, C. 1972. *A Preface to Psychology*. 2d ed. New York: Harper & Row

Flavell, J.H. 1963. *The Developmental Psychology of Jean Piaget*. Princeton,
NJ: Van Nostrand

Foppa, K. 1967. 'Das Dilemma der Lerntheorien,' in *Bericht über den 25.
Kongress der Deutschen Gesellschaft für Psychologie*. Göttingen: Hogrefe

Fowler, H.W., and Fowler, F.G. eds. 1964. *The Concise Oxford Dictionary
of Current English*. Oxford: Clarendon Press

Fraisse, P. 1963. 'La méthode expérimentale,' in P. Fraisse and J. Piaget
eds, *Traité de psychologie expérimentale*, vol. 1. Paris: Presses
Universitaires de France

Freud, A. 1937. *The Ego and the Mechanisms of Defence*. London: Hogarth

Freud, S. 1945. *Gesammelte Werke*. London: Imago

- 1950 (1895). *Aus den Anfängen der Psychoanalyse.* London: Imago
- 1910. *Über den Gegensinn der Urworte.* In *Gesammelte Werke*, vol. 8
- 1912. *Ratschläge für den Arzt bei der psychoanalytischen Behandlung.* G.W., vol. 8
- 1913. *Das Interesse an der Psychoanalyse.* G.W., vol. 8
- 1920. *Jenseits des Lustprinzips.* G.W., vol. 13
- 1923. *Das Ich und das Es.* G.W., vol. 13
- 1927. *Die Zukunft einer Illusion.* G.W., vol. 14
- 1930. *Das Unbehagen in der Kultur.* G.W., vol. 14
- 1932. *Warum Krieg? G.W., vol. 16*
- 1937a. *Konstruktionen in der Analyse.* G.W., vol. 16
- 1937b. *Die endliche und die unendliche Analyse.* G.W., vol. 16
- 1940. *Abriss der Psychoanalyse.* G.W., vol. 17

Gaines, B.R. 1976. 'Foundations of Fuzzy Reasoning,' *International Journal of Man-Machine Studies* 8: 623-68

Giorgi, A. 1970. *Psychology as a Human Science.* New York: Harper & Row

Goethe, J.W. 1917 (1795.) 'Erster Entwurf einer allgemeinen Einleitung in die vergleichende Anatomie, ausgehend von der Osteologie,' in Goethe, *Werke*, vol. 16. Leipzig: Insel
- (1810.) *Zur Farbenlehre*. Tübingen: Cottasche Buchhandlung
- 1917. *Faust. Werke*, vol. 6

Gouldner, A.W. 1970. *The Coming Crisis of Western Sociology.* New York: Basic Books

Graumann, C.F. 1960. *Grundlagen einer Phänomenologie und Psychologie der Perspektivität.* Berlin: de Gruyter
- 1966. 'Bewusstsein und Bewusstheit,' in W. Metzger ed

Greenspoon, J. 1955. 'Reinforcing Effect of Two Spoken Sounds on Frequency of Two Responses,' *American Journal of Psychology* 68: 409-16

Grinker, R.R., sr ed. 1967. *Toward a Unified Theory of Human Behavior.* 2d ed. New York: Basic Books

Habermas, J. 1971. *Knowledge and Human Interest.* Translated by J.J. Shapiro. Boston: Beacon

Hall, C.S. 1954. *A Primer of Freudian Psychology.* New York: World

Hall, C.S., and Lindzey, G. 1957. *Theories of Personality.* New York: Wiley

Hanson, N.R. 1969. *Perception and Discovery.* San Francisco: Freeman, Cooper & Co.

Harms, E. 1967. *Origins of Modern Psychiatry.* Springfield, Ill.: Thomas

Hart, J.D., and Gohdes, C. 1955. *America's Literature.* New York: Holt

Hartmann, H. 1958 (1939). *Ego Psychology and the Problem of Adaptation.* Translated by D. Rapaport. New York: International Universities Press

Hastorf, A.H., Richardson, A., and Dornbusch, S.M. 1958. 'The Problem of Relevance in the Study of Person Perception,' in R. Tagiuri and L. Petrullo eds, *Person Perception and Interpersonal Behavior*. Stanford, Calif.: Stanford University Press

Hayek, F.A. 1964. 'The Theory of Complex Phenomena,' in M. Bunge ed, *The Critical Approach to Science and Philosophy*. London: Collier-Macmillan

- 1975. 'The Pretence of Knowledge,' *Swedish Journal of Economics* 77: 433-42

Hein, T.C., II. 1979. 'Reifying Thinking: A Critique of Cognitive Behaviorism and the Stimulus-Cognition-Response (S-C-R) Model in Psychological Theory' PHD thesis, University of Regina (Canada)

Heisenberg, W. 1958. *The Physicist's Conception of Nature*. London: Hutchinson

- 1971a. 'Der Begriff der kleinsten Teilchen in der Entwicklung der Naturwissenschaft,' in *Meyers enzyklpädisches Lexikon*. Mannheim: Bibliographisches Institut

- 1971b. 'The Completion of Physics as a Science?' *Universitas* 13: 97-103

- 1971c. 'Die Bedeutung des Schönen in der exakten Naturwissenschaft,' *Physikalische Blätter* 27: 97-107

- 1974. *Across the Frontiers*. Translated by P. Heath. New York: Harper & Row

Hilgard, E.R. 1972. 'Behaviorismus,' in W. Arnold, H.J. Eysenck and R. Meili eds

Hilke, R., and Kempf, W. 1973. 'Kann Aggressionsforschung objektiv sein?' Forschungsbericht 39 des Sonderforschungsbereiches 22. Nürnberg: Sozialwissenschaftliches Forschungszentrum

Hofstätter, P.R. 1956. 'Behaviorismus als Anthropologie,' *Jahrbuch für Psychologie und Psychotherapie* 4: 357-69

Holzkamp, K. 1964. *Theorie und Experiment in der Psychologie*. Berlin: de Gruyter

- 1968. *Wissenschaft als Handlung*. Berlin: de Gruyter

- 1970. 'Zum Problem der Relevanz psychologischer Forschung für die Praxis,' *Psychologische Rundschau* 21: 1-22

- 1972. *Kritische Psychologie*. Frankfurt: Fischer

Hornstein, H.A. 1973. 'The Social Psychology of Change,' *American Psychologist* 28: 191-4

Horton, R.W., and Edwards, H.W. 1967. *Backgrounds of American Literary Thought*. New York: Appleton-Century-Crofts

Humboldt, W. von. 1917 (1836). *Linguistic Variability and Intellectual Development*. University of Miami Press

Irle, M. 1975. 'Eine Flaute in der Sozialpsychologie?' *Zeitschrift für Sozialpsychologie* 6: 96-102

Iwanowa, I.I., and Assejew, V.G. 1974. 'Methodologie und Methoden der psychologischen Forschung,' in E.W. Schorochowa ed

James, W. 1890. *Principles of Psychology*. New York: Holland

Jaspers, K. 1963. *Allgemeine Psychopathologie*. Berlin: Springer

Jones, E. 1957. *The Life and Work of Sigmund Freud*. New York: Basic Books

Jung, C.G. 1934. 'Zur gegenwärtigen Lage der Psychotherapie,' *Zentralblatt für Psychotherapie* 7: 1-16

Kadushin, C. 1969. *Why People Go to Psychiatrists*. New York: Atherton

Kaiser, H.J., and Werbik, H. 1977. 'Der "Telefonzellenversuch" – Ein erstes Experiment zur Überprüfung einer Theorie sozialen Handelns,' *Zeitschrift für Sozialpsychologie* 8: 115-29

Kaminski, G. 1959. *Das Bild vom anderen*. Berlin: Lüttke

– 1963. 'Die Beurteilung unserer Mitmenschen als Prozess,' in *Bericht über den 23. Kongress der Deutschen Gesellschaft für Psychologie*. Göttingen: Verlag f. Psychologie

– 1970. *Verhaltenstheorie und Verhaltensmodifikation*. Stuttgart: Klett

Katz, D. 1969. *Gestaltpsychologie*. Basel: Schwabe

Kaufmann, H. 1967. 'The Price of Obedience and the Price of Knowledge,' *American Psychologist* 22: 321-2

Kaufmann, W. 1961. 'Nietzsche,' in *Encyclopaedia Britannica*. Chicago: W. Benton

Keiler, P. 1970. 'Ansätze zu einer Ideologiekritik von Wahrnehmungstheorien,' *Zeitschrift für Sozialpsychologie* 1: 211-24, 311-35

Kelly, G.A. 1955. *The Psychology of Personal Constructs*. New York: Norton

Kempf, W.F. 1972. 'Zur Bewertung der Faktorenanalyse als psychologische Methode,' *Psychologische Beiträge* 14: 610-25

Kety, S. 1969. 'New Perspectives in Psychopharmacology,' in A. Koestler and J.R. Smythies eds, *Beyond Reductionism*. Boston: Beacon

Klein, M.H., Dittman, A.T., Parloff, M.M., and Gill, M.M. 1969. 'Behaviour Therapy: Observations and Reflections,' *Journal of Consulting and Clinical Psychology* 33: 259-66

Koch, S. 1961. 'Behaviorism,' in *Encyclopaedia Britannica*. Chicago: Benton

– 1964. 'Psychology and Emerging Conceptions of Knowledge as Unitary,' in T.W. Wann ed, *Behaviourism and Phenomenology*. Chicago: University of Chicago Press

Koestler, A. 1967. *The Ghost in the Machine*. London: Pan

– 1973. *The Call Girls*. New York: Random House

Kohler, I. 1961. *The Formation and Transformation of the Perceptual World*. New York: International Universities Press

Köhler, W. 1925 (1917). *The Mentality of Apes.* Translated by E. Winter. New York: Harcourt

− 1920. *'Die physischen Gestalten in Ruhe und im stationären Zustand.* Braunschweig: Vieweg

Kohut, H. 1971. *The Analysis of the Self.* New York: International Universities Press

− 1977. *The Restoration of the Self.* New York: International Universities Press

Korzybski, A. 1933. *Science and Sanity.* Lakeville, Conn.: International Non-Aristotelian Library

Kostjuk, G.S. 1974. 'Das Entwicklungsprinzip in der Psychologie,' in E.W. Schorochowa ed

Krauch, H. 1969. *Wege und Aufgaben der Systemforschung.* Dortmund: Arbeitsgemeinschaft f. Rationalisierung des Landes Nordrhein-Westfalen

Krauch, H., Feger, H., and Opgenoorth, W. 1970. 'Forschungsplan I,' *Zeitschrift für Sozialpsychologie* 1: 155-66

Krech, D., and Crutchfield, R.S. 1960. *Elements of Psychology.* New York: Knopf

Kuhn, T.S. 1970a. *The Structure of Scientific Revolutions.* Chicago: University of Chicago Press

− 1970b. 'Reflections on My Critics,' in I. Lakatos and A. Musgrave eds

Kvale, S. 1973. 'The Technological Paradigm of Psychological Research,' *Journal of Phenomenological Psychology* 3: 143-59

La Fave, L. 1966. 'Essay vs. Multiple-Choice: Which Test Is Preferable?' *Psychology in the Schools* 3 (1), 65-9

Lakatos, I. and Musgrave, A. eds. 1970. *Criticism and the Growth of Knowledge.* Cambridge, Eng.: Cambridge University Press

Langenheder, W. 1975. 'Determinanten der Berufswahl: Versuch zu einer "integrierenden" Theorie,' Unpublished manuscript. Nürnberg

Laucken, U. 1973. *Naive Verhaltenstheorie.* Stuttgart: Klett

Lee, D. 1959. *Freedom and Culture.* Englewood Cliffs, NJ: Prentice-Hall

Lewin, K. 1935. *A Dynamic Theory of Personality.* New York: McGraw-Hill

Lichtenberg, G.C. n.d. *Aphorismen.* Leipzig: Insel

London, P. 1972. 'The End of Ideology in Behavior Modification,' *American Psychologist* 27: 913-20

Lorenz, K. 1977. *Behind the Mirror.* London: Methuen

Lorenzen, P. 1974. *Konstruktive Wissenschaftstheorie.* Frankfurt: Suhrkamp

Lorenzer, A. 1970. *Kritik des psychoanalytischen Symbolbegriffs.* Frankfurt: Suhrkamp

− 1973. *Über den Gegenstand der Psychoanalyse, oder: Sprache und Interaktion.* Frankfurt: Suhrkamp

- 1976. *Die Wahrheit der psychoanalytischen Erkenntnis.* Frankfurt: Suhrkamp
Lumpkin, M. 1970. 'Walden I and II: A Plea for Renewed Balance in the Psychological Pursuit of Science,' *American Psychologist* 25: 1087-90
Lyons, J. 1963. *Psychology and the Measure of Man.* New York: Free Press
MacLeod, R.B. 1964. 'Phenomenology: A Challenge to Experimental Psychology,' in T.W. Wann ed, *Behaviorism and Phenomenology.* Chicago: University of Chicago Press
Mannheim, K. 1964 (1927). 'Das konservative Denken,' in *Wissenssoziologie.* Neuwied: Luchterhand
- 1969. (1929). *Ideologie und Utopie.* Frankfurt: Schulte-Bulmke
- (1936.) *Ideology and Utopia.* New York: Harcourt, Brace & World
McGuire, W.J. 1967. 'Some Impending Reorientation in Social Psychology,' *Journal of Experimental Social Psychology* 3: 124-39
Menninger, K. 1958. *The Theory of Psychoanalytic Technique.* New York: Basic Books
Merton, R.K. 1949. *Social Theory and Social Structure.* New York: Free Press
Metzger, W. 1962. *Schöpferische Freiheit.* Frankfurt: W. Kramer
- 1963. *Psychologie.* Darmstadt: Steinkopf
- 1965. *'The Historical Background for National Trends in Psychology: German Psychology,' *Journal of the History of the Behavioral Sciences* 1: 109-15
- ed. 1966. *Handbuch der Psychologie. 1. Band Allgemeine Psychologie 1. Halbband: Wahrnemung und Bewusstsein.* Göttingen: Verlag für Psychologie
- 1966a. 'Der Ort der Wahrnehmungslehre im Aufbau der Psychologie,' ibid.
- 1966b. 'Das einäugige Tiefensehen,' ibid.
Meyer, M.F. 1911. *The Fundamental Laws of Human Behavior.* Boston: Badger
- 1921. *The Psychology of the Other One.* Columbia, Mo.: Missouri Book Publishing Co.
Milgram, S. 1963. 'Behavioral Study of Obedience,' *Journal of Abnormal and Social Psychology* 67: 371-8
- 1964. 'Issues in the Study of Obedience,' *American Psychologist* 19: 848-52
- 1965. *Obedience.* Film. Graduate Center, City University of New York
- 1969. 'The Lost-Letter Technique,' *Psychology Today* 3 (3), 30-3, 68
Mischel, T. 1974. 'Understanding Neurotic Behavior,' in T. Mischel ed, *Understanding Other Persons.* Oxford: Blackwell

Mitscherlich, A. 1970. 'Dangers in Psychosomatic Adaptation,' *Universitas* 12: 347-57

– 1971. 'Eine Chance für die Psychologie?' *Frankfurter Rundschau*, 21 December 1971

Moore, O.K., and Anderson, A.R. 1962. 'Some Puzzling Aspects of Social Interaction, *Review of Metaphysics* 15: 409-33

Murphy, G. 1951. *An Introduction to Psychology*. New York: Harper

Neisser, U. 1967. *Cognitive Psychology*. New York: Appleton-Century-Crofts

Newberry, B.H. 1973. 'Truth Telling in Subjects with Information about Experiments,' *Journal of Personality and Social Psychology* 25: 369-74

Nietzsche, F. 1906. 'Die fröhliche Wissenschaft,' *Werke*, vol. 6. Leipzig: Naumann

Orne, M.T., and Holland, C.H. 1968. 'On the Ethological Validity of Laboratory Deceptions,' *International Journal of Psychiatry* 6: 282-93

Osgood, C.E. 1964. 'Semantic Differential Technique in the Comparative Study of Cultures,' *American Anthropologist* 66: 171-200

Osgood, C.E., Suci, G.J., and Tannenbaum, P.H. 1957. *The Measurement of Meaning*. Urbana: University of Illinois Press

Overton, W.F., and Reese, H.W. 1973. 'Models of Development,' in J.R. Nesselroade and H.W. Reese eds, *Life-Span Developmental Psychology*. London: Academic Press

Park, D. 1964. *Contemporary Physics*. New York: Harcourt, Brace & World

Pasztor (Brandt), E.H. 1960. 'A Study of Invariance under Transformation in a German-English Translation.' PHD dissertation. University of Denver. Ann Arbor: University microfilms (1964)

Penfield, W., and Roberts, L. 1959. *Speech and Brain-Mechanisms*. Princeton, NJ: Princeton University Press

Peters, R.S. 1969. 'Motivation, Emotion, and the Conceptual Schemes of Common Sense,' in T. Mischel ed, *Human Action*. London: Academic Press

Piaget, J. 1923. *Le langage et la pensée chez l'enfant*. Neuchâtel: Delachaux & Niestlé

– 1930. *The Child's Conception of Physical Causality*. Translated by M. Gabain. London: Routledge & Kegan Paul

– [1947]. *La psychologie de l'intelligence*. Paris: Colin

– 1957. *Logic and Psychology*. New York: Basic Books

– 1968. 'Explanation in Psychology and Psychophysiological Parallelism,' in P. Fraisse and J. Piaget eds, *Experimental Psychology*, vol. 1. London: Routledge & Kegan Paul

– 1969. *The Mechanisms of Perception*. Translated by G.N. Seagrim. London: Routledge & Kegan Paul

Pickenhain, L. 1970. 'The Higher Nervous Activity of Man,' in W.H. Gantt and C. Zwingmans eds, *Pavlovian Approach to Psychopathology*. Leipzig: Pergamon

Polanyi, M. 1958. *Personal Knowledge*. New York: Harper & Row

Pongratz, L.J. 1967. *Problemgeschichte der Psychologie*. Bern: Francke

Popper, K.R. 1935 (1934). *Logik der Forschung*. Vienna: Springer

- 1959. *The Logic of Scientific Discovery*. New York: Harper & Row
- 1970. 'Normal Science and Its Dangers,' in I. Lakatos and A. Musgrave eds
- 1973. 'Indeterminism Is Not Enough,' *Encounter* 40 (4), 20-6
- 1976. *Unended Quest*. La Salle, Ill.: Open Court

Pribram, K.H. 1976. 'Problems Concerning the Structure of Consciousness,' in G.G. Globus, G. Maxwell, and I. Savodnik eds, *Consciousness and the Brain*. New York: Plenum

Radnitzky, G. 1971. 'Theorienpluralismus – Theorienmonismus,' in A. Diemer ed, *Der Methoden – und Theorienpluralismus in den Wissenschaften*. Meisenheim am Glan: Hain

- 1973. *Contemporary Schools of Metascience*. Chicago: Henry Regnery

Rapaport, D. 1951. 'Toward a Theory of Thinking,' in D. Rapaport ed, *Organization and Pathology of Thought*. New York: Columbia University Press

- 1960. *The Structure of Psychoanalytic Theory*. New York: International Universities Press

Reese, H.W., and Overton, W.F. 1970. 'Models of Development and Theories of Development,' in L.W. Goulet and P.B. Baltes eds, *Life-Span Developmental Psychology*. New York: Academic Press

Resnick, J.H., and Schwartz, T. 1973. 'Ethical Standards as an Independent Variable in Psychological Research,' *American Psychologist* 28: 134-9

Riecken, H.W. 1962. 'A Program for Research on Experiments in Social Psychology,' in N.F. Washburne ed, *Decisions, Values and Groups*, vol. 2. New York: Pergamon

Riesman, D. 1950. *The Lonely Crowd*. New Haven, Conn.: Yale University Press

Ritter, R.N. 1972. 'A Study of the Limitations in Experimental Design.' MA thesis, University of Saskatchewan, Regina Campus

Rokeach, M. 1960. *The Open and the Closed Mind*. New York: Basic Books

- 1968. *Beliefs, Attitudes and Values*. San Francisco: Jossey-Bass

Rosenhan, D.L. 1973. 'On Being Sane in Insane Places,' *Science* 179: 250-8

Rosenthal, R. 1966. *Experimenter Effects in Behavioral Research*. New York: Appleton-Century-Crofts

- 1969. 'Interpersonal Expectations,' in R. Rosenthal and R.L. Rosnow eds, *Artifact in Behavioral Research*. London: Academic Press

Rubinstein, S.L. 1958. *Grundlagen der allgemeinen Psychologie.* Berlin: Volk & Wissen

– 1973. *Sein und Bewusstsein.* Berlin: Akademie

– 1974. 'Mensch und Welt,' in E.W. Schorochowa ed

– 1977. *Das Denken und die Wege seiner Erforschung.* Berlin: VEB Deutscher Verlag der Wissenschaften

Ruesch, J., and Bateson, G. 1951. *Communication: The Social Matrix of Society.* New York: Norton

Russell, W.A., and Roth, E. 1958. 'Psychologie in Deutschland und Amerika: Eine Studie in Gegensätzen,' *Psychologie und Praxis* 2: 223-31

Rychlak, J.F. 1968. *A Philosophy of Science for Personality Theory.* Boston: Houghton Mifflin

Sarbin, T.R., Taft, R., and Bailey, D.E. 1960. *Clinical Inference and Cognitive Theory.* New York: Holt, Rinehart & Winston

Sartre, J.P. 1946. *Réflexions sur la question juive.* Paris: Morihien

Schefflen, A.E. 1961. *Psychotherapy of Schizophrenia: Direct Analysis.* Springfield, Ill.: Thomas

Schmidt, H. 1934. *Philosophisches Wörterbuch.* Leipzig: Kröner

Schorochowa, E.W. ed, 1974. *Methodologische und theoretische Probleme der Psychologie.* Berlin: VEB Deutscher Verlag der Wissenschaften

– 'Das Prinzip des Determinismus in der Psychologie,' ibid.

Schrödinger, E. 1963 (1960). 'Was ist Wirklichkeit?' in E. Schrödinger, *Meine Weltansicht.* Frankfurt: Fischer

Schultz, D. 1971. 'Psychology: A World with Man Left Out,' *Journal for the Theory for Social Behaviour* 1: 99-107

Scripture, E.W. 1895. *Thinking, Feeling, Doing.* Meadville, Pa.: Flood & Vincent

Sherif, C.W., Sherif, M., and Nebergall, R.E. 1965. *Attitude and Attitude Change.* Philadelphia: Saunders

Siegel, S. 1956. *Nonparametric Statistics for the Behavioral Sciences.* New York: McGraw-Hill

Silverman, I. 1971. 'Crisis in Social Psychology,' *American Psychologist* 26: 583-4

Singer, C. 1961. 'Science,' in *Encyclopaedia Britannica.* Chicago: Benton

Skinner, B.F. 1959. *Cumulative Record.* New York: Appleton-Century-Crofts

– 1971. Beyond Freedom and Dignity. New York: Knopf

Sprung, L. 1976. 'Relevanz der Repräsentanz,' in H. Helm ed, *Neurosenpsychologie.* Berlin: VEB Deutscher Verlag der Wissenschaften

Stevens, S.S. 1935. 'The Operational Definition of Psychological Concepts,' *Psychological Review* 42: 517-27

Sullivan, H.S. 1953. *The Interpersonal Theory of Psychiatry.* New York: Norton

Szasz, T.S. 1961. *The Myth of Mental Illness.* New York: Harper

Tagiuri, R. 1969. 'Person Perception,' in G. Lindzey and E. Aronson eds, *The Handbook of Social Psychology.* Reading, Mass.: Addison-Wesley

Taylor, C. 1970. 'The Explanation of Purposive Behaviour,' in R. Borger and F. Cioffi eds, *Explanation in the Behavioural Sciences.* Cambridge, Eng.: Cambridge University Press

Thomae, H. 1960. *Der Mensch in der Entscheidung.* Munich: Barth

- 1968. *Das Individuum und seine Welt.* Göttingen: Verlag f. Psychologie

- 1969. 'Die Psychologie als ein pluralistisches System,' in H. Thomae and H. Feger eds, *Einführung in die Psychologie,* vol. 7. Bern: Huber

- 1974. *Konflikt, Entscheidung, Verantwortung.* Stuttgart: Kohlhammer

Thurstone, L.L. 1923. 'The Stimulus-Response Fallacy in Psychology,' *Psychological Review* 30: 354-69

Toulmin, S. 1970. 'Reasons and Causes,' in R. Borger and F. Cioffi eds, *Explanation in the Behavioural Sciences.* Cambridge, Eng.: Cambridge University Press

Traxel, W. 1968. *Über Gegenstand und Methode der Psychologie.* Bern: Huber

Warr, P.B., and Knapper, C. 1968. *The Perception of People and Events.* London: Wiley

Watson, J.D. 1968. *The Double Helix.* Toronto: McClelland & Stewart

Watzlawick, P., Beavin, J.H., and Jackson, D.D. 1967. *Pragmatics of Human Communication.* New York: Norton

Wentworth, H., and Flexner, S.B. 1960. *Dictionary of American Slang.* New York: Crowell

Werbik, H. 1976. 'Grundlagen einer Theorie sozialen Handelns,' *Zeitschrift für Sozialpsychologie* 7: 248-61, 310-26

Wertheimer, Max. 1959. *Productive Thinking.* New York: Harper

Wertheimer, Michael. 1965. 'Relativity and Gestalt,' *Journal of the History of the Behavioral Sciences* 1: 86-7

- 1972. *Fundamental Issues in Psychology.* Toronto: Holt, Rinehart & Winston

Whorf, B.L. 1956. *Language, Thought, and Reality.* New York: Wiley

Witte, W. 1966. 'Das Problem der Bezugssysteme,' in W. Metzger ed

Wyss, D. 1961. *Die tiefenpsychologischen Schulen von den Anfängen bis zur Gegenwart.* Göttingen: Vandenhoeck & Ruprecht

Zborowski, M. 1969. *People in Pain.* San Francisco: Jossey-Bass

Zborowski, M., and Herzog, E. 1952. *Life Is with People.* New York: International Universities Press

Zellinger, E. 1970. 'Probleme der Psychologie,' *Jahrbuch für Psychologie, Psychotherapie und medizinische Anthropologie* 18: 71-143, 194-259
- 1972. 'Psychologie nach behavioristisch-reflexologischer Fasson,' *Zeitschrift für klinische Psychologie und Psychotherapie* 20: 99-114, 199-230
Zimmer, E. 1940. *Umsturz im Weltbild der Physik.* Munich: Knorr & Hirth

Index

abilities 75

acting out 103, 214

action / activity 27, 50, 53, 55, 61, 63, 71
74, 77, 118, 124, 146, 155, 156, 165, 168,
171-3, 175, 181, 189, 191, 196, 201,
207-11 passim, 214, 219, 222, 226, 239,
245, 248, 250, 260; vs. behaviour 50; in
behaviourism 108; in diamat psychology 94-5, 107, 119, 205; in genetic
psychology 44-5, 92, 108; in gestalt-
phenomenology 89-90; in psychoanalysis 81, 85

actualize 159, 166, 167, 169; defined 159n.

adaptation 92, 201; see also Adjustment

adaptive viewpoint 103-4

address, forms of 35-6, 172, 243

ad hominem argument 121, 124, 235, 243

adjustment 182, 194, 204, 208-10 passim,
218-19, 221, 243

ad maiorem scientiae gloriam 120,
127n., 260

adultomorphizing 228

aesthetics 18, 52, 208, 216, 251-7

aggression 26, 27, 87-8, 126-8, 245, 229;
defined 126; behaviourist's 103;
psychoanalyst's 26, 86

Albert, H. 257

alienation 182, 226-46; author's 16,
26-8, 226

allopsychology: defined 72

Allport, G.W. 43, 198, 200, 201, 219

America(n) 21n.; *see also* U.S.; Yankee

American Association for the Advancement of Science 241

American Psychoanalytic Association
23, 121, 194

American Psychological Association 27,
28, 228, 240, 260

Amundson, N.E. 180-1

anal stage 15, 30, 102

Anastasi, A. 33

Anderson, A.R. 177n.

Anderson, R. 136-7

anger, expression of 15, 209; in various
languages 36; *see also* Aggression

animals, experiments with 37, 55, 131,
209, 222, 232, 234; *see also* Human
being vs. animals, rats

anthropomorphizing 7, 111n., 218, 232

anxiety 57, 103, 105, 122, 215, 243-5

archaeology, method of 25-6, 82, 249

Argyris, C. 156, 218

Ariadne's thread 143-4

Aristotle 67

arm-chair psychology 4, 54, 106, 136, 196, 200, 212n.; critique of term 54n.
art 13, 15, 16, 18, 19, 21-6 passim, 30, 248, 249, 252-4, 255n., 257
Asch, S.E. 24
aspects 5, 14, 24, 26, 51, 74, 90-2, 149-51, 166n., 221, 227, 229, 234, 235; *see also* Perspective
Assejew, V.G. 183
assessment 171-6, 210; *see also* Diagnosis
assumptions 6, 69, 80, 96-7, 120, 123-4, 127-8, 135, 156n., 173, 196, 198, 204, 215, 216, 231, 232, 239, 243-5 passim, 251; *see also* Taken-for-granted
attention, focus of 171, 174, 176, 203, 253
attitudes 72, 75; dialectics of 73
attribution 73, 123, 177, 232, 241-2
Ausdruckspsychologie: defined 200
Austria 23, 197-8n.
authenticity 30, 234
authority 127; defined 126
autism 232
autokinetic effect 133, 233
autopsychology *see* Observation of self
autotelic: defined 260-1

Bailey, D.E. 166
Bakan, D. 3, 212n., 217, 220
Bandura, A. 98n.
Bannister, D. 3, 217, 238
Barber, T.X. 141
Bassin, F.V. 202
Bateson, G. 127n.
Battegay, R. 29, 190n.
Baxter, R. 218
beauty 251-2, 255-7, 263; defined 252
Beavin, J.H. 177n.
behaviour 7, 18, 182, 208, 213-14, 218, 228, 233, 237, 243; vs. activity 50,

89-90n.; expressive 200; mistranslated from Piaget 44-5; subject of all sciences 53-4; verbal 98, 109; as word magic 103; *see also* Practice
behaviourism / behaviourists 4, 24, 26, 27, 77, 95-106, 120-8, 145, 156n., 161n., 201-4, 206-22, 237, 263; defined 95, 209; and alienation 228, 242; cognitive 95-6, 182, 209, 263; major contribution of 222; evaluated 102-6, 108; and happiness 120, 232; as ideology 204; leap 126n.; methodological 210; research in 133-43; as measure of theories 108-9; *see also* Conditioning, Experiment, Experimenter, Interest (cognitive, technical), Psychologist, Psychology, Science, Scientism, Scientist
behaviourization 89n.; of gestalt psychology 217; of Piaget 44-5, 217; of psychoanalysis 44, 217
behaviour modification 92n., 123, 215; as mere technology 54
Bekker, K. 202
belief 120, 137, 145, 155-6, 188, 195, 249, 250; ambiguity in system of 40-1; knowledge as 3
Benedetti, G. 29
Bertalanffy, L.v. 201
bias 120; *see also* Experimenter (effect), Perspective
Bible 189, 197, 212; quoted 15
Bieri, J. 135
Bischof, N. 55, 230n.
black box 220
Block Lewis, H. 24
Bohr, N. 58, 66, 71
Boring, E.G. 185, 206-7, 210, 217
Born, M. 76; on *Gestalten* 78
bourgeois 107, 194, 200, 201, 204
bracket 5, 14, 157, 161n.; defined 156n.

counter-transference: defined 163; analysis of 27, 115, 131, 202

creativity 25, 249, 253; in diamat psychology 94-5; in psychoanalysis 87; *see also* Science (as human creation), Theories (construction of)

critique (critical) 3, 4, 24, 25, 29, 30, 51-5 passim, 79, 101, 110, 121, 124, 135, 151, 177, 187, 188, 191-3 passim, 196, 200, 201, 205, 217, 254, 263; defined 40n.; of experimenter-subject inequality 123-8; lack of 54, 124n., 125n., 228, 251n.; *see also* Theories (evaluation of)

Crutchfield, R.S. 217

Dadaism 253

Danziger, K. 210

Darwin, C. 201, 217, 237

data 27, 89, 96, 119, 123, 136, 152n., 178, 227, 231, 232, 234n., 239, 249; collection of 121, 130-3, 200, 202; grouped 122, 136, 219, 236, 239; production 147-50; relativity of 70, 75; theory laden 150, 210; *see also* Measurement, Observation, Quantification

dataism 253

debriefing 103

deception 18, 59, 103, 116, 118, 121-3 passim, 139, 140, 170, 178, 257; sanctified 260; by 'subjects' 100, 139

'decide' 37

decision making 24, 77

defences 26, 85, 191, 201, 245-6; behaviourist's 102-3, 123; psychoanalyst's 86-7; *see also* individual defence mechanisms

definition 72; vagueness of 41, 126-7; importance of 55, 91, 196, 211

deism 207n.

Delaunay, R. 14

democratization 188, 206

denial 102, 227, 245, 246

depersonalization 227

description vs. explanation 243

'determine' 37

determinism 76; in psychoanalysis 79-81, 87

development 77, 81, 85, 105, 106, 108, 158, 191, 201, 203, 219, 246, 263

diagnosis 92n., 160-2, 172-3, 176, 181, 202, 222, 228, 231, 233, 240; defined 161

dialectic(s) 4, 115, 202-3, 205; defined 6; of activity and consciousness 94, 107, 119; of alienation 234-6; of behaviourism and positivism 217; of body and mind 79; of carriers and fields 79; of conceptualizations and mistranslations 44-6; with environment 106, 201; of impressions 170-2, 182; of interests 58, 63-4; of measurements 75, 202, 205; of observations 73; of problems 140-50; of science and art 252; of science and technology 53; of theories and impressions 157; of theory and practice 43, 158, 201-2, 205

dialectic-materialist psychology 93-4; *see also* Diamat psychology, Marxism

dialogue 60, 90, 108; *see also* Communication

diamat psychology (dialectical-materialist) 4, 14, 62, 80n., 93-5, 119-20, 201-6; described 93-4; and author's identity 14; evaluated 102, 104, 106, 108; as ideology 205-6; as measure of theories 107-8; pluralistic 74; on relativity 77-8; research in 132-3; *see also* Marxism

displacement 127n.; psychoanalyst's 87

Dölle, E.A. 256-7

dogmatism 216; scale 40-1, 137

doing vs. thinking 55, 102, 208; *see also* Action / activity

ignored 120; naïve 108, 177; *see also*
    Behaviourism / behaviourist, Psy-
    chologist, Science, Scientist, 'Subject'
explanation 18, 80, 101-2, 149-50, 218,
    223, 237, 243, 245, 246, 251, 255;
    defined 245; *see also* Aesthetics,
    Beauty, Elegance, Uncertainty
extraversion 136
Eysenck, H.J. 77, 121, 136, 137

Fachidiot: defined 257
'fact' 39, 74, 120, 121, 130n., 227, 232n.;
    always interpreted 115, 150
factor analysis 236, 239
faith 30, 195-6, 210, 211, 214, 216
false consciousness 187, 202-3, 205, 214,
    222, 227
falsification 123, 141, 212n.; evasion of
    58, 63, 76, 110n., 177, 211; immunity
    to 80
Farthing, G.R. 28
Faust see Goethe, J.W.v.
feelings 15, 39, 58, 71, 122, 145-9, 155,
    160, 169, 172, 176, 186, 191, 209, 214,
    227, 231-3, 237, 238, 242-3, 245-6,
    250, 255; in diamat psychology 94;
    disregarded 102, 104, 209-16 passim,
    220, 229, 232n., 243, 246; *see also*
    Retrospection
Feyerabend, P.K. 80, 110, 121n., 253
fields 69, 73, 78-9, 81; and carriers 79
Fincher, C. 237
Foppa, K. 40
Fraisse, P. 238
frame of reference / framework 3, 5-8,
    14, 89, 109; defined 50
free association 29, 44, 168, 192, 203
freedom 67n., 77, 123, 211, 257; *see*
    also Emancipation
freemasonry 207n.
French language 15, 34-7 passim, 40, 41,

43-5 passim; author's study of 16, 18-20
    passim
Freud, A. 195n.
Freud, S. 4, 22, 26, 43, 58, 64, 74, 77,
    79-82, 87-8, 115-17, 188-95, 201-4,
    244-5, 254; committed to knowing 61n.;
    mistranslated 42-4; precursors of 190;
    as translator 190
frontier *see* Pioneer mentality
functionalism 212; defined 206
fuzzy concepts / logic / reasoning / sets
    17, 75, 77n., 80, 91, 255-6

Galilei, G. 254
game 76, 237, 254, 256-7, 261, 263
Gardner, M. 232n.
Geisteswissenschaft 7, 52, 60, 82, 197,
    211; explained 52
genetic psychology 4, 62, 92-3, 118-19,
    162, 201, 219, 238; defined 92; author
    introduced to 24; evaluated 101, 102,
    104, 108; as measure of theories 105-6;
    research in 92-3, 132; *see also* Piaget
Geneva School *see* Genetic psychology,
    Piaget
German: author's identity 13-22 passim,
    25, 226; language 15, 19, 20, 34-7,
    40, 42-4, 195, 197, 221; *see also* psy-
    chology (German-language)
Germany 13-22 passim, 197, 198n., 220;
    see also Nazi, Psychology (East
    German, German-language, West
    German)
gestalt-phenomenology 4, 78, 89-92,
    117-18, 195, 201, 210, 219; evaluated
    101, 102, 106-8; vs. existential pheno-
    menology 89n.; as ideology and utopia
    200; as measure of theories 104-5;
    precursors and founders of 195, 199;
    research in 90, 131-2; *see also* Bracket,
    Gestalt psychology, Interest (cognitive,

individual differences 144, 117, 124, 149, 219, 228, 233, 235, 241
induction 238, 239
industrialization 206-8 passim, 213, 219, 220, 221, 228, 230
infinite regress 141n., 144
information 165, 172, 175, 233-6 passim, 241; loss of 135; theory 74
insight *see* Understanding (of self)
instinct: mistranslated 44
instructions 175; as independent variable 120, 134-9, 241
intellectualization: psychoanalyst's 87; psychologist's 102
intelligence 171, 173; in Piaget 43-4, 132; quality vs. quantity 44
intention 73, 99, 123-4, 245
interaction 180; *see also* Dialectics, Relationship, Research
interest 71, 233, 235, 236, 238, 253, 257; cognitive 18, 51-2, 56, 59; defined 53; emancipatory 51-5, 60, 64, 79-82, 182, 194; hermeneutic 45, 51-6, 60-4, 70, 114-20, 131, 169, 229; technical 51-64, 66, 70, 73, 75, 78-80, 99, 109, 120-8, 169, 182, 200, 216, 229, 243
International Psychoanalytic Association 204
International Psychoanalytic Society 17, 192
interpersonal relations 113-28, 163; *see also* Relationship
interpretation 6, 80, 123, 189, 191, 194, 235, 241; in analysis 25, 89, 167-9; of data, 148, 234n.; of history 185; in human sciences 52, 120; in physics 80; by s 115, 127n; *see also* Hermeneutic(s)
intersubjectivity 51, 97, 110, 143, 195, 209, 213, 214, 217, 234n., 251
interview 131, 238, 240
intimacy 16, 27, 28, 35, 230
intolerance 216

introspection 96, 145, 196, 211, 227; by behaviourists 121-2; *see also* Observation (of self), Self-reflection
invariance 53, 78, 91, 133, 159n.
IQ *see* Intelligence
isolation (defence mechanism) 102, 245-6; defined 245
Iwanowa, I.I. 183

Jackson, D.D. 177n.
Jacoby (author's maternal forebears) 16; Hans (author's uncle) 30, 263; William (author's grandfather) 15, 20, 30
James, W. 34n., 254
Japanese 36, 172
Jaspers, K. 237
Jew(s) 30, 164n., 188-93, 195, 212n., 223, 227, 260; author's identity as 14-18, 30, 226; original synthesis by 189
Judaism 26, 30, 189
judgment 54, 167-8, 179, 248, 253, 256n., 257
Jung, C.G. 18, 20, 192, 221

Kaminski, G. 3, 29, 55, 92n., 159n., 160n., 162, 182
Kaufmann, H. 121
Kaufmann, W. 188
Keiler, P. 79
Kekule, F.A. 145
Kelly, G.A. 61, 91, 201
Kepler, J. 252
Kety, S. 73n.
Knapper, C. 179
'to know': in various languages 37
knowledge 3, 52, 61, 67, 68, 88, 150, 155-6, 159n., 167, 182, 212n., 219, 223, 230, 235, 237-8, 254, 260; defined 3, 250, 252; articulate vs. tacit 74, 156; of nature 82; 'objective': in diamat 95; *see also* Sociology of knowledge

Koch, S. 89n., 95, 99, 217
Koehler, W. 78
Kohler, I. 29, 91, 240
Kohut, H. 29
Korzybski, A. 38
Kostjuk, G.S. 106-7
Krech, D. 217
Kris, E. 195n.
Kuhn, T.S. 6, 54, 58, 238

La Fave, L. 173
language(s) 15-20 passim, 23, 26, 33-47, 103, 149, 155-6, 197, 198n., 216-17, 222, 235, 240-1, 250, 257; development of 94; and Jews 30, 190-1; *see also* Translation, Verbalization; individual languages
Laucken, U. 91, 157n.
learning 77, 209, 210, 218-19, 222, 239; theory 210, 215
Lehre: explained 199n.
Lewin, K. 77, 195, 237, 243
Lichtenberg, G.C. 58
life: everyday / real 24, 39, 55, 61, 62, 76, 122, 155-7, 167, 180-1, 243; *see also* Alienation
life-space 105, 117, 233; defined 90
limits: of psychoanalysis 64n., 72; of psychologist 161; of psychology 46-7, 150-2; of reports 174; of science 72, 82, 147, 150, 152, 251-7
Lindzey, G. 248, 249, 253
Linnaeus, C. 237
logic 56, 77-8, 130, 188, 238-9, 249, 255-6, 263; of science 212n, 248, 254; *see also* Causality, Determinism, Epistemology, Falsification, Induction, Positivism, Proof, Theories (construction of), Truth, Uncertainty (principle)
logical empiricism *see* Positivism
London, P. 54

Lorenz, K. 36, 37n.
Lorenzen, P. 50n.
Lorenzer, A. 29
lost-letter technique 229, 233
Lucretius 254
Luther, M. 195, 197
Lutheran 15, 30, 188, 195-6, 199, 200, 210-11

McGuire, W. 102, 206
MacLeod, R. 34n., 89, 217
magic 103
Maltzmann, I. 132
Mannheim, K. 5, 185-90, 200-1, 203, 205-6, 213, 221-3, 226-7, 231, 232, 237
marriage counselling 170-1
Marx, K. 187-9, 194, 206
Marxism 193, 223, 230; defined 202; author introduced to 19-21 passim; similarity with psychoanalysis 202-3; *see also* Dialectic-materialist psychology
Maslow, A. 43
materialist 94, 206, 217
mathematics 74, 76, 232n., 239, 252; *see also* Quantification, Statistics
Maya 145
meaning 7, 14, 26, 40-1, 63-4, 80, 89-91, 120, 143, 148-9, 167, 186, 191, 195, 196, 200, 213, 223, 226-35, 263; in diamat 74, 94; measurement of 42; multiple 230n.
means and ends 50, 121, 229, 260; *see also* Values
measurement 44, 53-4, 68-70, 75, 80, 95, 103, 106, 109, 122, 133-6, 139, 143, 173, 196, 202-3, 209, 211–14, 222, 239, 250-1; derivation unknown 75; no requirement of science 213, 240; theory laden 75; *see also* Dialectics, Method, Quantification, Statistics, Uncertainty

melting pot 29, 207, 208, 214, 216, 218, 219, 228
memory 77, 145, 147-9 passim, 164-9, 175, 228, 232-3, 239
Menninger, K. 86, 115, 116
Mensch 34, 35, 155; *see also* Human being
meta-experiment 126-7, 138-40, 177
meta-perspective 6
meta-psychology 3
meta-science 7, 82, 101
method 3-8, 25-7 passim, 52, 53, 54, 63, 70, 71, 74, 81, 82, 119, 130-52, 161, 162, 186, 192, 198-200, 202, 210, 219, 227, 238-40, 245, 249, 253; experimental 59; 'scientific' 7, 100, 209, 237, 254, 257; *see also* Bracket, Conditioning, Content analysis, Experiment, Interest (cognitive), Introspection, Observation, Operational definition, Phenomenal analysis, Phenomenology, Practice, Psychoanalysis, Quantification, Science, Scientism, Self-reflection, Thought experiment
metromania 103, 213; *see also* Measurement
Metzger, W. 13, 24, 39, 46, 55, 76, 117, 198-9, 230n., 242, 255, 263
Mexico 21n., 219
Meyer, M.F. 72, 120
Meyer (author's paternal forefathers) 16
Milgram, S. 121, 124-8, 177, 229
mind 7, 13, 18, 23, 25, 60, 79, 81, 148, 156n., 182, 191, 196, 200, 210, 215, 217 229; vs. body 79; not reducible to brain 73
Mischel, T. 201
Mitscherlich, A. 29, 79, 204
models 133-8, 182, *see also* World (models of)
monism 67, 68, 73-4, 80
Montessori School 17, 18

Moore, O.K. 177n.
motivation 4, 15, 72, 74, 80, 81, 85-7 passim, 102, 136, 142-3, 170-1, 173, 214, 232-3, 243, 245-6; relational to observer 73
Müller-Lyer illusion 250-1
multiculturalism *see* Canada
multideterminism 81
Murphy, G. 24
myomorphizing *see* Ratomorphizing

naïve: experimenter 108, 177; psycho-analyst 167, 170, 204; psychologist 72, 151, 167, 169, 170, 174; reporter 174; 'subject' 92, 98-100, 121, 176, 209, 218, 219; theories 91, 157n., 244; *see also* Pre-scientific
narcissism, psychoanalyst's 29, 86, 87
National Socialist *see* Nazi
Naturwissenschaft 7, 52, 82, 197; *see also* Physics, Science
Nazi 13-22 passim, 28, 30, 192, 198n., 210, 221, 227
Nebergall, R.E. 125
negation of the negation 202-3, 205, 206
Nelson, M.C. 24
neurotic 136, 172-3, 236; *see also* Psychopathology
Newberry, B.H. 99-100
New School for Social Research 23-4, 254
Nietzsche, F. 23, 25, 30, 42, 43n., 187-8
nomothetic 4, 122, 206

obedience: defined 126; vs. helping vs. meddling 127n.; of 'subjects' 59-60, 124-7
objectivity 14, 67, 70, 109-10, 119, 132, 137, 143, 173, 199, 209-13 passim, 237-8, 243, 251, 253, 257; defined 14, 105, 109-10, 237; of science denied 66-8; *see also* Reality, Truth, Uncertainty

observation 80, 90, 130, 132, 135, 175, 203, 215, 249, 250, 251; in behaviourism 120; influencing data 70-73, 89, 143, 145-6, 149-52, 241; 'objective' 95; of self 72, 116-17, 119, 136, 145, 151; systematic 155; *see also* Uncertainty

Occam's razor 216; *see also* Consistency, Parsimony

observer *see* Experimenter, Psychoanalyst, Psychologist

omnipotence 67n., 246, 248-9; *see also* Control, Power

one-armed bandit 111

operational definition 58, 71, 75, 105, 109, 122, 126, 209, 217, 260; demonstrating relativity 70; *see also* Behaviourism, Logic (of science), Measurement, Method, Positivism, Quantification

operations: concrete 106; formal 74, 92, 93, 106, 119; *see also* Genetic psychology, Piaget, Thinking

Orne, M.T. 103, 124n., 125, 177

Orozco, J. 254

Osgood, C.E. 41-2; unilingual 41

other-directed 194, 228, 242

Papini, G. 70n.

paradox 14-17, 27, 143, 248, 255, 263; alienation 242-3; creation of theories 249; diamat 95; evaluation of theories 108-9; experimenter-effect 141; gestalt-phenomenological 92; linguistic 46; Marxist 206; positivist 234n.; psychoanalytic 193; *see also* Contradiction

parents 86, 162; author's *see* Brandt, O.L. *and* Brandt-Jacoby, M.; in various languages 34-5

Park, D. 69, 72, 80, 81

parsimony 127n., 209, 213, 216-18, 251-2, 255

participant 261; *see also* 'Subject'

Pasztor, E.H. *see* Brandt, E.P.

Pauli, W. 67-71 passim

Pavlov, I.P. 74, 93, 205, 206

Penfield, W. 73

perceive 4, 5, 134, 139, 165, 168, 175, 180, 250; *see also* Conceive, Perception

perception 44, 71, 74, 75, 78, 81, 90, 132, 151, 240, 242, 250; *see also* Gestalt-phenomenology, Gestalt psychology

'person': defined 157, 161n., 163; change of 160, 169

person perception *see* Personicating

personality 85, 172, 239, 241-2; theories of 72, 75, 77, 158, 181, 199, 238; traits 75

personicatee: defined 157

personicating 16, 29, 147-50 passim, 155-82, 194, 227, 255, 257; defined 157; first-hand 158-65; defined 158; vs. second-hand 179-81; research on 139, 178, 180-2, 233, 241-2; second-hand 164-76; defined 158; variables in 170

personicator: defined 157

perspective 3, 5, 6, 8, 14, 45-6, 64, 81, 89-92, 110, 117, 132, 151, 186-7, 195, 200-1, 203, 207, 213, 216, 222-3, 228, 237, 243, 253, 257; *see also* Aspects, Gestalt-phenomenology, Objectivity, Phenomenology

Peters, R.S. 55

phenomenal analysis 90, 92n., 158-80, 182, 210-11; defined 6; of 'alienation' 227-34; of 'belief' 41, 254; of 'identity' 227-30; *see also* Content analysis, Gestalt-phenomenology

phenomenology 25, 26, 146, 185, 187, 216, 248; described 4-5, 88-9; *see also* Bracket, Gestalt-phenomenology, Phenomenal analysis

misunderstood in English 42-4, 81; of psychoanalysts 115-16, 163, 203; research in 85, 131; only self-reflective science 55; in U.S.S.R. 194n., 202, 203, 204n.; as utopia 204; *see also* Interest (cognitive)

psychoanalyst 22, 23, 115-17, 204, 242; anonymity of 87, 163, 164n.; author as 13, 14, 17, 23, 160n., 164, 177, 240n.; defences of 86-7; Marxist 193, 201; naïve 167, 170, 204; non-medical 195n., 204; North-American 194, 202, 204; small number of 193; reluctant to abandon theory 58; technical interest of 182; utopian thinking of 204; West German 193, 205

psycho-logic 125n., 130, 170, 230, 249, 253, 255-6, 263

psychologist: average 236; status of 229-30, 244; *see also* Experimenter, Interest (cognitive), Limits of, Naïve

psychology: defined 7, 50n., 257; by behaviourists 53-4, 232; by diamat psychologists 95; by French psychologists 238; by gestalt-phenomenologists 51, 55, 117; by lay persons 193n., 244; aim of 64, 237, 243; Anglo-American vs. European 64, 200, 206, 219; East German 205-6; emancipatory 53; as game 260-1; as *Geisteswissenschaft* 82; German-language 6-7, 26, 29, 199, 210, 221, 230n., 256-7; hermeneutic 53; mechanistic 226, 231, 232, 236, 244; relevance of 223; 'schools' of 117, 195, 197; Soviet 93, 201-4; technical 53; uniqueness of 55, 238; West German 79, 220-1; *see also* Cognitive psychology, Interest (cognitive), Limits, individual schools

psychopathology 72, 158, 173; *see also* Diagnosis, Neurotic, Schizophrenic

psychophysics 90

psychosomatic 7n., 78, 79

psychotherapist 96

psychotherapy 161-2, 192, 214-15, 219, 222, 228, 233; *see also* Counselling, Psychoanalysis

publications 26, 151, 176, 178, 181, 194, 204, 205, 212, 213, 217, 218, 221, 256-7; and alienation 234-6, 241

publishing: meaning of 87, 90, 93, 96

punishment 18, 26, 120, 124-5, 209, 215-16, 219, 230n.

puritans 191, 207-18, 246; *see also* Calvinism, Pioneer mentality

purpose *see* motivation

Pythagoras 252

qualities vs quantities 68, 75, 78, 81, 94, 102, 202, 213, 222, 240

quantification 44, 45, 102, 122, 212-13, 239-40; in diamat psychology 94; *see also* Measurement, Statistics

quantum mechanics *see* Physics

questionnaire 119, 121, 130, 133, 136, 149, 227, 239, 257

Radnitzky, G. 75, 217

Raths, L.E. 27-8

Rapaport, D. 87, 195n.

rationality 18, 253

rationalization 79, 127n., 245; behaviourist's 103; psychoanalyst's 87

ratomorphizing 7, 218

rats 24, 35, 61, 99n., 108, 110-11, 114, 117, 120, 128, 138n., 199, 212, 214, 215, 217-18, 222, 246; related to psychologists 128, 218; slang meaning of 218; no taste for 24, 199

reaction formation 102-3, 245

reality 13, 94, 104, 120, 166, 169, 202-3, 205, 222, 230n., 255; 'objective'

66-7, 70, 89, 133; ordering of 63; reality$_1$ 156n., reality$_2$ 64, 152; principle 192; testing 163; unknowable 88; *see also* World

reason: in German 37; vs. cause 91; Jews and 188; *see also* Logic, Rationality, Thinking

reductionism 73, 248; rejected by diamat psychology 94; *see also* Physiology, Positivism

reflection: in diamat psychology 94-5, 151; *see also* Objectivity, Reality, World

reflexive psychology 3, 244

reflexology 78, 93; *see also* Conditioning, Rats, Stimulus

reification 104, 106; in SAE 38; hampering scientific progress 39; *see also* Behaviourism (cognitive), Operational definition

Reik, T. 23, 195n.

reinforcement 216; history of 219; *see also* Conditioning, Learning, Stimulus

relationism 91, 222-3, 263; defined 109, 187; *see also* Perspective, Sociology of knowledge

relationship 16, 17, 19, 28, 220; expressed in various languages 35-6, 38; between psychologist and others 71-2, 79, 114-28, 235, 241, 245; making sense out of 61; *see also* Alienation, Control

relativism 3, 110, 222-3

relativity 77-8, 81

relevance 141, 252; of psychology 51, 55-63, 223; *see also* Interest, Value

religion 15, 188, 193-200 passim, 207-16

Renyi, A. 254

report 122, 134-5, 139, 141, 147, 149, 151-2, 158, 171, 174-6, 179, 227, 234-6, 240-1; *see also* Publications

reportee / reporter 164-5, 174, 179; defined 158; 'naïve' reporter 174

representativeness 104-5, 136, 142-3

repression 203

research 130-52, 214; aim of 81; non-experimental 43-4, 238-40; in U.S. 97n.; *see also* Experiment, Interest (cognitive), Method, Psychoanalysis, Representativeness, individual areas and schools

resistance 115, 163, 167-8, 191, 192, 203, 213-14; analysis of: defined 167n.

Resnick, J.H. 59, 62-3, 98

response 233; mistranslated in Piaget 44-5; as word magic 103; *see also* Behaviourism, Conditioning, Learning, Stimulus, 'Writing behaviour'

responsibility 52, 60; *see also* Ethics

retrospection 146-52 passim

reversibility 92; defined 105

reward *see* Cost and pay-off, Product of one's labour, Punishment

Riesman, D. 194

Ritter, R.N. 136-7

ritual 103

Rock, I. 24

Roheim, G. 195n.

Rokeach, M. 120, 137, 212; 'belief' misused 40-1

role 55, 114, 119, 140, 172, 204, 214, 229-30, 233n., 234, 235, 242

Roman Catholic 190, 197-8, 210, 248

Romanticism 199-200

Rosen, J. 96

Rosenhan, D.L. 173

Rosenthal, R. 110, 138-42, 211

Rousseau, J.J. 23

Rubinstein, S.L. 46, 51, 55, 77-8, 93-4, 119, 132

Ruesch, J. 207, 208, 212-13, 241

rule 52, 72, 76, 208, 237, 251, 254, 256,

tions (formal), Retrospection, Self-reflection

Thomae, H. 3, 61, 63, 77, 131, 199, 238, 239

thought experiment 70, 98-9, 133, 144-5, 148, 149, 249; example of 70n.

Thurstone, L.L. 218

time 67, 159n., 165, 167, 168, 175, 192, 255; dimension 5; relativity of 69, 77-8; subjective 77, 81

Titchener, E.B. 237

tool for scientific observation 71

Torah 14, 189, 190-1

transference 162-3, 166-9, 191; defined 162; see also Counter-transference

translation: of Bible 197, 212n.; errors of: Freud, 42-4; Piaget 42, 43-5; semantic differential 41-2; behaviourists' unawareness of, 103-4; dearth of English 46, 93, 217

translator: author as 16, 20, 25, 26; equal traitor 26

'truth' 3, 58, 82, 151, 195, 207, 211-13 passim, 216, 222, 223, 240, 248-57, 263; feeling of 250; in psychoanalysis 116, 195; see also 'Fact,' Relationism, Uncertainty

uncertainty 103, 131, 136, 143, 146, 147, 151-2; principle 68, 70-3, 80; illustrated 70n; see also Prediction, Relativity

unconscious 24, 27, 85, 187, 190, 192, 203, 204n., 230n., 243; collective 186, 221, 222; communication 161; conviction of 116; motivation 80, 87, 102, 243, 245-6; see also Defences, Self-reflection

understanding 53, 55, 61-2, 81, 88, 190, 200, 219, 223, 229, 236, 237, 240, 243; defined 178n.; goal of psychoanalysis 107; as opposed to control 27; of self 22, 27, 64, 115, 187, 203, 214, 244, 245,

255; see also Explanation, Knowledge

undoing 102-3

unilingualism 34-47, 103, 216-17, 236; see also Language(s)

uniqueness 81; see also Individual differences, History (individual)

universities 24, 25, 28, 193, 197, 204, 241, 257; German-speaking 52, 195, 197, 221; U.S. 217, 221

universe 151-2, 189; see also World

'unscientific' 101, 210, 244

U.S. 21, 22, 27, 28, 206-9, 218, 220; see also Yankee

utopian thinking 194, 200, 204, 221-2; defined 190

value: empirical 104; free science 54, 109, 222

value(s) 22, 28, 40, 50-64, 72, 155, 186, 213, 216, 219, 235, 243, 248, 257; author's father's 17; Jewish 188, 189, 190-2; questioned 64; romantic 200; survival as 56-8, 63-4; Yankee 22, 64, 207-8, 210, 220; see also Interest, Means and ends, Relevance

variables 106, 151, 170, 211; independent 104, 120, 136; intervening 96, 100, 214; intrapersonal 135; uncontrolled 72-3; see also Data, Experimenter, Factor analysis, Instructions, Stimulus

verbalization 92, 93, 119, 132, 148-52, 156, 166, 174, 190, 214, 237; see also Communication, Language

Verhaltenszirkus 231n.

verification 212n., 217; as fuzzy concept 80; see also Falsification, Logic (of science), Objectivity, Truth, Uncertainty

Victorian 190, 202

volition 145-9, 186, 231, 240; see also Motivation, Wishes

voyeurism, psychoanalyst's 86

Wallach, H. 24
Warr, P.B. 179
Watson, J.B. 206
Watson, J.D. 252
Watzlawick, P. 142, 177n.
'we': for author 155n., 235
Werbik, H. 118
Wertheimer, Max 24, 195
Wertheimer, Michael 89n., 235
West Germany 220-1, 238
whole vs. parts 14, 78, 88, 90, 195-6,
    198-200, 227, 232, 233, 235, 238, 240,
    242, 250, 252; *see also* Gestalt
    psychology
Wiener Kreis see Positivism
wishes, unconscious 86-7; *see also*
    Volition
Wissenschaft 261; *see also* Science
work 25, 181, 203, 210, 212n., 227, 230-1,
    235, 238, 246, 260; in diamat psy-
    chology 94, 107, 205; psychoanalytic
    107, 115; in puritanism 207, 208, 211-13

passim, 215, 219-21; *see also* Practice
world 22, 81, 187; external 88, 119; of
    fields 69; individual 63-4, 91, 233, 238;
    beyond laboratory 59-60; material
    107, 145, 229, 257; models of 56, 78,
    82, 95; objective 94; observable 151-2;
    perceptual: naïve vs. measured 90;
    phenomenal 89; physical 53; ver-
    balizable 151-2; *see also* Life, Reality
'World 1,' 'World 2,' 'World 3' *see*
    Popper, K.R.
'Writing behaviour' 61, 96, 98
Wundt, W. 151, 197, 210

Yankee 189, 206-21; use of term ex-
    plained 21n.; resistance to anything
    foreign 26; *see also* Bourgeois, Capital-
    ism, Industrialization, Melting pot,
    Pioneer mentality, Puritan,
    Unilingualism

Zborowski, M. 189
Zellinger, E. 201-3